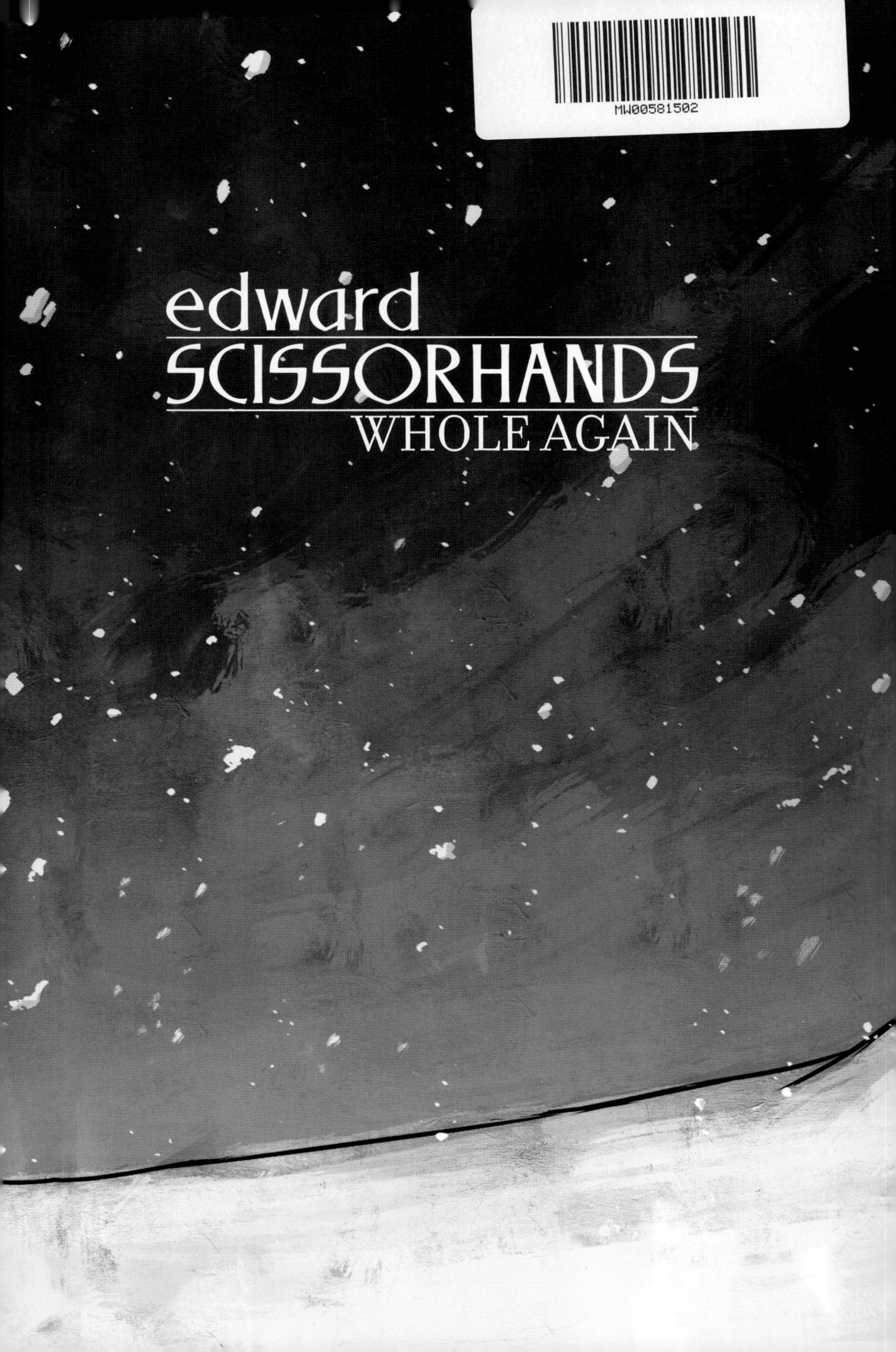
edward
SCISSORHANDS
WHOLE AGAIN

COVER ART BY
DREW RAUSCH

COLLECTION EDITS BY
JUSTIN EISINGER
AND ALONZO SIMON

COLLECTION DESIGN BY
GILBERTO LAZCANO

Facebook **facebook.com/idwpublishing**
Twitter **@idwpublishing**
YouTube **youtube.com/idwpublishing**
Tumblr: **tumblr.idwpublishing.com**
Instagram **instagram.com/idwpublishing**

978-1-63140-440-5   19 18 17 16 15   1 2 3 4 5

Originally published as EDWARD SCISSORHANDS issues #6-10.

Ted Adams, CEO & Publisher
Greg Goldstein, President & COO
Robbie Robbins, EVP/Sr. Graphic Artist
Chris Ryall, Chief Creative Officer/Editor-in-Chief
Matthew Ruzicka, CPA, Chief Financial Officer
Alan Payne, VP of Sales
Dirk Wood, VP of Marketing
Lorelei Bunjes, VP of Digital Services
Jeff Webber, VP of Digital Publishing & Business Development

IDW founded by Ted Adams, Alex Garner,
Kris Oprisko, and Robbie Robbins

Special thanks to Joshua Izzo and
Nicole Spiegel of Fox.

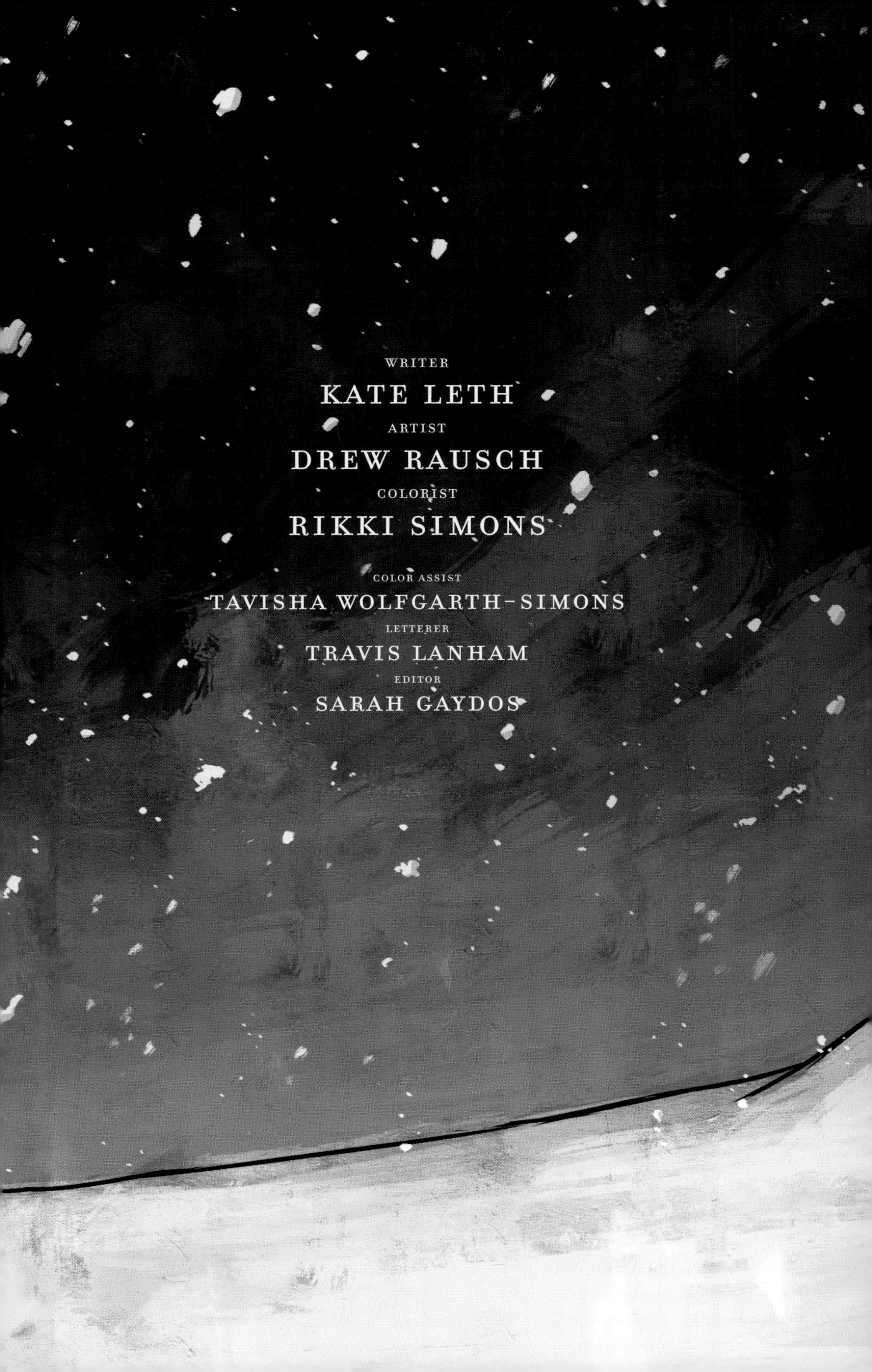

WRITER
KATE LETH
ARTIST
DREW RAUSCH
COLORIST
RIKKI SIMONS

COLOR ASSIST
TAVISHA WOLFGARTH-SIMONS
LETTERER
TRAVIS LANHAM
EDITOR
SARAH GAYDOS

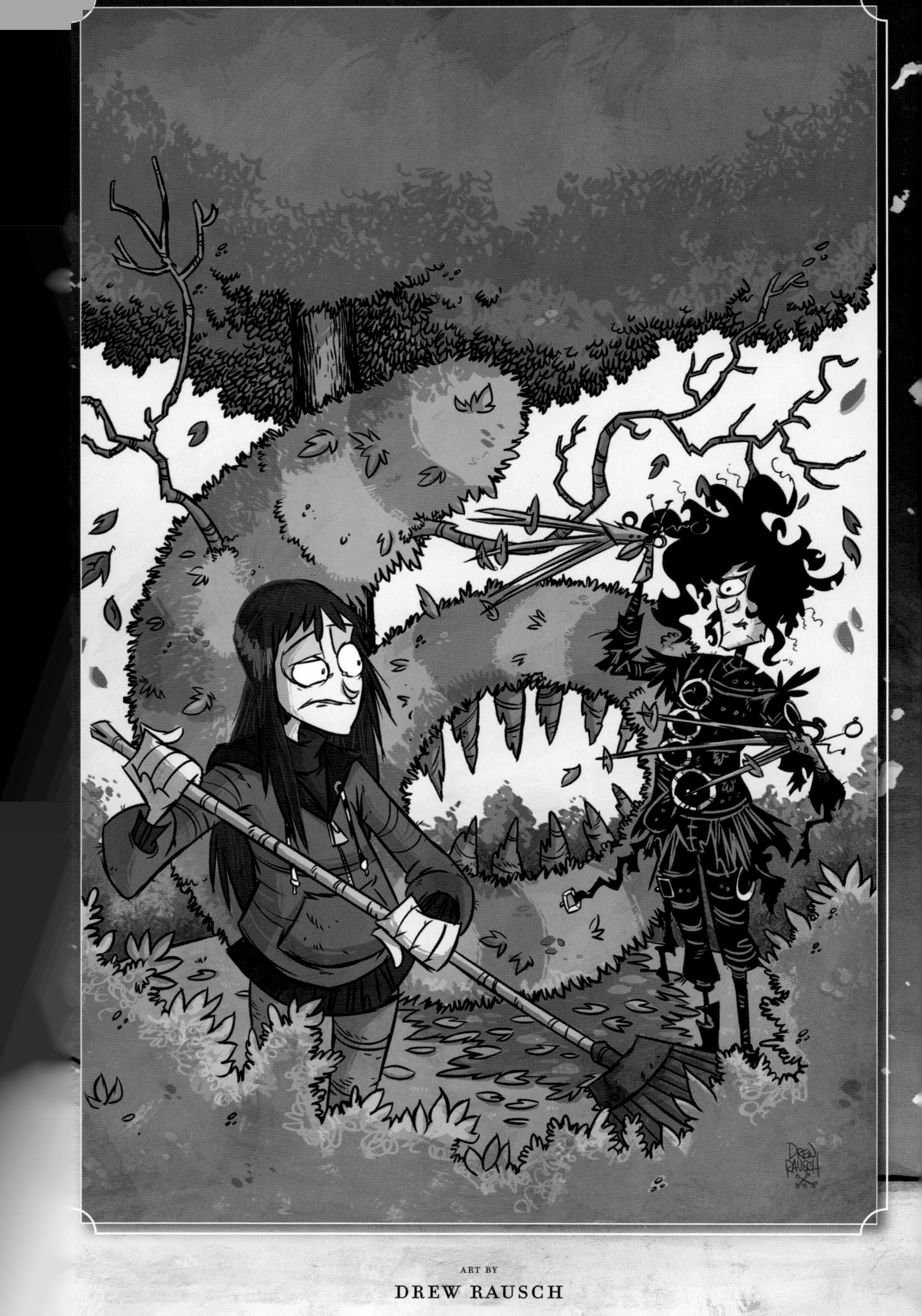
DREW RAUSCH

ART BY

DREW RAUSCH

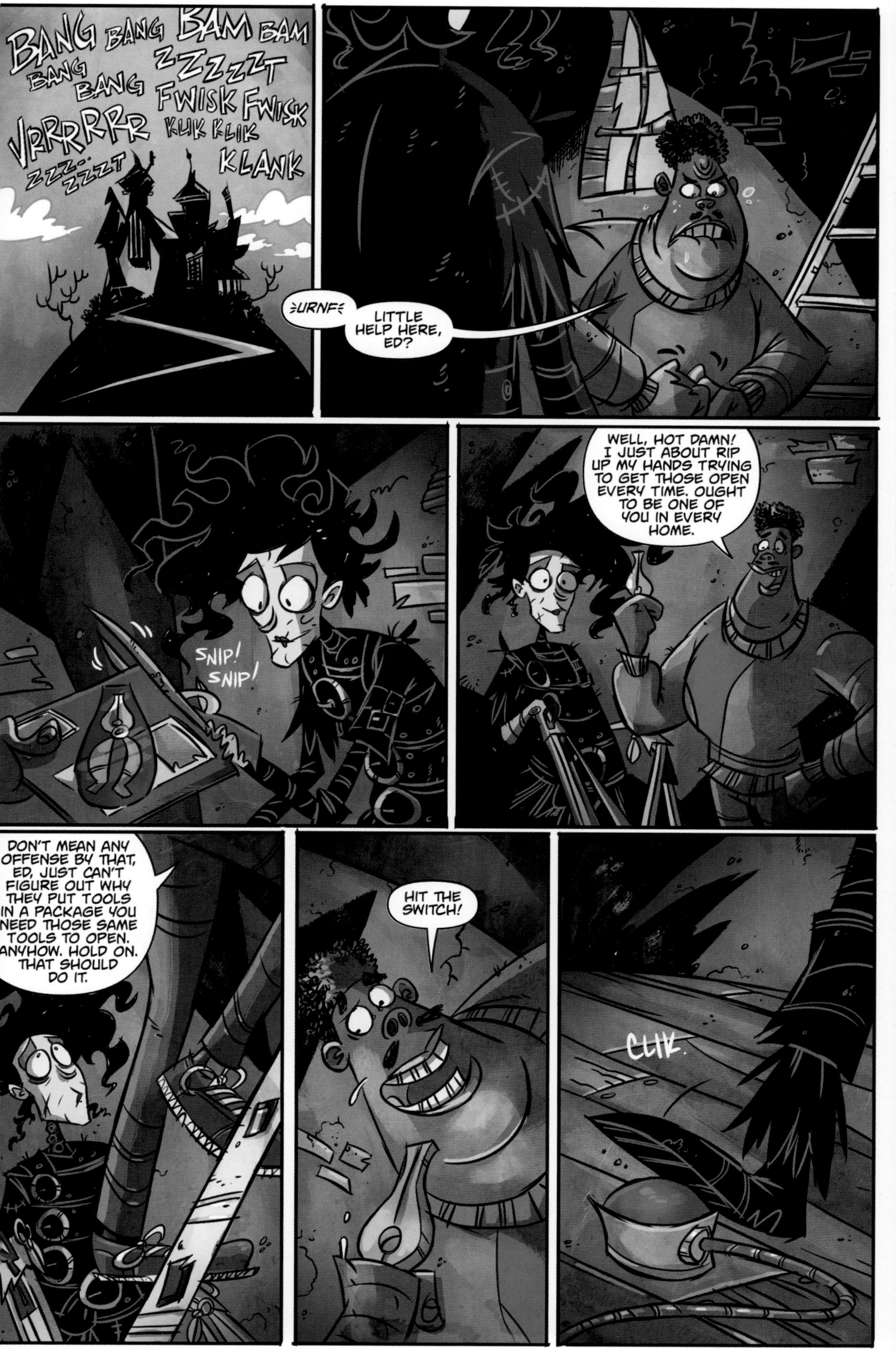
BANG BANG BAM BAM
BANG
BANG
ZZZZZT
FWISK FWISK
VRRRRRR
KLIK KLIK
ZZZ..
ZZZT
KLANK
URNF
LITTLE HELP HERE, ED?
SNIP! SNIP!
WELL, HOT DAMN! I JUST ABOUT RIP UP MY HANDS TRYING TO GET THOSE OPEN EVERY TIME. OUGHT TO BE ONE OF YOU IN EVERY HOME.
DON'T MEAN ANY OFFENSE BY THAT, ED, JUST CAN'T FIGURE OUT WHY THEY PUT TOOLS IN A PACKAGE YOU NEED THOSE SAME TOOLS TO OPEN. ANYHOW. HOLD ON. THAT SHOULD DO IT.
HIT THE SWITCH!
CLIK.

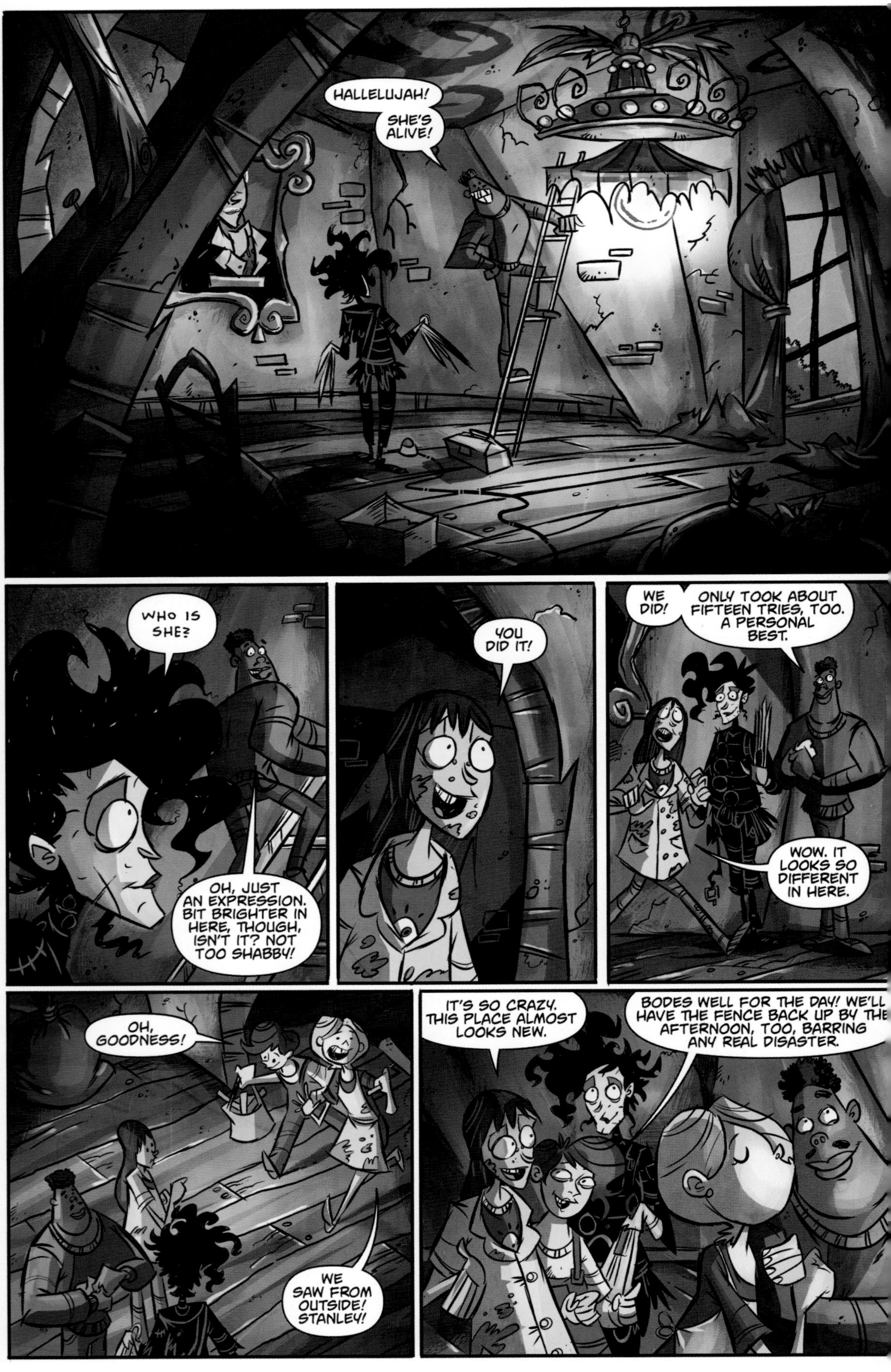
HALLELUJAH!
SHE'S ALIVE!
WHO IS SHE?
OH, JUST AN EXPRESSION. BIT BRIGHTER IN HERE, THOUGH, ISN'T IT? NOT TOO SHABBY!
YOU DID IT!
WE DID!
ONLY TOOK ABOUT FIFTEEN TRIES, TOO. A PERSONAL BEST.
WOW. IT LOOKS SO DIFFERENT IN HERE.
OH, GOODNESS!
WE SAW FROM OUTSIDE! STANLEY!
IT'S SO CRAZY. THIS PLACE ALMOST LOOKS NEW.
BODES WELL FOR THE DAY! WE'LL HAVE THE FENCE BACK UP BY THE AFTERNOON, TOO, BARRING ANY REAL DISASTER.

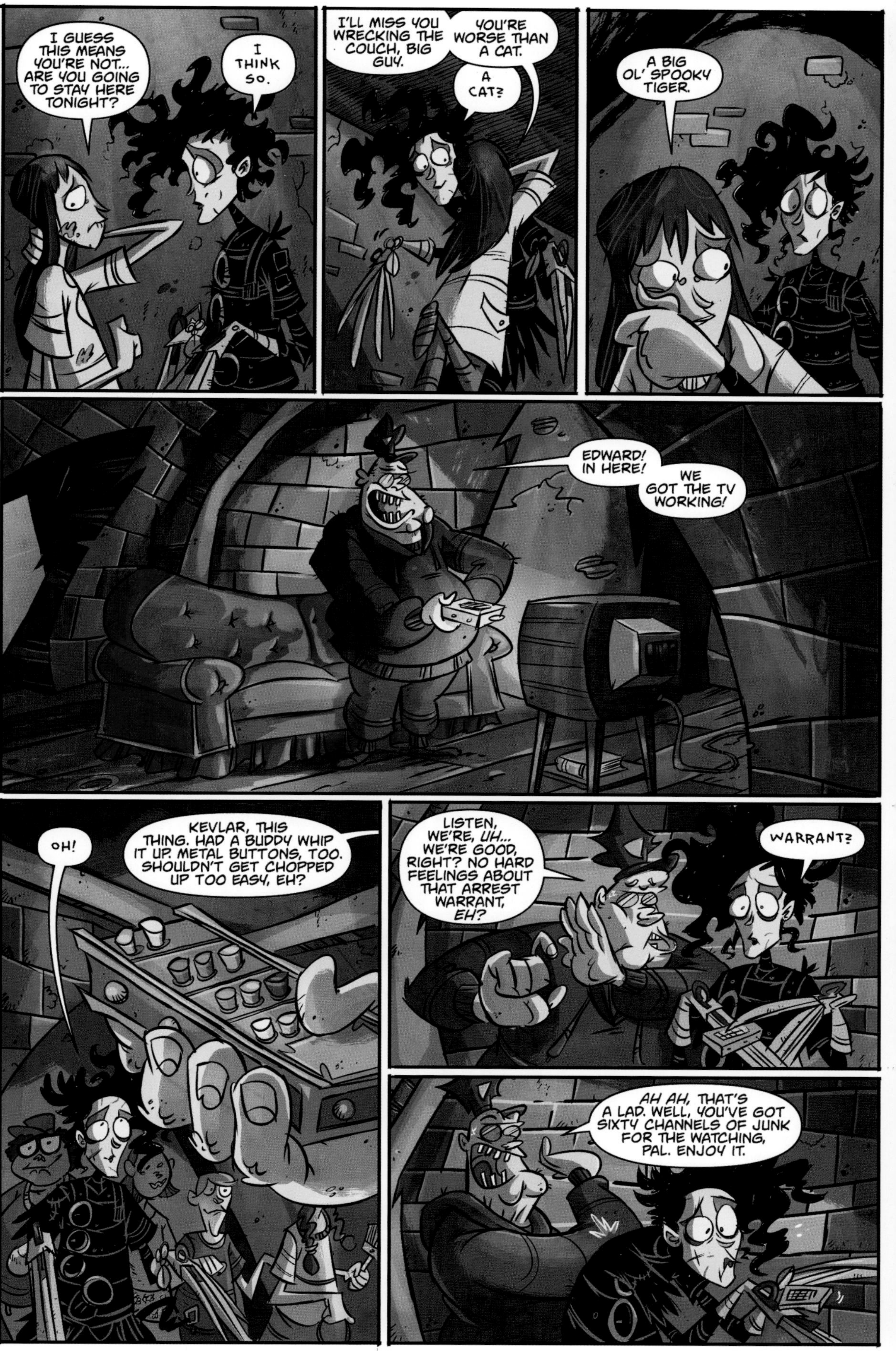
I GUESS THIS MEANS YOU'RE NOT... ARE YOU GOING TO STAY HERE TONIGHT?
I THINK SO.
I'LL MISS YOU WRECKING THE COUCH, BIG GUY.
YOU'RE WORSE THAN A CAT.
A CAT?
A BIG OL' SPOOKY TIGER.
EDWARD! IN HERE!
WE GOT THE TV WORKING!
OH!
KEVLAR, THIS THING. HAD A BUDDY WHIP IT UP. METAL BUTTONS, TOO. SHOULDN'T GET CHOPPED UP TOO EASY, EH?
LISTEN, WE'RE, UH... WE'RE GOOD, RIGHT? NO HARD FEELINGS ABOUT THAT ARREST WARRANT, EH?
WARRANT?
AH AH, THAT'S A LAD. WELL, YOU'VE GOT SIXTY CHANNELS OF JUNK FOR THE WATCHING, PAL. ENJOY IT.

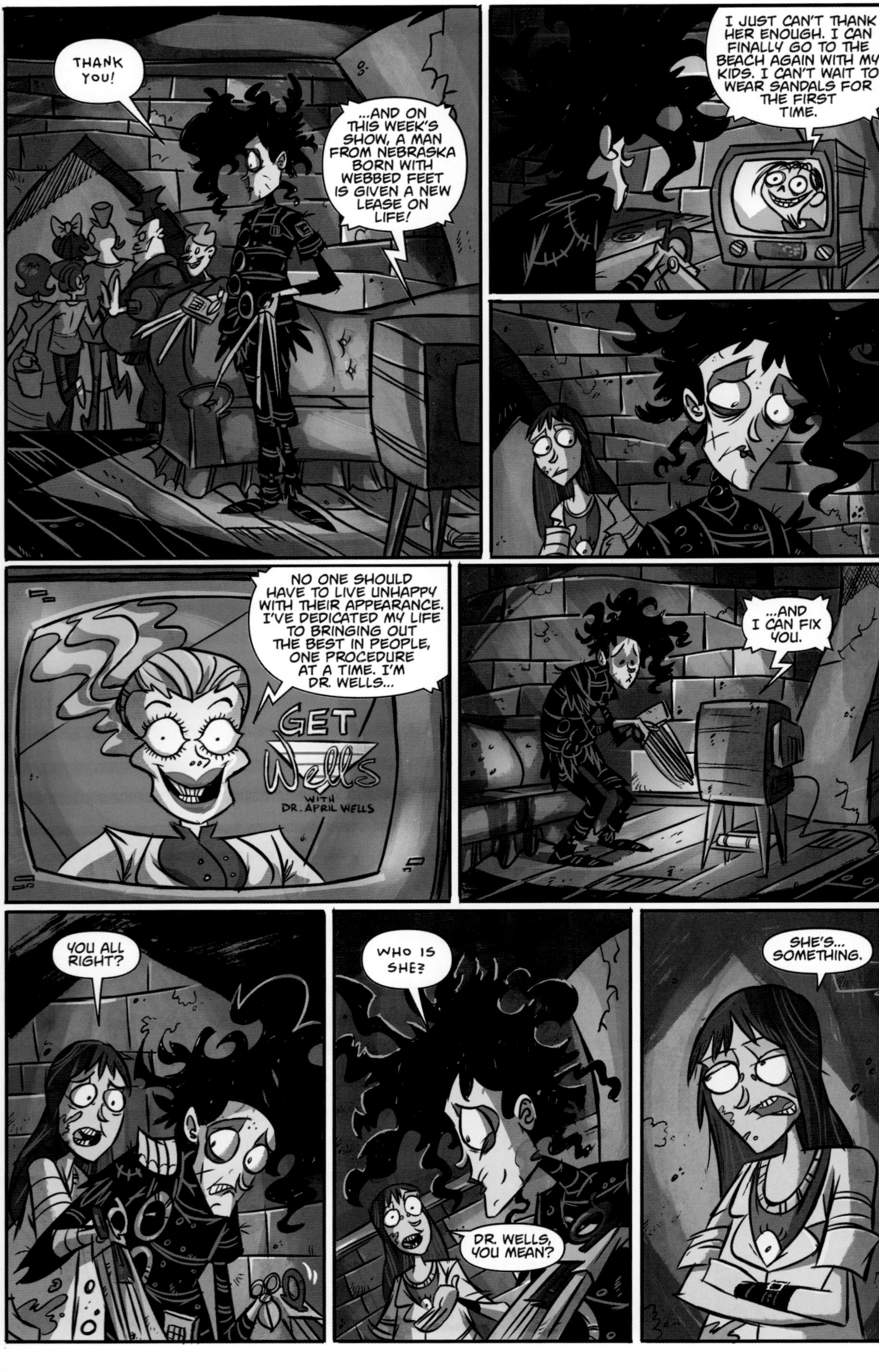
THANK YOU!
...AND ON THIS WEEK'S SHOW, A MAN FROM NEBRASKA BORN WITH WEBBED FEET IS GIVEN A NEW LEASE ON LIFE!
I JUST CAN'T THANK HER ENOUGH. I CAN FINALLY GO TO THE BEACH AGAIN WITH MY KIDS. I CAN'T WAIT TO WEAR SANDALS FOR THE FIRST TIME.
NO ONE SHOULD HAVE TO LIVE UNHAPPY WITH THEIR APPEARANCE. I'VE DEDICATED MY LIFE TO BRINGING OUT THE BEST IN PEOPLE, ONE PROCEDURE AT A TIME. I'M DR. WELLS...
GET Wells
WITH DR. APRIL WELLS
...AND I CAN FIX YOU.
YOU ALL RIGHT?
WHO IS SHE?
DR. WELLS, YOU MEAN?
SHE'S... SOMETHING.

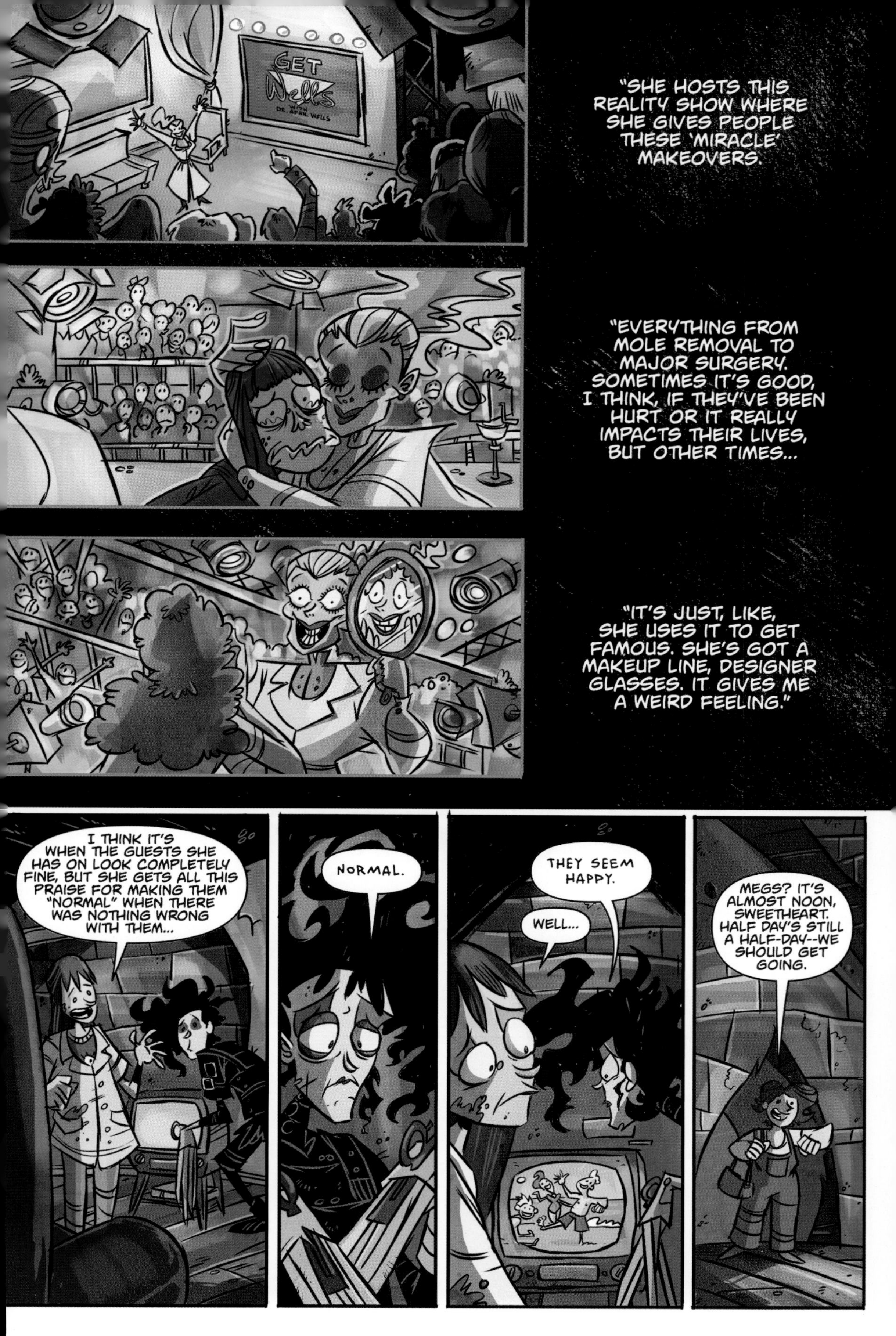
GET Wells
WITH DR. APRIL WELLS
"SHE HOSTS THIS REALITY SHOW WHERE SHE GIVES PEOPLE THESE 'MIRACLE' MAKEOVERS.
"EVERYTHING FROM MOLE REMOVAL TO MAJOR SURGERY. SOMETIMES IT'S GOOD, I THINK, IF THEY'VE BEEN HURT OR IT REALLY IMPACTS THEIR LIVES, BUT OTHER TIMES...
"IT'S JUST, LIKE, SHE USES IT TO GET FAMOUS. SHE'S GOT A MAKEUP LINE, DESIGNER GLASSES. IT GIVES ME A WEIRD FEELING."
I THINK IT'S WHEN THE GUESTS SHE HAS ON LOOK COMPLETELY FINE, BUT SHE GETS ALL THIS PRAISE FOR MAKING THEM "NORMAL" WHEN THERE WAS NOTHING WRONG WITH THEM...
NORMAL.
THEY SEEM HAPPY.
WELL...
MEGS? IT'S ALMOST NOON, SWEETHEART. HALF DAY'S STILL A HALF-DAY--WE SHOULD GET GOING.

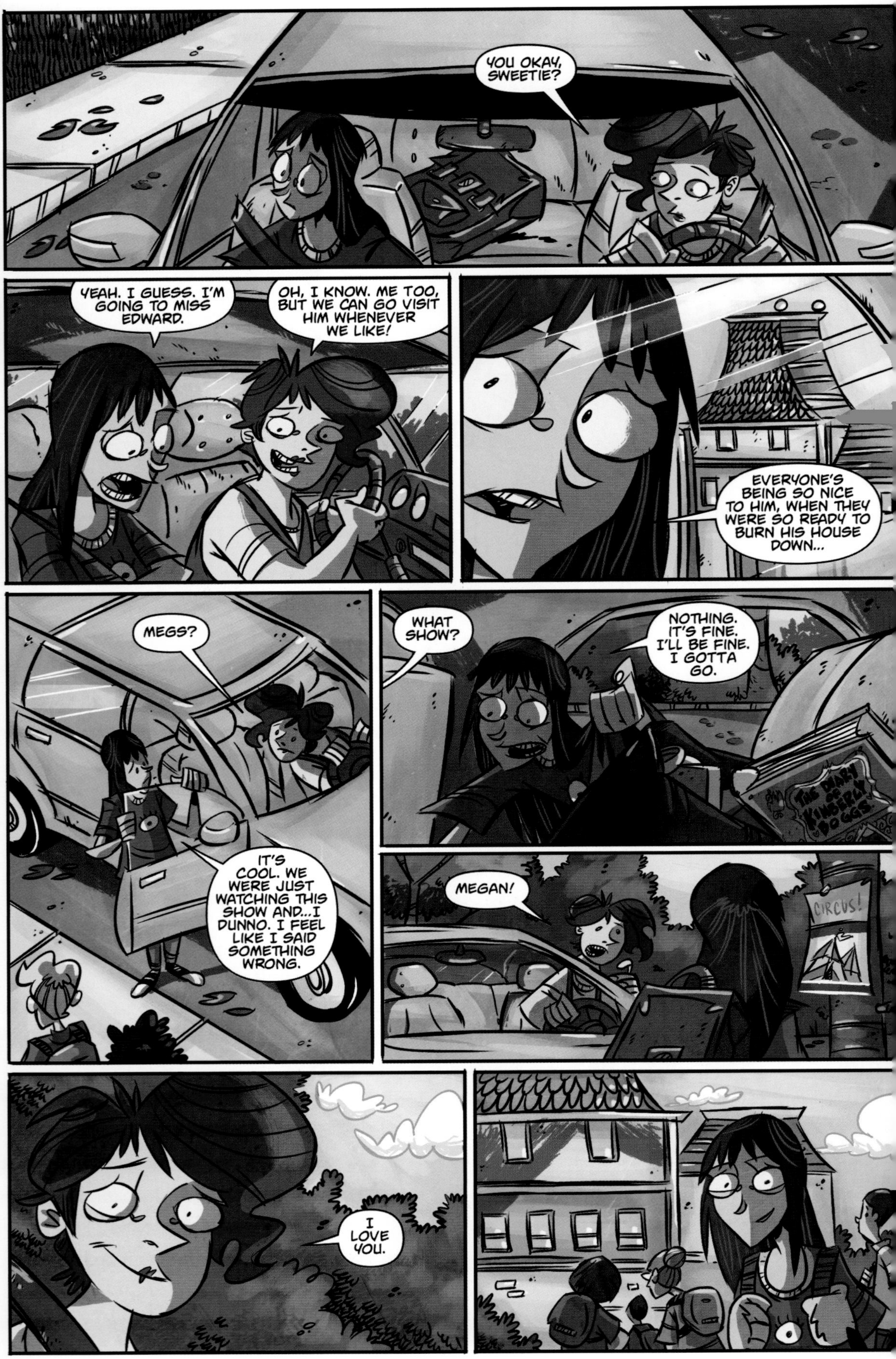

YOU OKAY, SWEETIE?
YEAH. I GUESS. I'M GOING TO MISS EDWARD.
OH, I KNOW. ME TOO, BUT WE CAN GO VISIT HIM WHENEVER WE LIKE!
EVERYONE'S BEING SO NICE TO HIM, WHEN THEY WERE SO READY TO BURN HIS HOUSE DOWN...
MEGS?
IT'S COOL. WE WERE JUST WATCHING THIS SHOW AND...I DUNNO. I FEEL LIKE I SAID SOMETHING WRONG.
WHAT SHOW?
NOTHING. IT'S FINE. I'LL BE FINE. I GOTTA GO.
THE DIARY OF KIMBERLY DOGGS
MEGAN!
CIRCUS!
I LOVE YOU.

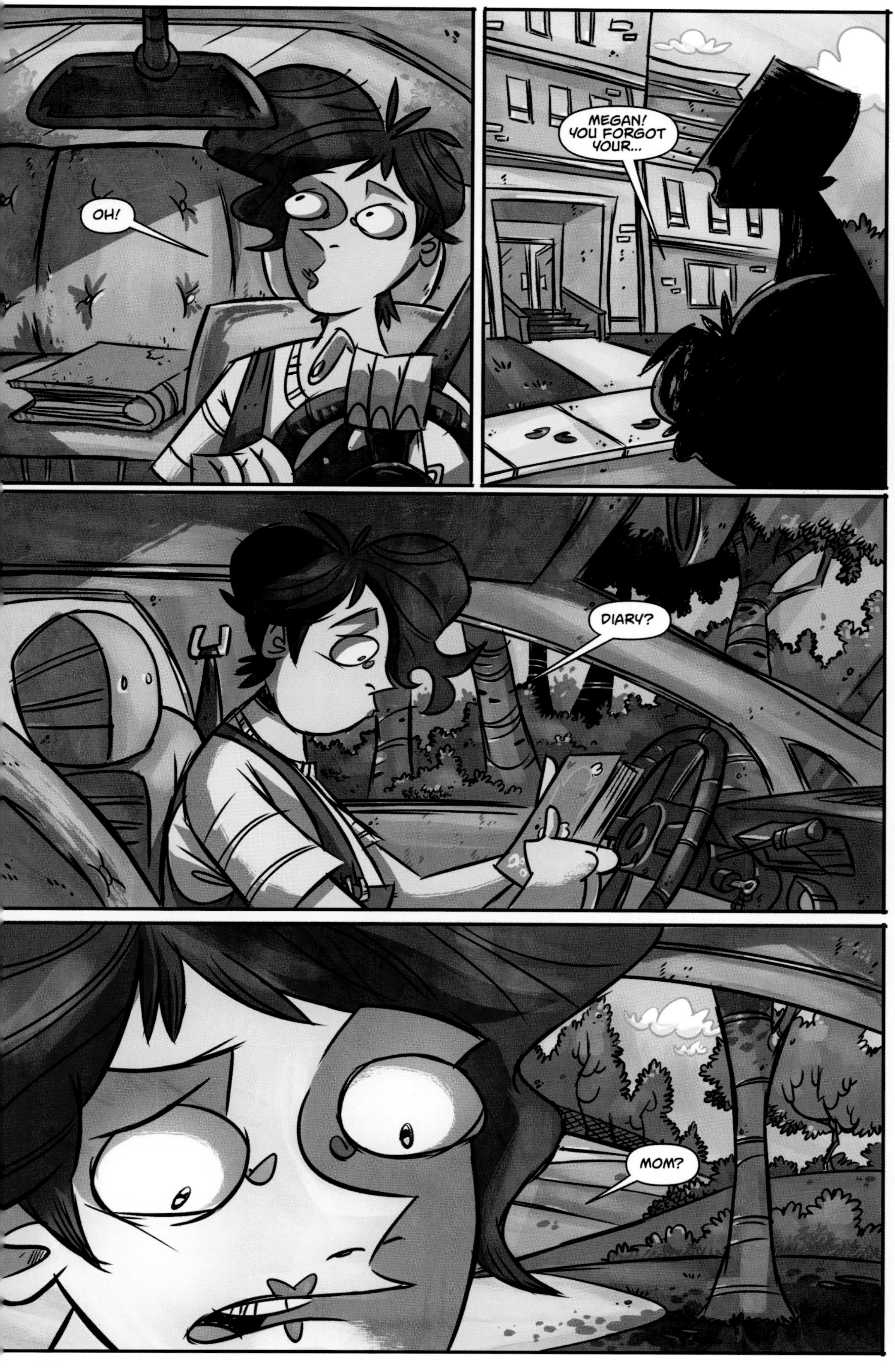
OH!
MEGAN! YOU FORGOT YOUR...
DIARY?
MOM?

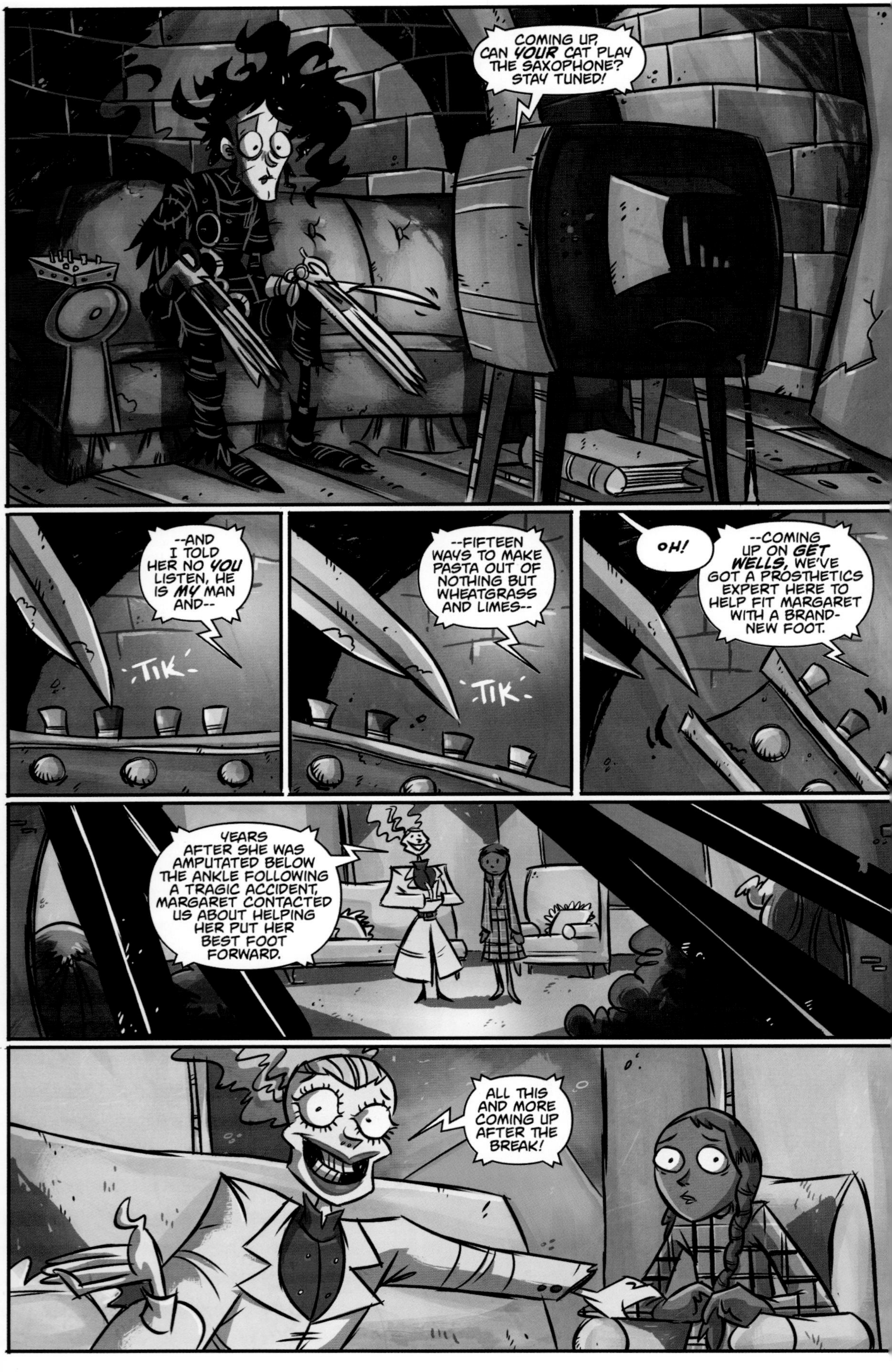
COMING UP, CAN YOUR CAT PLAY THE SAXOPHONE? STAY TUNED!
--AND I TOLD HER NO YOU LISTEN, HE IS MY MAN AND--
TIK
--FIFTEEN WAYS TO MAKE PASTA OUT OF NOTHING BUT WHEATGRASS AND LIMES--
TIK
OH!
--COMING UP ON GET WELLS, WE'VE GOT A PROSTHETICS EXPERT HERE TO HELP FIT MARGARET WITH A BRAND-NEW FOOT.
YEARS AFTER SHE WAS AMPUTATED BELOW THE ANKLE FOLLOWING A TRAGIC ACCIDENT, MARGARET CONTACTED US ABOUT HELPING HER PUT HER BEST FOOT FORWARD.
ALL THIS AND MORE COMING UP AFTER THE BREAK!

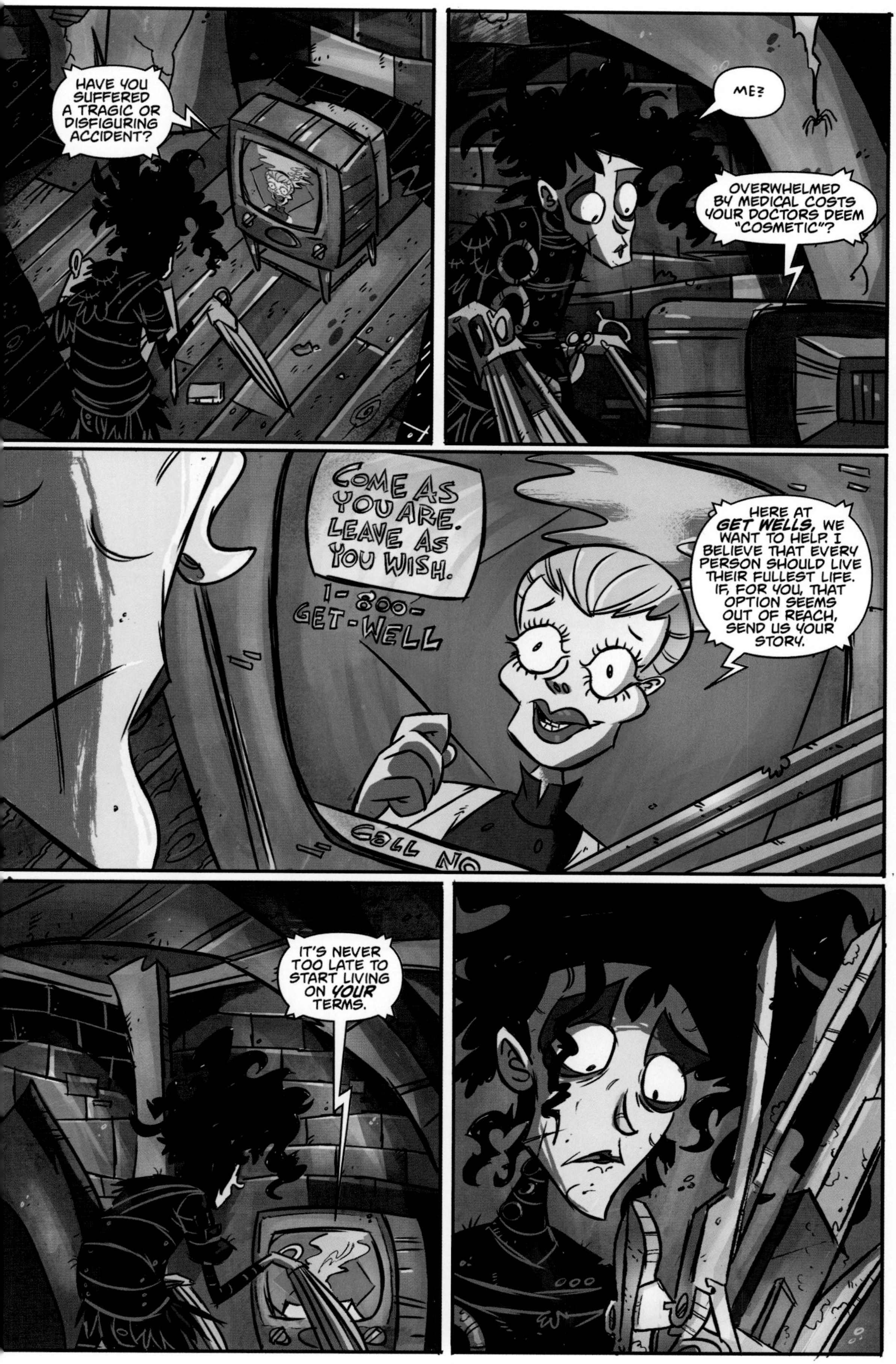
HAVE YOU SUFFERED A TRAGIC OR DISFIGURING ACCIDENT?
ME?
OVERWHELMED BY MEDICAL COSTS YOUR DOCTORS DEEM "COSMETIC"?
COME AS YOU ARE. LEAVE AS YOU WISH.
1-800-GET-WELL
HERE AT **GET WELLS**, WE WANT TO HELP. I BELIEVE THAT EVERY PERSON SHOULD LIVE THEIR FULLEST LIFE. IF, FOR YOU, THAT OPTION SEEMS OUT OF REACH, SEND US YOUR STORY.
CALL NO
IT'S NEVER TOO LATE TO START LIVING ON ***YOUR*** TERMS.

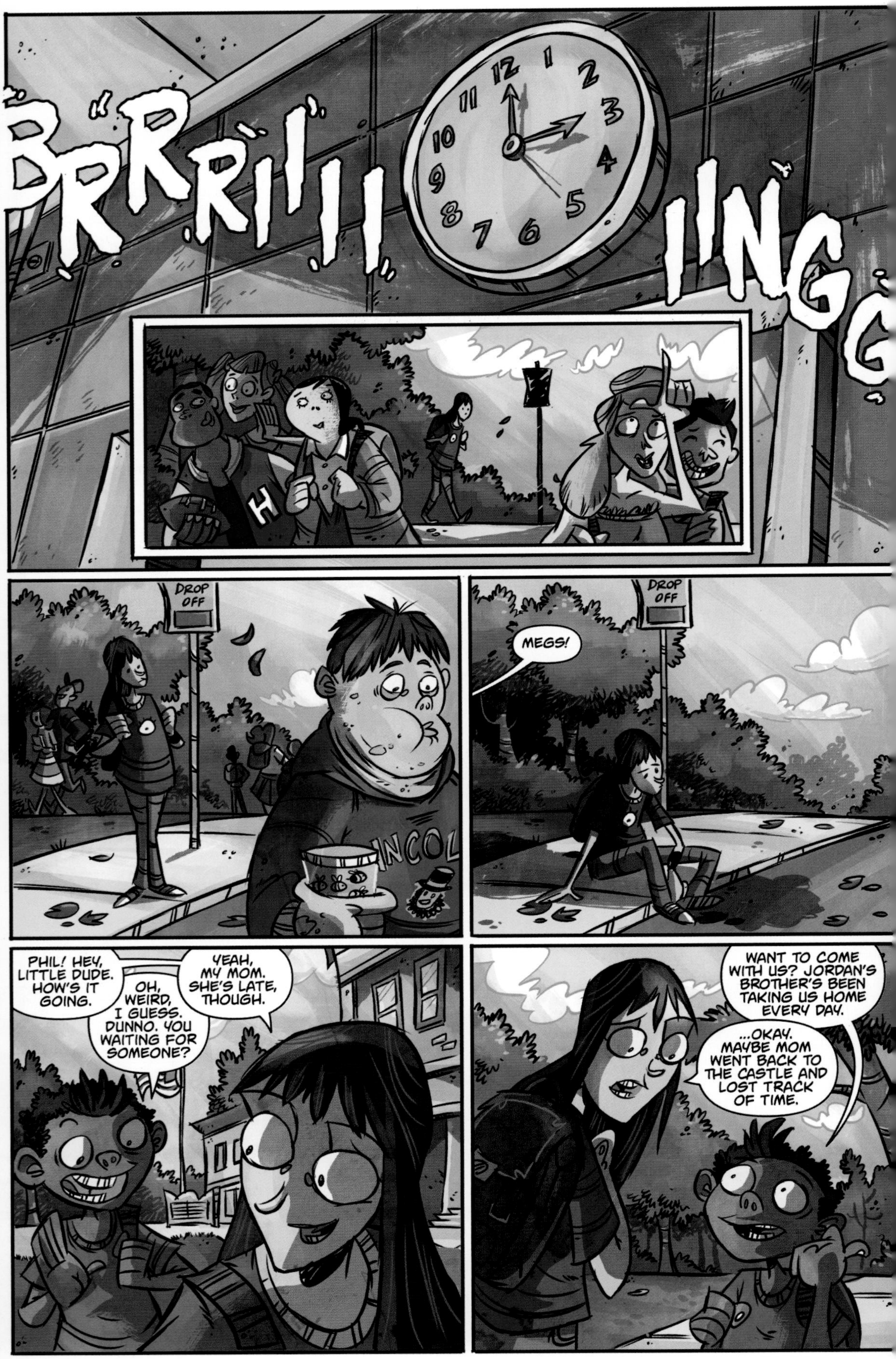

BRRRIIIIIINGG
DROP OFF
DROP OFF
MEGS!
PHIL! HEY, LITTLE DUDE. HOW'S IT GOING.
OH, WEIRD, I GUESS. DUNNO. YOU WAITING FOR SOMEONE?
YEAH, MY MOM. SHE'S LATE, THOUGH.
WANT TO COME WITH US? JORDAN'S BROTHER'S BEEN TAKING US HOME EVERY DAY.
...OKAY. MAYBE MOM WENT BACK TO THE CASTLE AND LOST TRACK OF TIME.

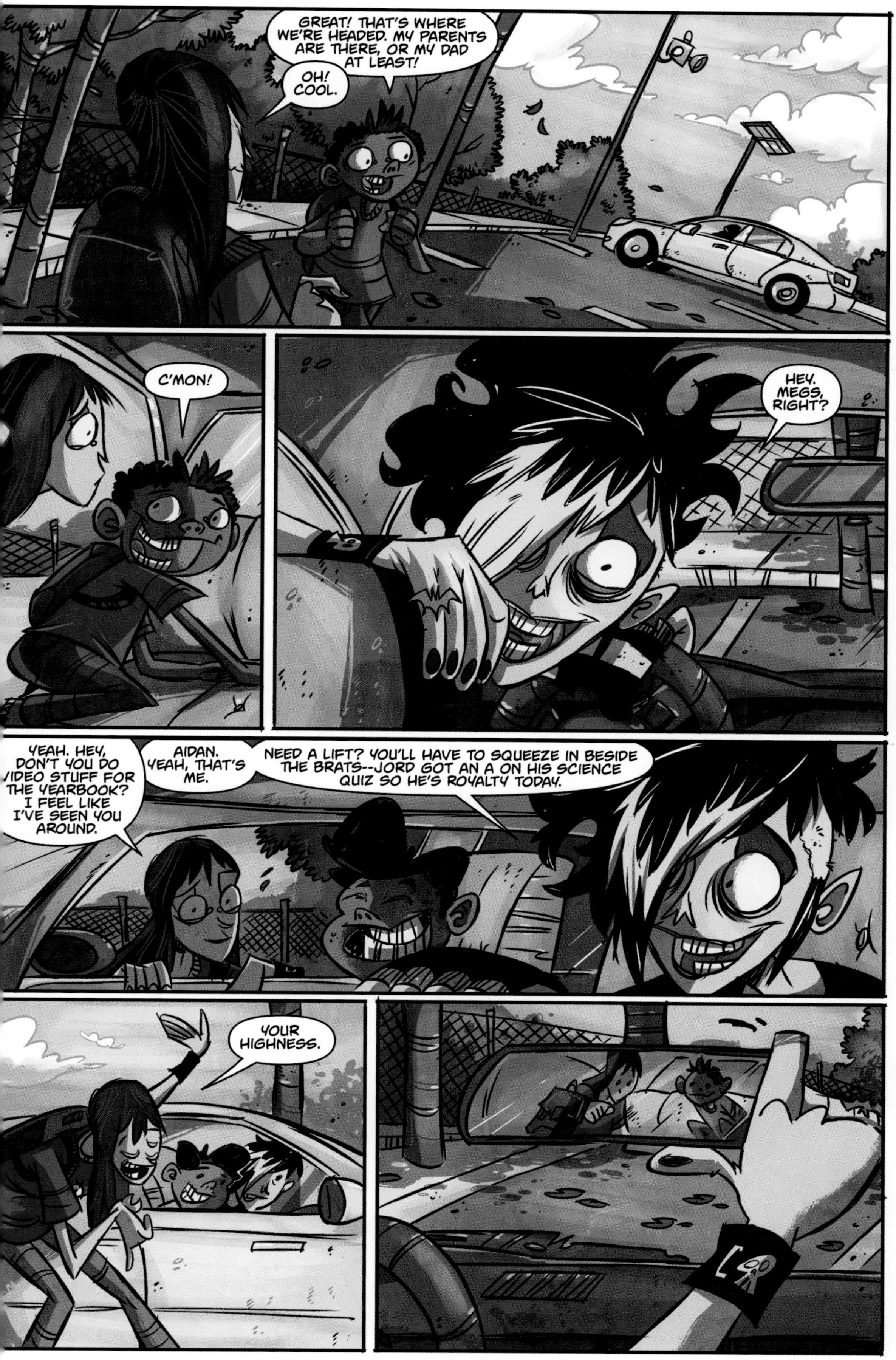
GREAT! THAT'S WHERE WE'RE HEADED. MY PARENTS ARE THERE, OR MY DAD AT LEAST!
OH! COOL.
C'MON!
HEY. MEGS, RIGHT?
YEAH. HEY, DON'T YOU DO VIDEO STUFF FOR THE YEARBOOK? I FEEL LIKE I'VE SEEN YOU AROUND.
AIDAN. YEAH, THAT'S ME.
NEED A LIFT? YOU'LL HAVE TO SQUEEZE IN BESIDE THE BRATS--JORD GOT AN A ON HIS SCIENCE QUIZ SO HE'S ROYALTY TODAY.
YOUR HIGHNESS.

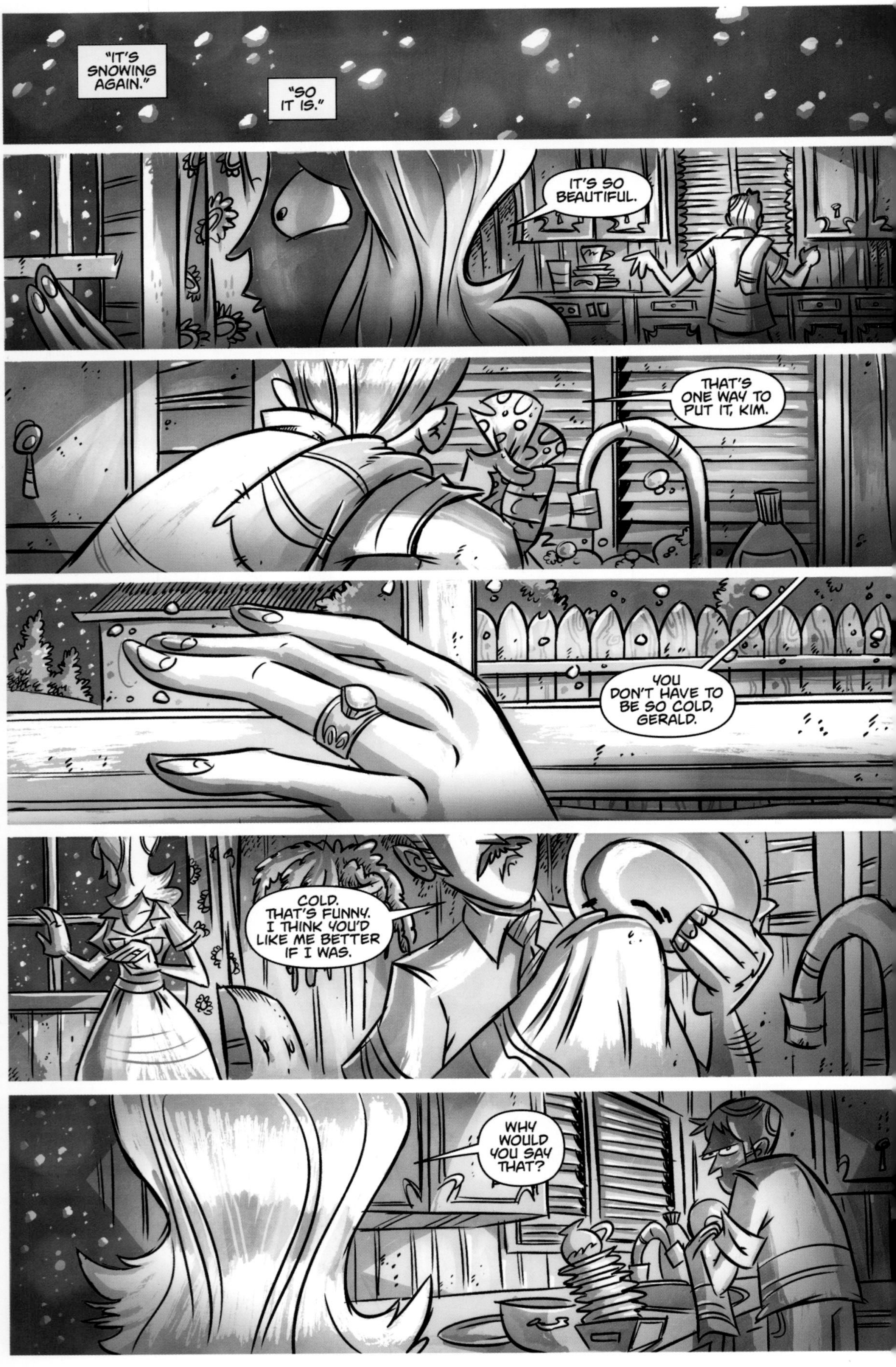
"IT'S SNOWING AGAIN."
"SO IT IS."
IT'S SO BEAUTIFUL.
THAT'S ONE WAY TO PUT IT, KIM.
YOU DON'T HAVE TO BE SO COLD, GERALD.
COLD. THAT'S FUNNY. I THINK YOU'D LIKE ME BETTER IF I WAS.
WHY WOULD YOU SAY THAT?

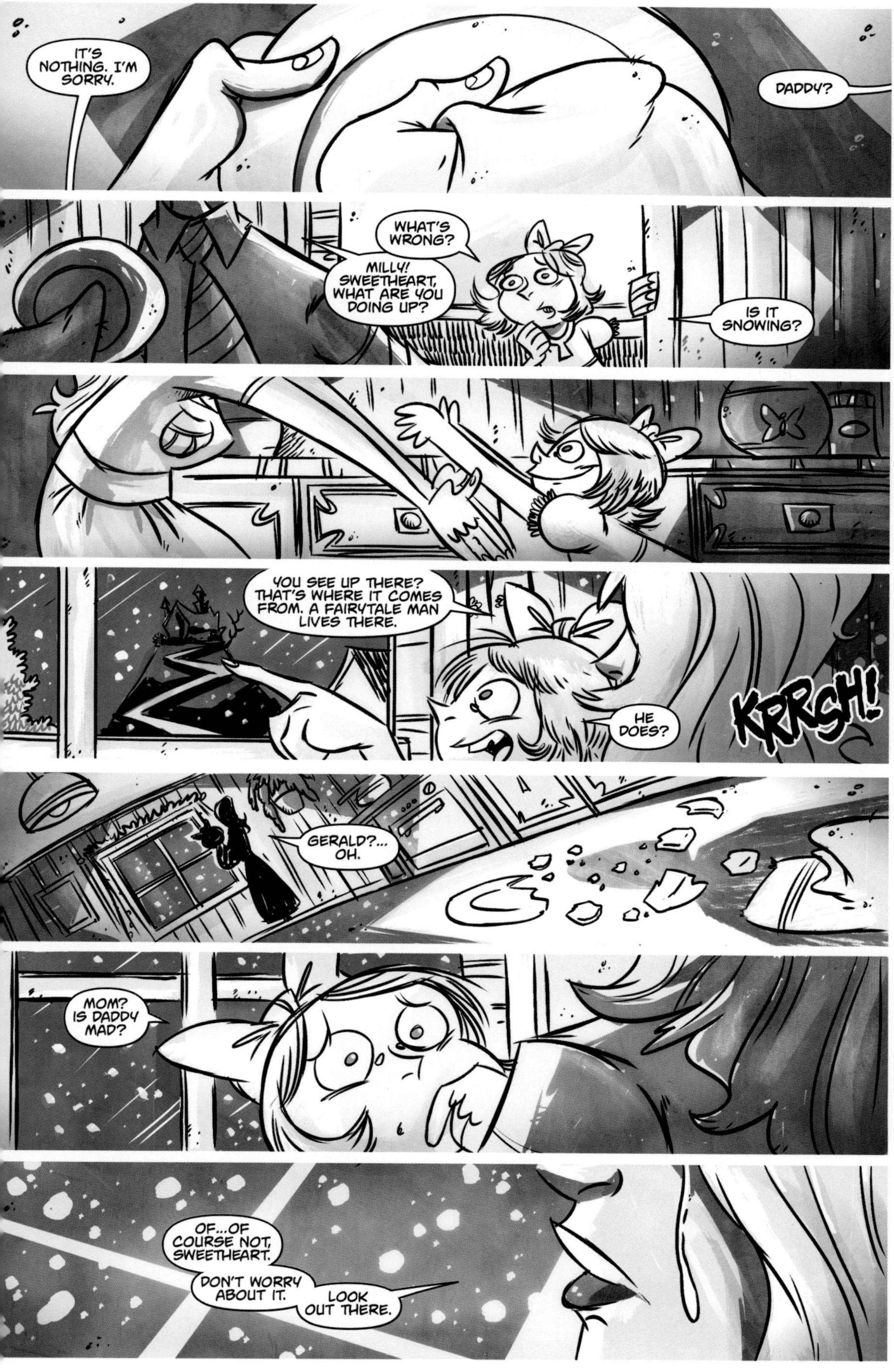
IT'S NOTHING. I'M SORRY.
DADDY?
WHAT'S WRONG?
MILLY! SWEETHEART, WHAT ARE YOU DOING UP?
IS IT SNOWING?
YOU SEE UP THERE? THAT'S WHERE IT COMES FROM. A FAIRYTALE MAN LIVES THERE.
HE DOES?
KRRSH!
GERALD?... OH.
MOM? IS DADDY MAD?
OF...OF COURSE NOT, SWEETHEART.
DON'T WORRY ABOUT IT.
LOOK OUT THERE.

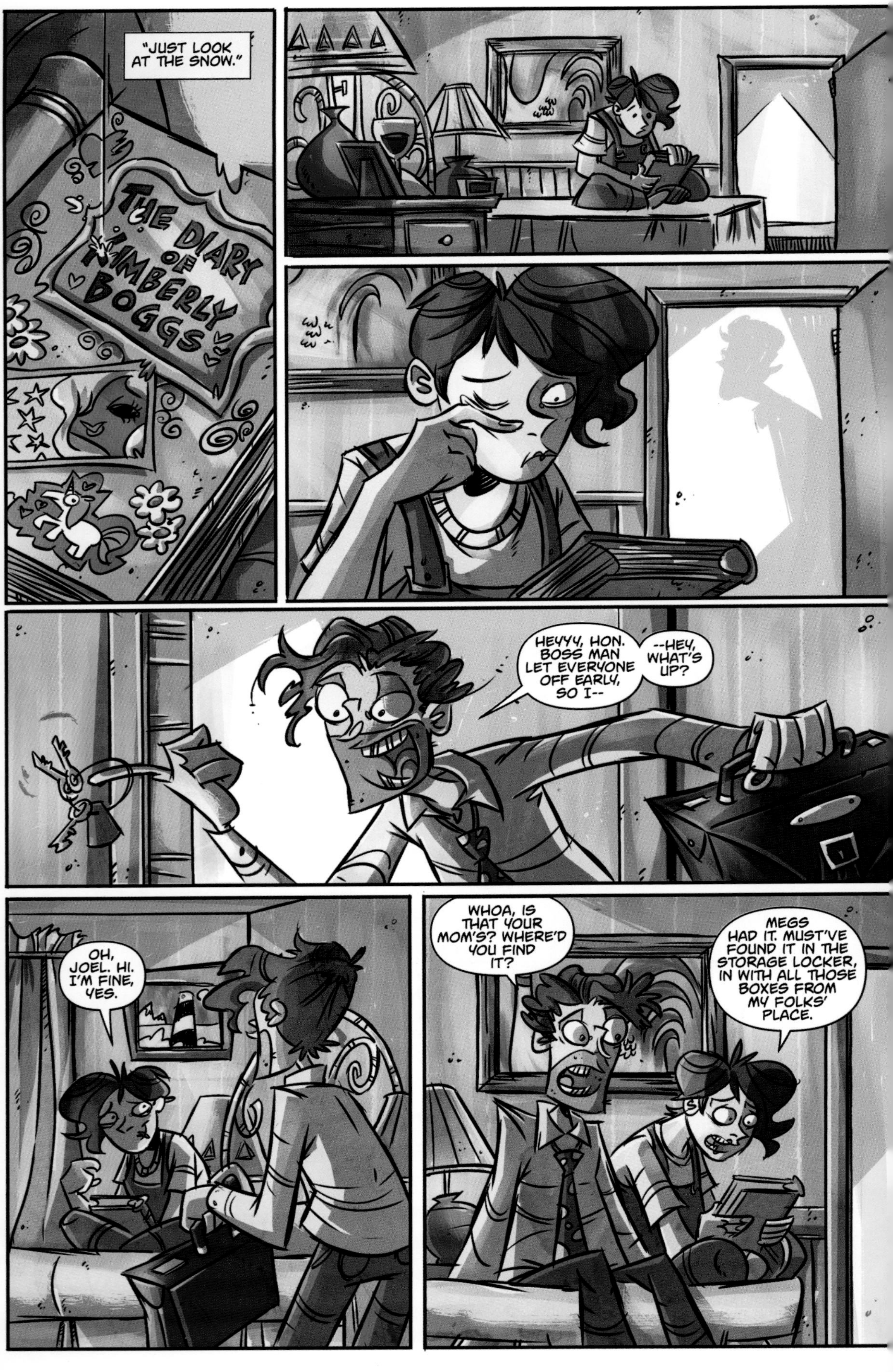
"JUST LOOK AT THE SNOW."
THE DIARY OF KIMBERLY BOGGS
HEYYY, HON. BOSS MAN LET EVERYONE OFF EARLY, SO I--
--HEY, WHAT'S UP?
OH, JOEL. HI. I'M FINE, YES.
WHOA, IS THAT YOUR MOM'S? WHERE'D YOU FIND IT?
MEGS HAD IT. MUST'VE FOUND IT IN THE STORAGE LOCKER, IN WITH ALL THOSE BOXES FROM MY FOLKS' PLACE.

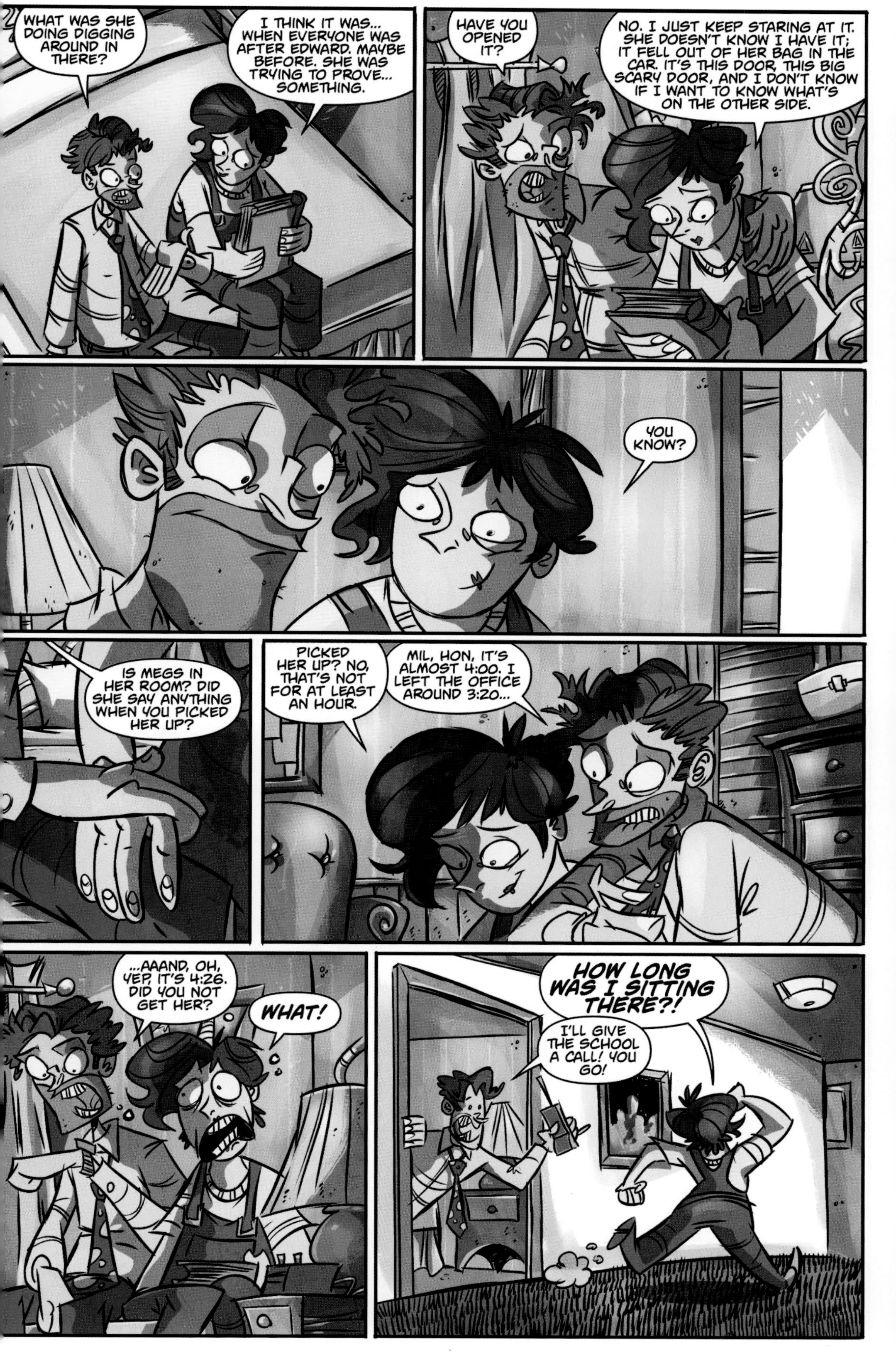
WHAT WAS SHE DOING DIGGING AROUND IN THERE?
I THINK IT WAS... WHEN EVERYONE WAS AFTER EDWARD. MAYBE BEFORE. SHE WAS TRYING TO PROVE... SOMETHING.
HAVE YOU OPENED IT?
NO. I JUST KEEP STARING AT IT. SHE DOESN'T KNOW I HAVE IT; IT FELL OUT OF HER BAG IN THE CAR. IT'S THIS DOOR, THIS BIG SCARY DOOR, AND I DON'T KNOW IF I WANT TO KNOW WHAT'S ON THE OTHER SIDE.
YOU KNOW?
IS MEGS IN HER ROOM? DID SHE SAY ANYTHING WHEN YOU PICKED HER UP?
PICKED HER UP? NO, THAT'S NOT FOR AT LEAST AN HOUR.
MIL, HON, IT'S ALMOST 4:00. I LEFT THE OFFICE AROUND 3:20...
...AAAND, OH, YEP, IT'S 4:26. DID YOU NOT GET HER?
WHAT!
HOW LONG WAS I SITTING THERE?!
I'LL GIVE THE SCHOOL A CALL! YOU GO!

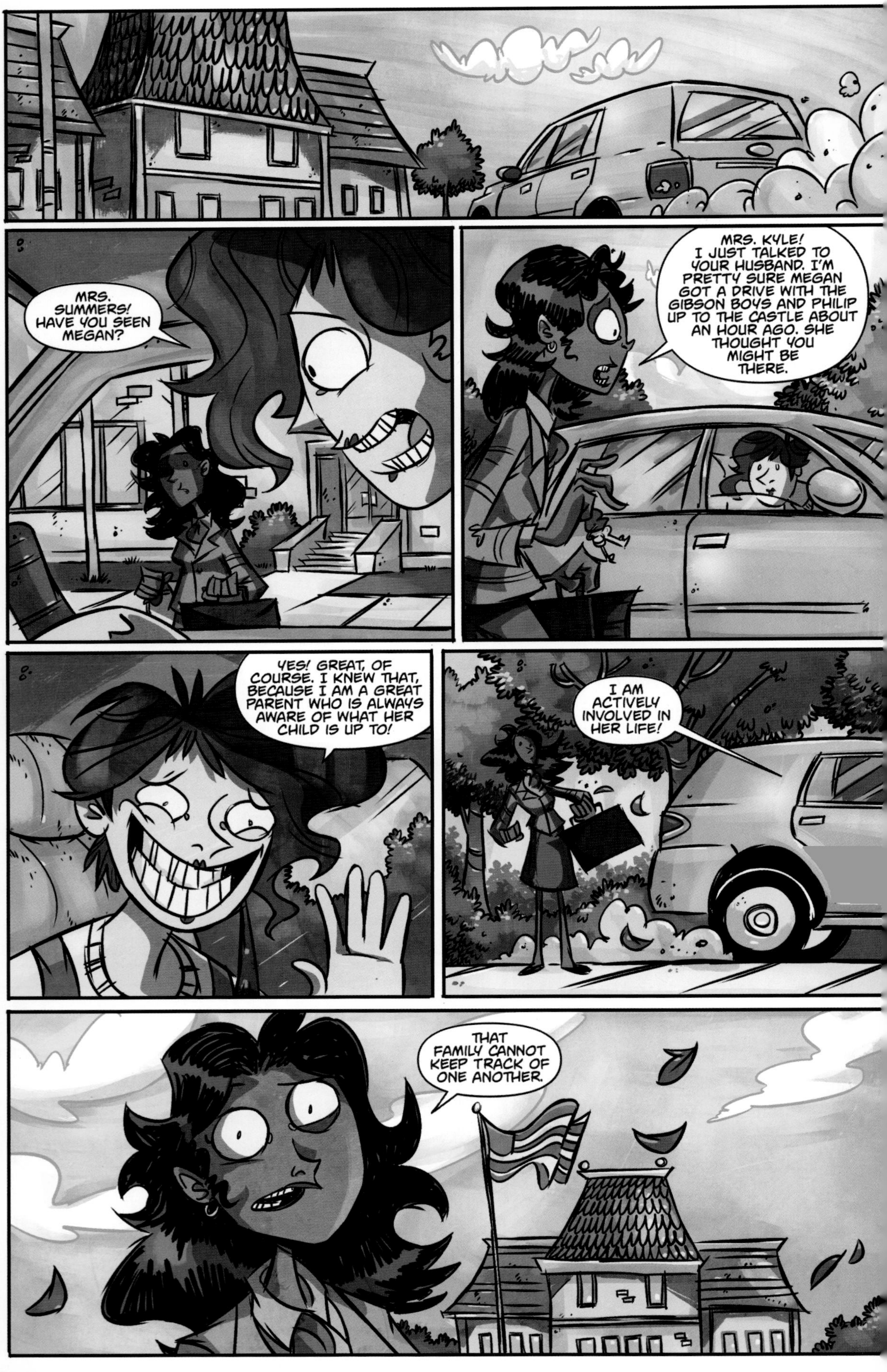
MRS. SUMMERS! HAVE YOU SEEN MEGAN?
MRS. KYLE! I JUST TALKED TO YOUR HUSBAND. I'M PRETTY SURE MEGAN GOT A DRIVE WITH THE GIBSON BOYS AND PHILIP UP TO THE CASTLE ABOUT AN HOUR AGO. SHE THOUGHT YOU MIGHT BE THERE.
YES! GREAT, OF COURSE. I KNEW THAT, BECAUSE I AM A GREAT PARENT WHO IS ALWAYS AWARE OF WHAT HER CHILD IS UP TO!
I AM ACTIVELY INVOLVED IN HER LIFE!
THAT FAMILY CANNOT KEEP TRACK OF ONE ANOTHER.

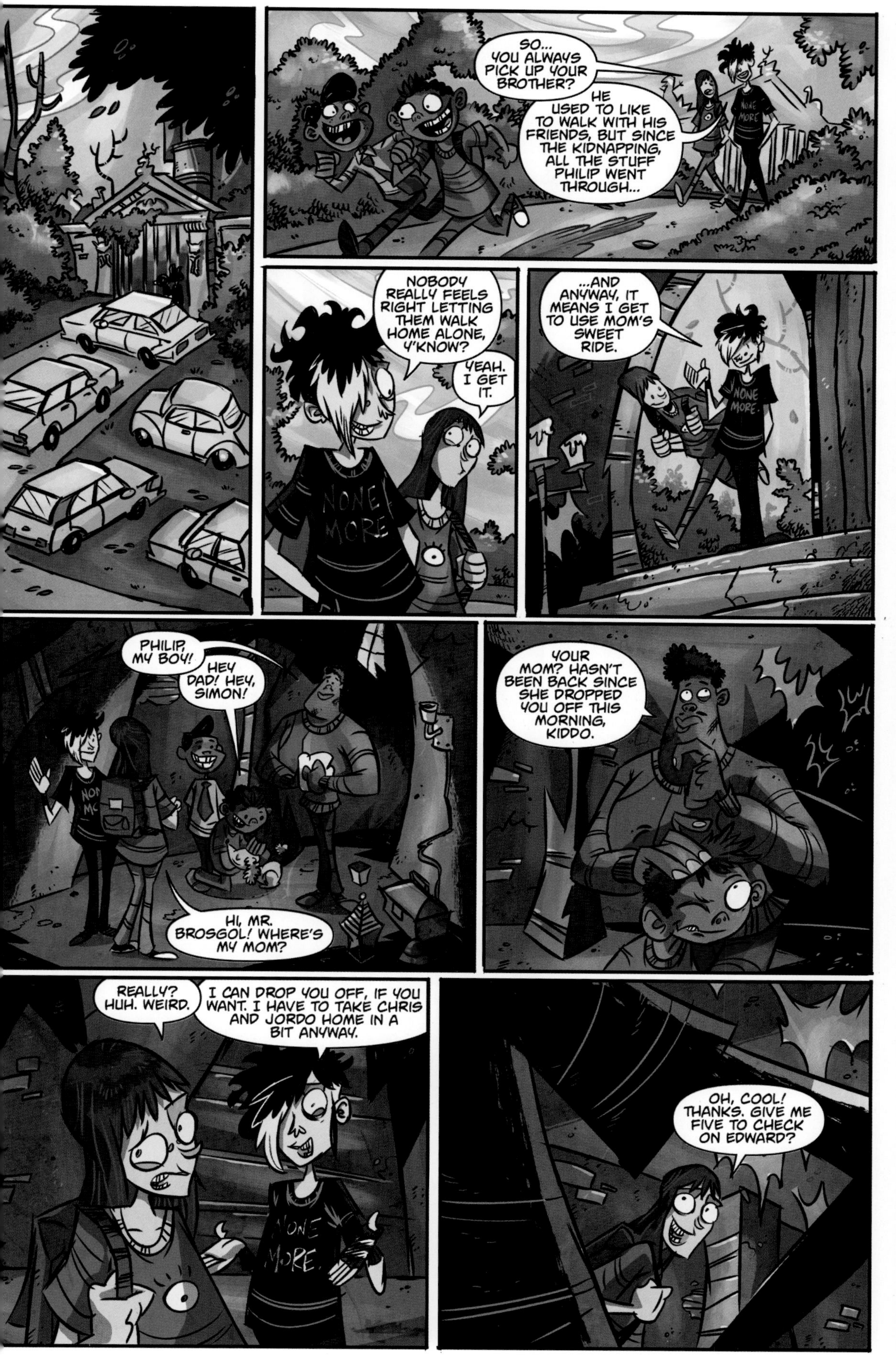

SO... YOU ALWAYS PICK UP YOUR BROTHER?
HE USED TO LIKE TO WALK WITH HIS FRIENDS, BUT SINCE THE KIDNAPPING, ALL THE STUFF PHILIP WENT THROUGH...
NONE MORE
NOBODY REALLY FEELS RIGHT LETTING THEM WALK HOME ALONE, Y'KNOW?
YEAH. I GET IT.
NONE MORE
...AND ANYWAY, IT MEANS I GET TO USE MOM'S SWEET RIDE.
NONE MORE.
PHILIP, MY BOY!
HEY DAD! HEY, SIMON!
HI, MR. BROSGOL! WHERE'S MY MOM?
YOUR MOM? HASN'T BEEN BACK SINCE SHE DROPPED YOU OFF THIS MORNING, KIDDO.
REALLY? HUH. WEIRD.
I CAN DROP YOU OFF, IF YOU WANT. I HAVE TO TAKE CHRIS AND JORDO HOME IN A BIT ANYWAY.
NONE MORE.
OH, COOL! THANKS. GIVE ME FIVE TO CHECK ON EDWARD?

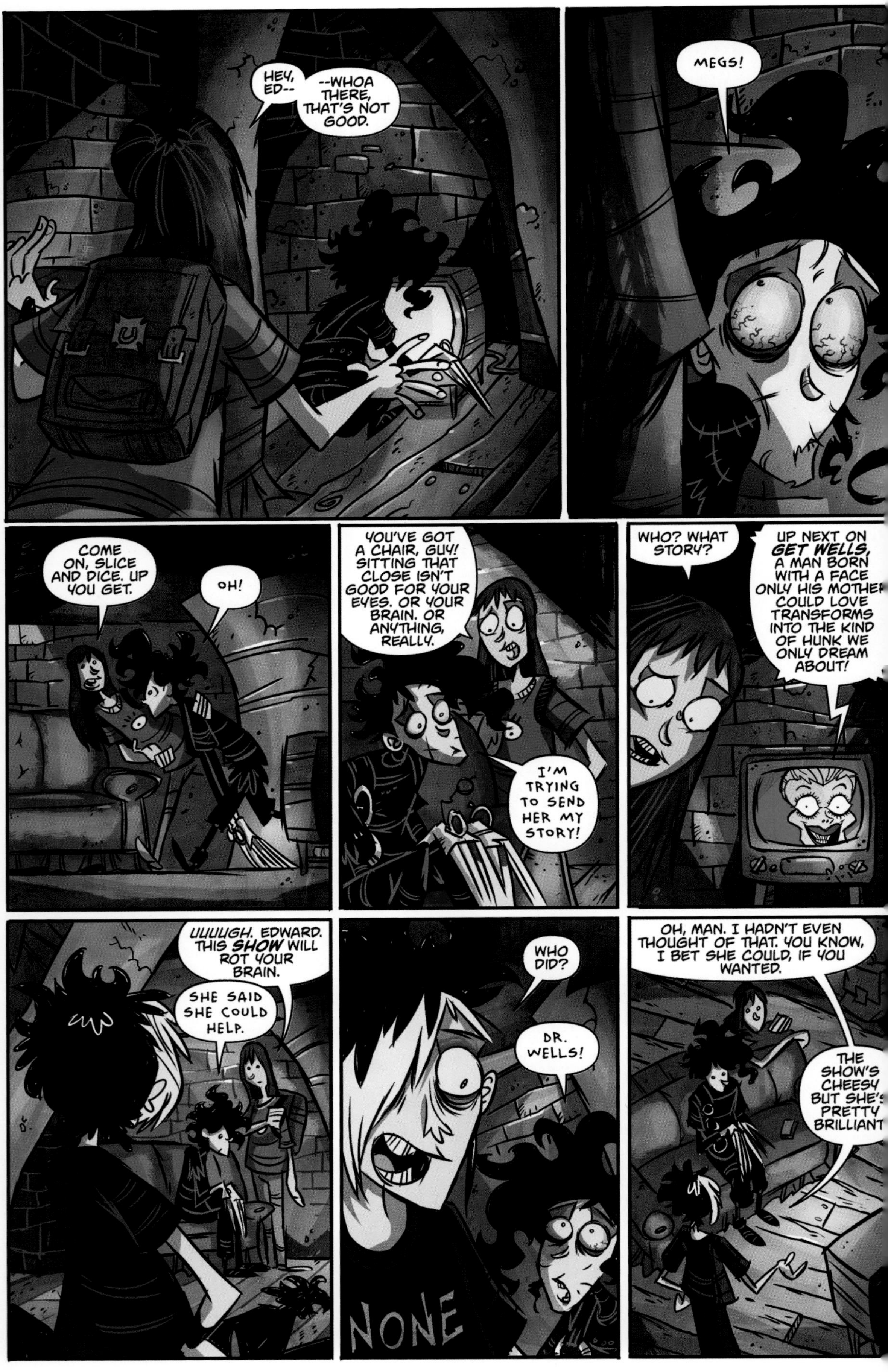
HEY, ED--
--WHOA THERE, THAT'S NOT GOOD.
MEGS!
COME ON, SLICE AND DICE. UP YOU GET.
OH!
YOU'VE GOT A CHAIR, GUY! SITTING THAT CLOSE ISN'T GOOD FOR YOUR EYES. OR YOUR BRAIN. OR ANYTHING, REALLY.
I'M TRYING TO SEND HER MY STORY!
WHO? WHAT STORY?
UP NEXT ON GET WELLS, A MAN BORN WITH A FACE ONLY HIS MOTHER COULD LOVE TRANSFORMS INTO THE KIND OF HUNK WE ONLY DREAM ABOUT!
UUUUGH. EDWARD. THIS SHOW WILL ROT YOUR BRAIN.
SHE SAID SHE COULD HELP.
WHO DID?
DR. WELLS!
NONE
OH, MAN. I HADN'T EVEN THOUGHT OF THAT. YOU KNOW, I BET SHE COULD, IF YOU WANTED.
THE SHOW'S CHEESY BUT SHE'S PRETTY BRILLIANT

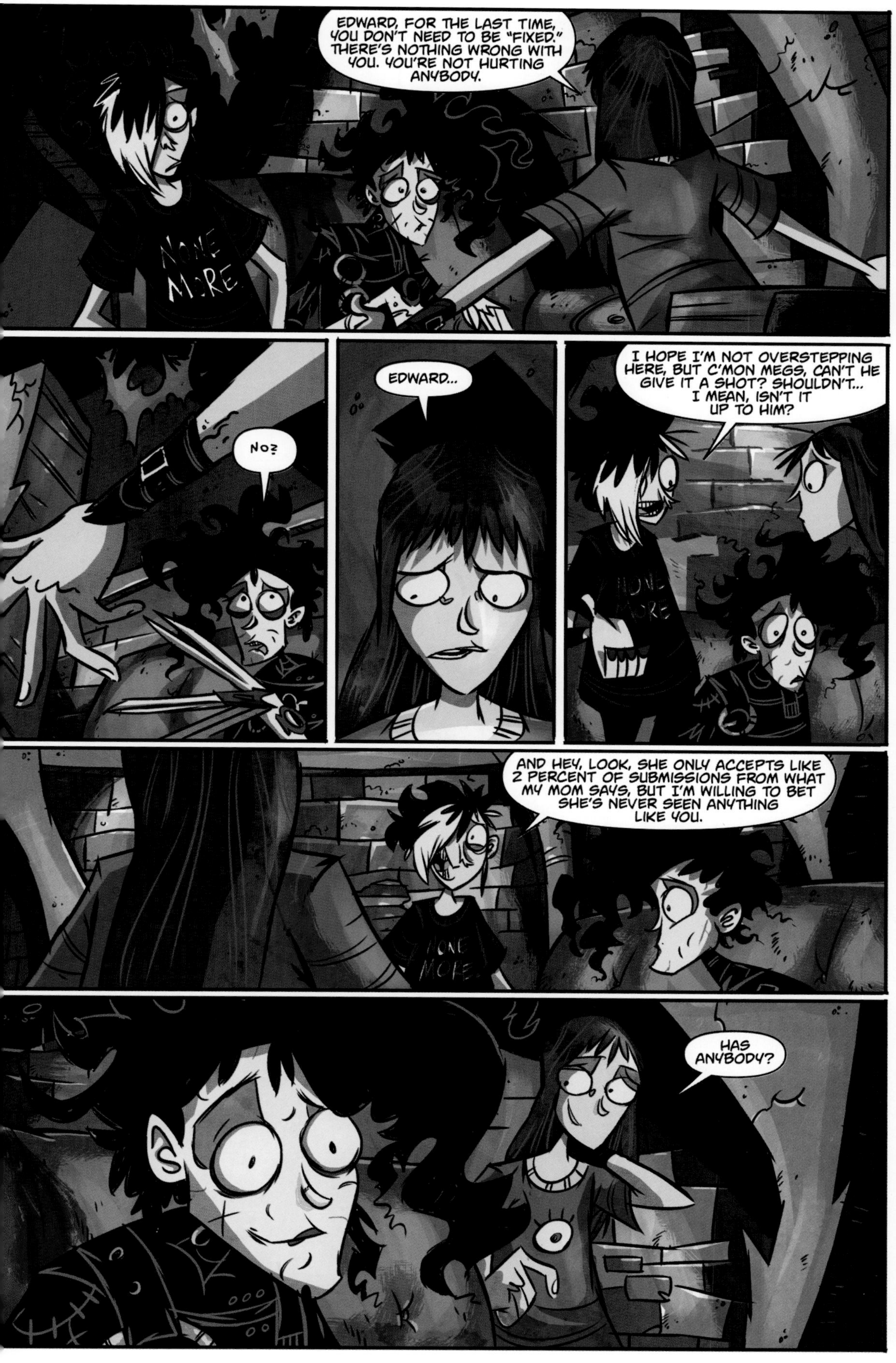
EDWARD, FOR THE LAST TIME, YOU DON'T NEED TO BE "FIXED." THERE'S NOTHING WRONG WITH YOU. YOU'RE NOT HURTING ANYBODY.
NO?
EDWARD...
I HOPE I'M NOT OVERSTEPPING HERE, BUT C'MON MEGS, CAN'T HE GIVE IT A SHOT? SHOULDN'T... I MEAN, ISN'T IT UP TO HIM?
NONE MORE
AND HEY, LOOK, SHE ONLY ACCEPTS LIKE 2 PERCENT OF SUBMISSIONS FROM WHAT MY MOM SAYS, BUT I'M WILLING TO BET SHE'S NEVER SEEN ANYTHING LIKE YOU.
HAS ANYBODY?

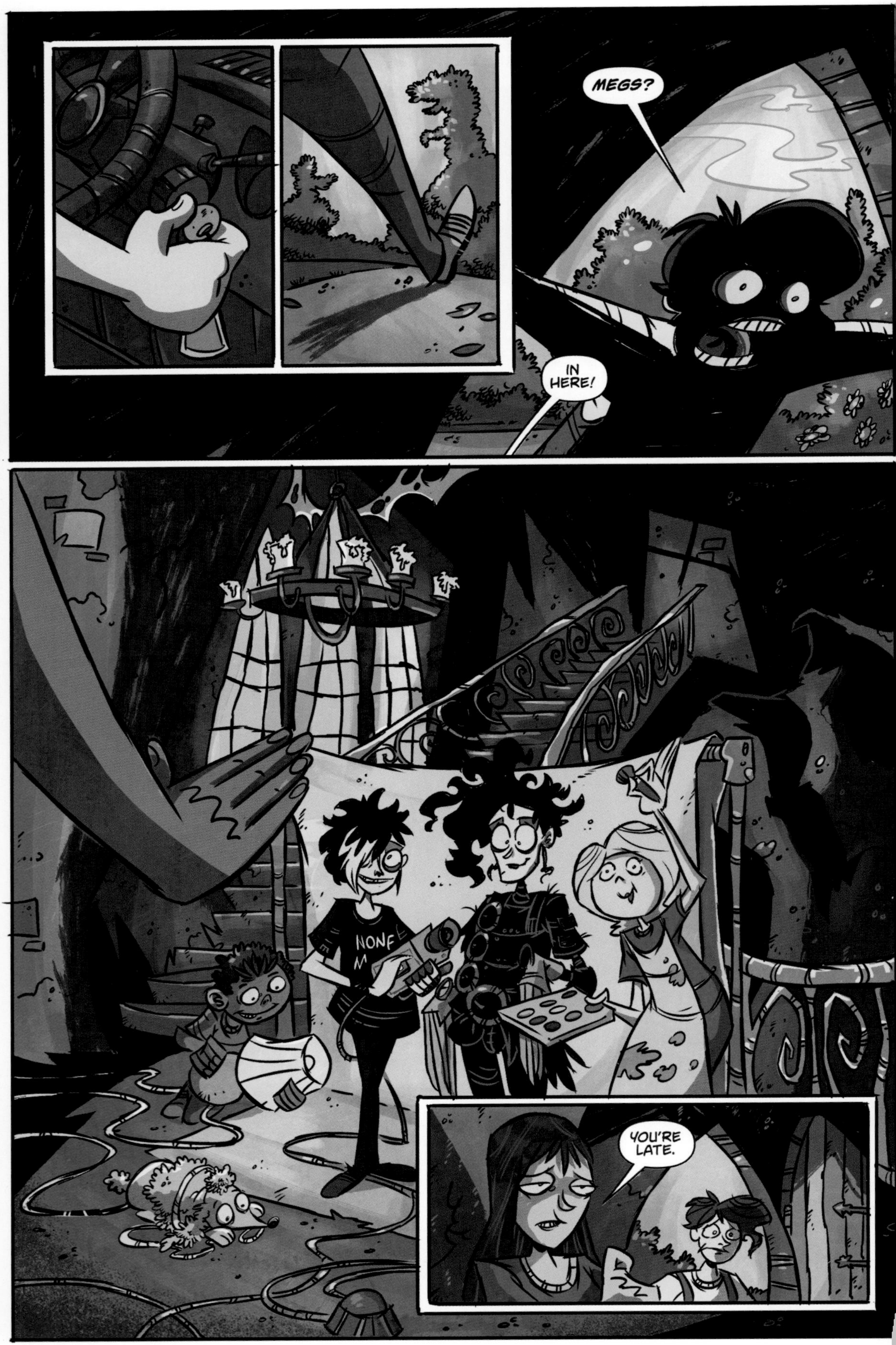
MEGS?
IN HERE!
NONF
M
YOU'RE LATE.

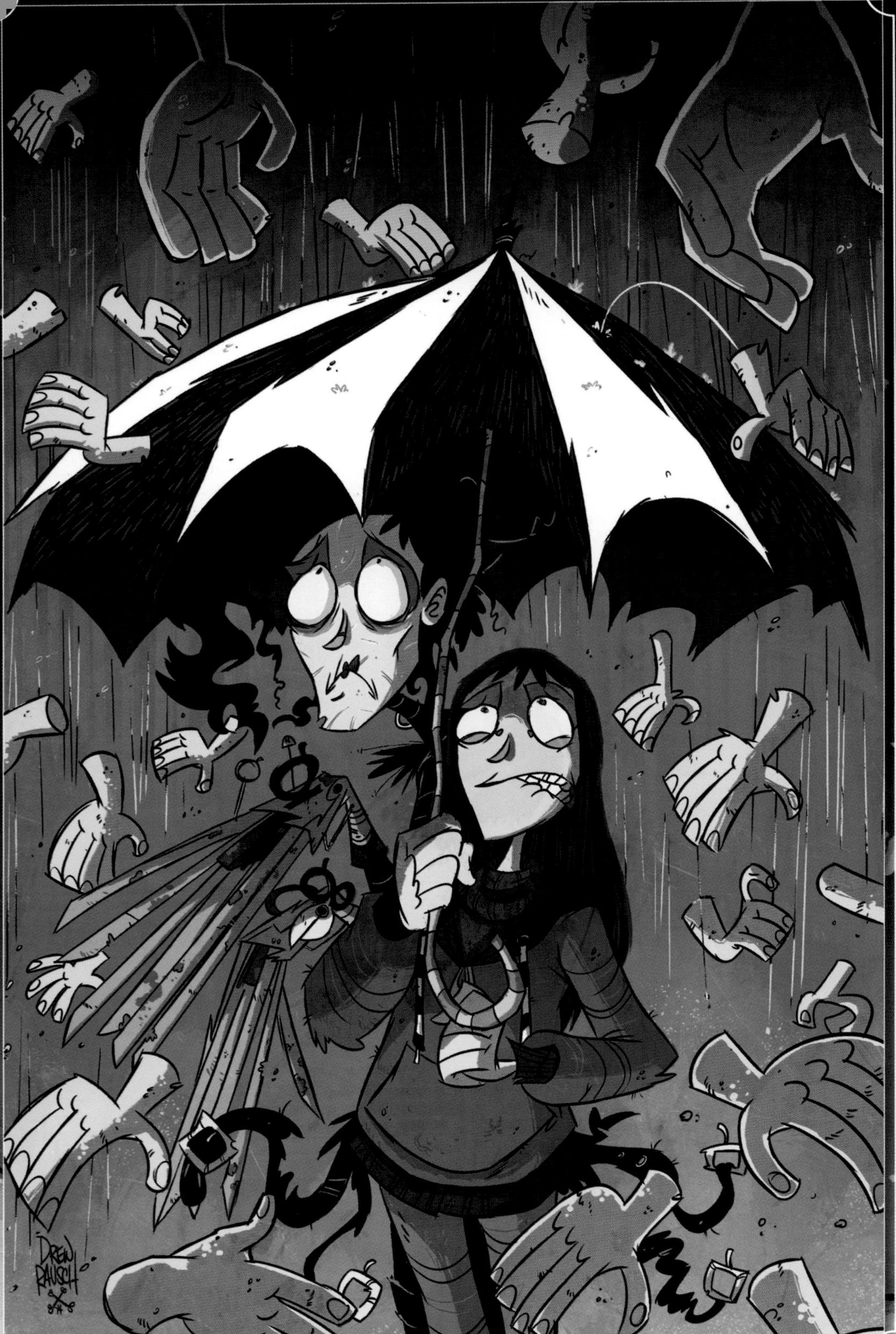
DREW RAUSCH

ART BY
DREW RAUSCH

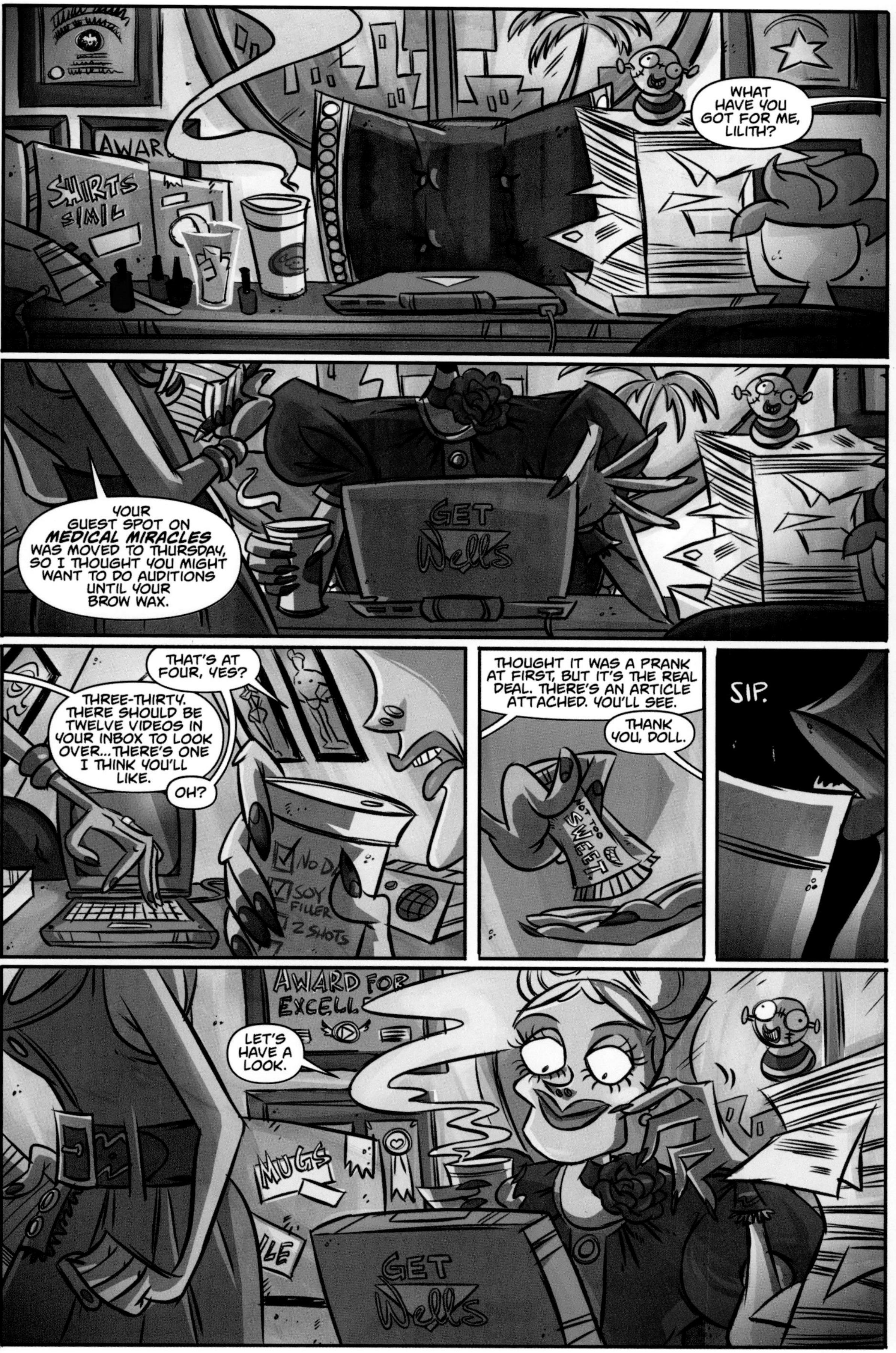

AWAR
SHIRTS
WHAT HAVE YOU GOT FOR ME, LILITH?
YOUR GUEST SPOT ON ***MEDICAL MIRACLES*** WAS MOVED TO THURSDAY, SO I THOUGHT YOU MIGHT WANT TO DO AUDITIONS UNTIL YOUR BROW WAX.
GET Wells
THAT'S AT FOUR, YES?
THREE-THIRTY. THERE SHOULD BE TWELVE VIDEOS IN YOUR INBOX TO LOOK OVER...THERE'S ONE I THINK YOU'LL LIKE.
OH?
SOY FILLER
2 SHOTS
THOUGHT IT WAS A PRANK AT FIRST, BUT IT'S THE REAL DEAL. THERE'S AN ARTICLE ATTACHED. YOU'LL SEE.
THANK YOU, DOLL.
NOT TOO SWEET
SIP.
AWARD FOR EXCELL
LET'S HAVE A LOOK.
MUGS
GET Wells

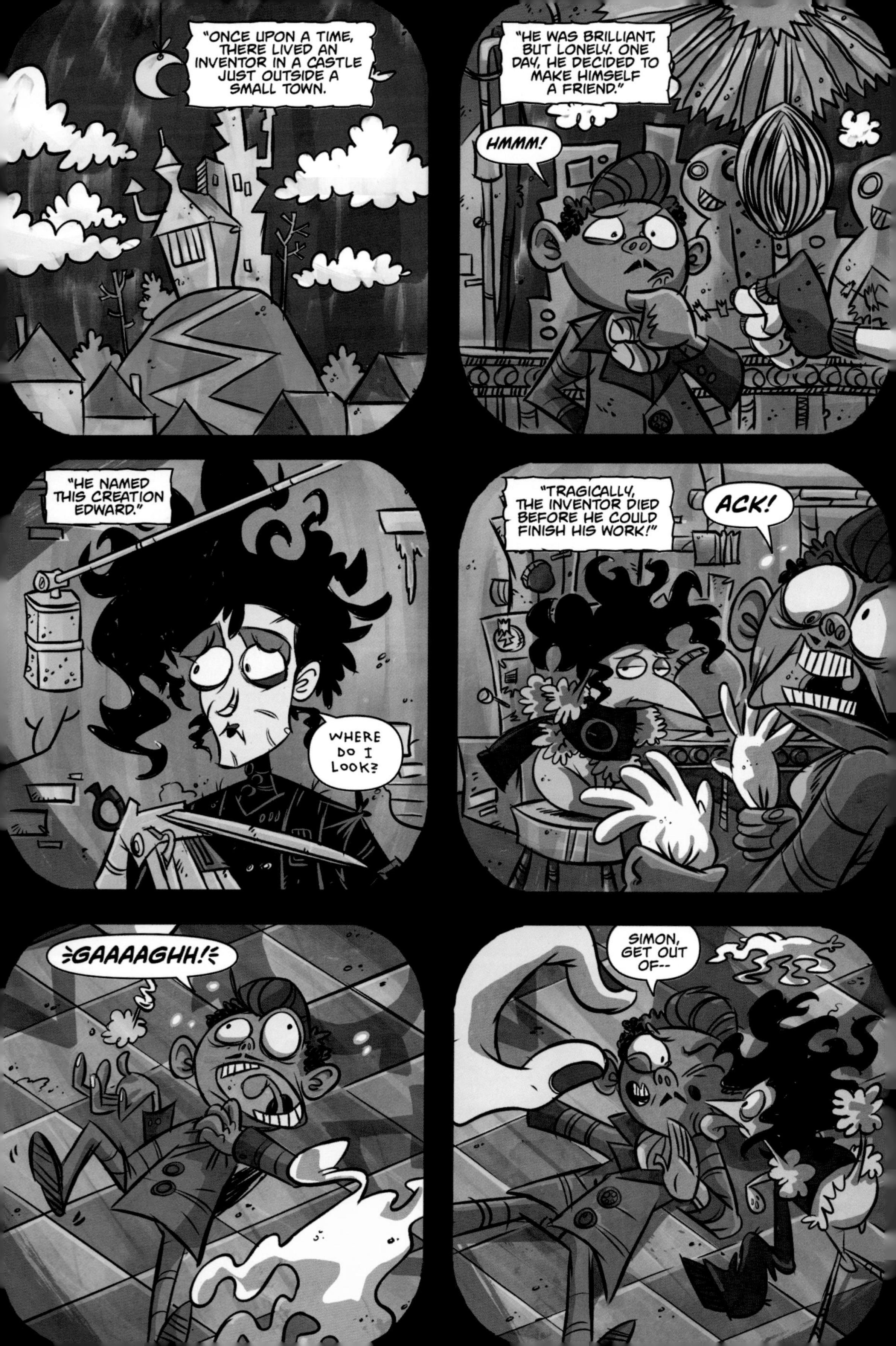
"ONCE UPON A TIME, THERE LIVED AN INVENTOR IN A CASTLE JUST OUTSIDE A SMALL TOWN.
"HE WAS BRILLIANT, BUT LONELY. ONE DAY, HE DECIDED TO MAKE HIMSELF A FRIEND."
HMMM!
"HE NAMED THIS CREATION EDWARD."
WHERE DO I LOOK?
"TRAGICALLY, THE INVENTOR DIED BEFORE HE COULD FINISH HIS WORK!"
ACK!
GAAAAGHH!
SIMON, GET OUT OF--

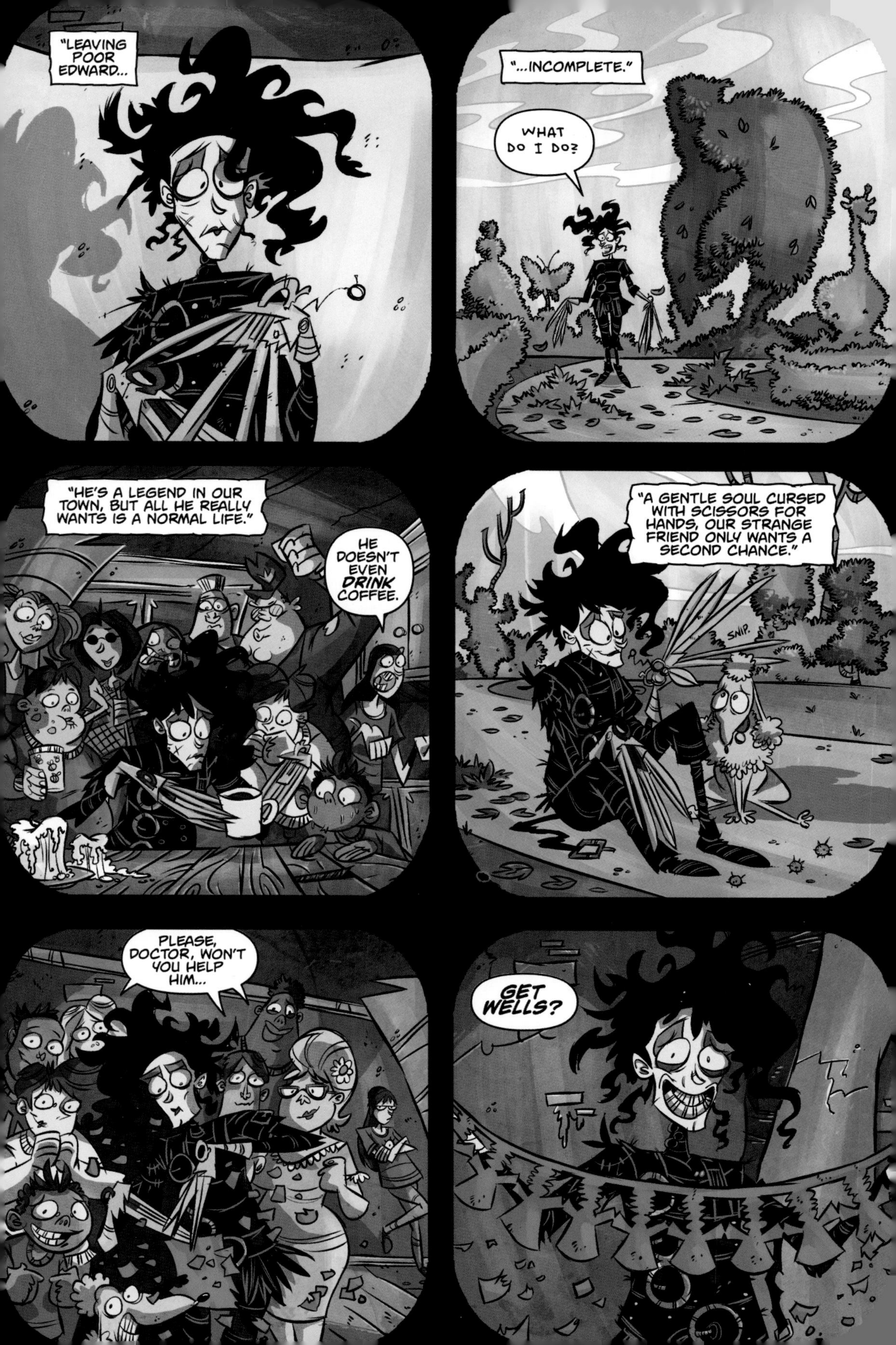
"LEAVING POOR EDWARD...
"...INCOMPLETE."
WHAT DO I DO?
"HE'S A LEGEND IN OUR TOWN, BUT ALL HE REALLY WANTS IS A NORMAL LIFE."
HE DOESN'T EVEN DRINK COFFEE.
"A GENTLE SOUL CURSED WITH SCISSORS FOR HANDS, OUR STRANGE FRIEND ONLY WANTS A SECOND CHANCE."
SNIP.
SNIP.
PLEASE, DOCTOR, WON'T YOU HELP HIM...
GET WELLS?

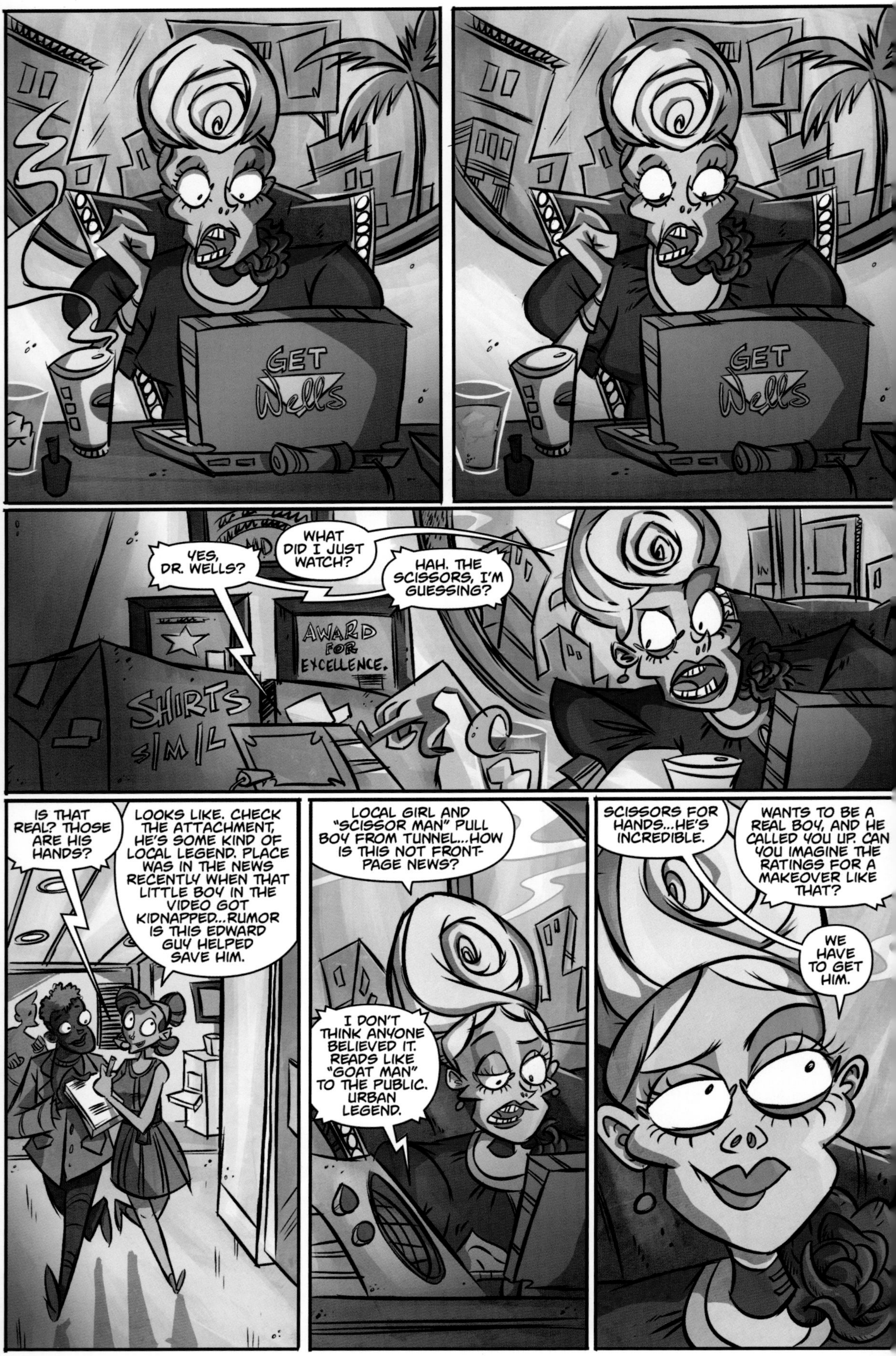
GET WELLS
GET WELLS
YES, DR. WELLS?
WHAT DID I JUST WATCH?
HAH. THE SCISSORS, I'M GUESSING?
AWARD FOR EXCELLENCE.
SHIRTS S/M/L
IS THAT REAL? THOSE ARE HIS HANDS?
LOOKS LIKE. CHECK THE ATTACHMENT, HE'S SOME KIND OF LOCAL LEGEND. PLACE WAS IN THE NEWS RECENTLY WHEN THAT LITTLE BOY IN THE VIDEO GOT KIDNAPPED...RUMOR IS THIS EDWARD GUY HELPED SAVE HIM.
LOCAL GIRL AND "SCISSOR MAN" PULL BOY FROM TUNNEL...HOW IS THIS NOT FRONT-PAGE NEWS?
I DON'T THINK ANYONE BELIEVED IT. READS LIKE "GOAT MAN" TO THE PUBLIC. URBAN LEGEND.
SCISSORS FOR HANDS...HE'S INCREDIBLE.
WANTS TO BE A REAL BOY, AND HE CALLED YOU UP. CAN YOU IMAGINE THE RATINGS FOR A MAKEOVER LIKE THAT?
WE HAVE TO GET HIM.

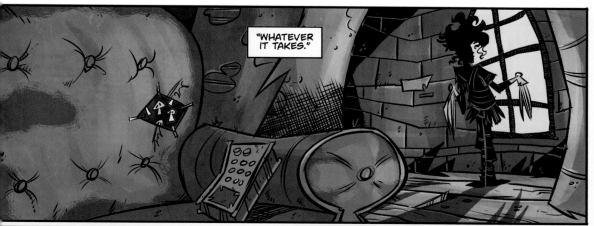

"WHATEVER IT TAKES."

YOU READY?

HM?

ZOMBIES IN THE SNOW. MOM SAID I COULD STAY TO WATCH IT WITH YOU.

OH. YES.

WHO ARE YOU WAITING FOR?

THE MAIL.

ARE YOU... IS IT BECAUSE OF THAT SHOW? EDWARD, LOTS OF PEOPLE APPLY FOR--

FRIENDS!

HELLO!

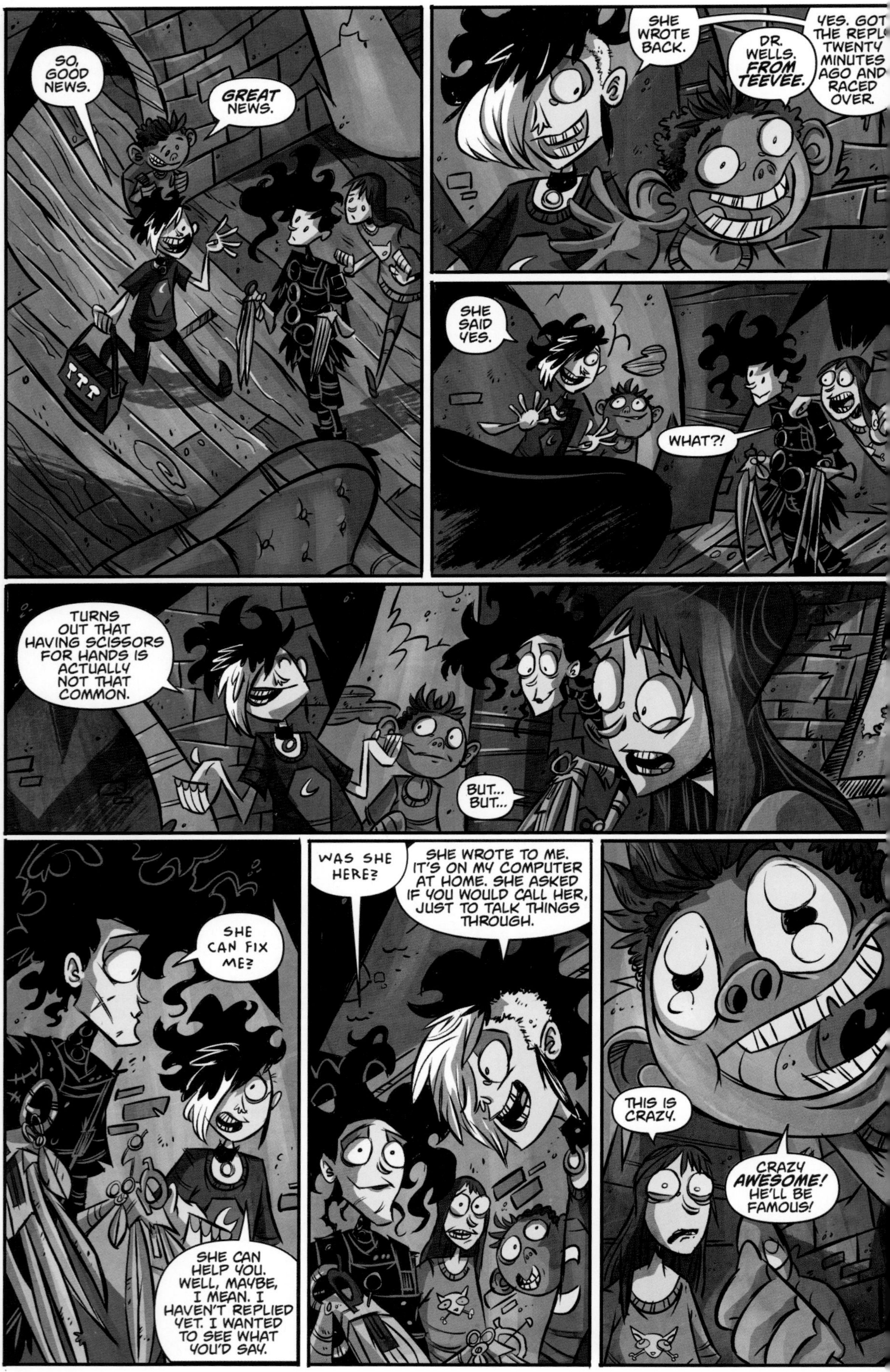
SO, GOOD NEWS.
GREAT NEWS.
SHE WROTE BACK.
DR. WELLS. FROM TEEVEE.
YES. GOT THE REPL[Y] TWENTY MINUTES AGO AND RACED OVER.
SHE SAID YES.
WHAT?!
TURNS OUT THAT HAVING SCISSORS FOR HANDS IS ACTUALLY NOT THAT COMMON.
BUT... BUT...
SHE CAN FIX ME?
SHE CAN HELP YOU. WELL, MAYBE, I MEAN. I HAVEN'T REPLIED YET. I WANTED TO SEE WHAT YOU'D SAY.
WAS SHE HERE?
SHE WROTE TO ME. IT'S ON MY COMPUTER AT HOME. SHE ASKED IF YOU WOULD CALL HER, JUST TO TALK THINGS THROUGH.
THIS IS CRAZY.
CRAZY AWESOME! HE'LL BE FAMOUS!

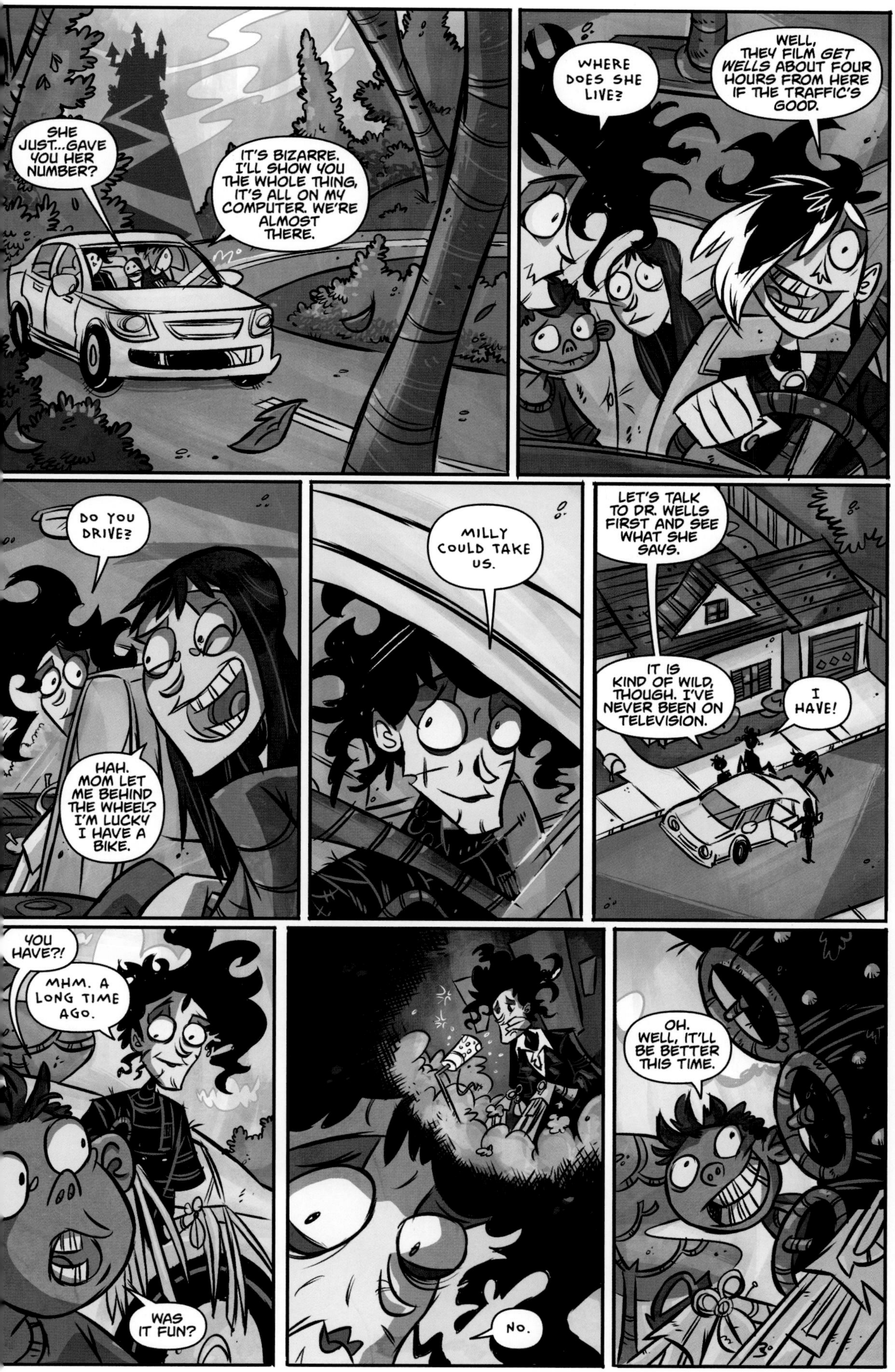

SHE JUST...GAVE YOU HER NUMBER?
IT'S BIZARRE. I'LL SHOW YOU THE WHOLE THING, IT'S ALL ON MY COMPUTER. WE'RE ALMOST THERE.
WHERE DOES SHE LIVE?
WELL, THEY FILM GET WELLS ABOUT FOUR HOURS FROM HERE IF THE TRAFFIC'S GOOD.
DO YOU DRIVE?
HAH. MOM LET ME BEHIND THE WHEEL? I'M LUCKY I HAVE A BIKE.
MILLY COULD TAKE US.
LET'S TALK TO DR. WELLS FIRST AND SEE WHAT SHE SAYS.
IT IS KIND OF WILD, THOUGH. I'VE NEVER BEEN ON TELEVISION.
I HAVE!
YOU HAVE?!
MHM. A LONG TIME AGO.
WAS IT FUN?
NO.
OH. WELL, IT'LL BE BETTER THIS TIME.

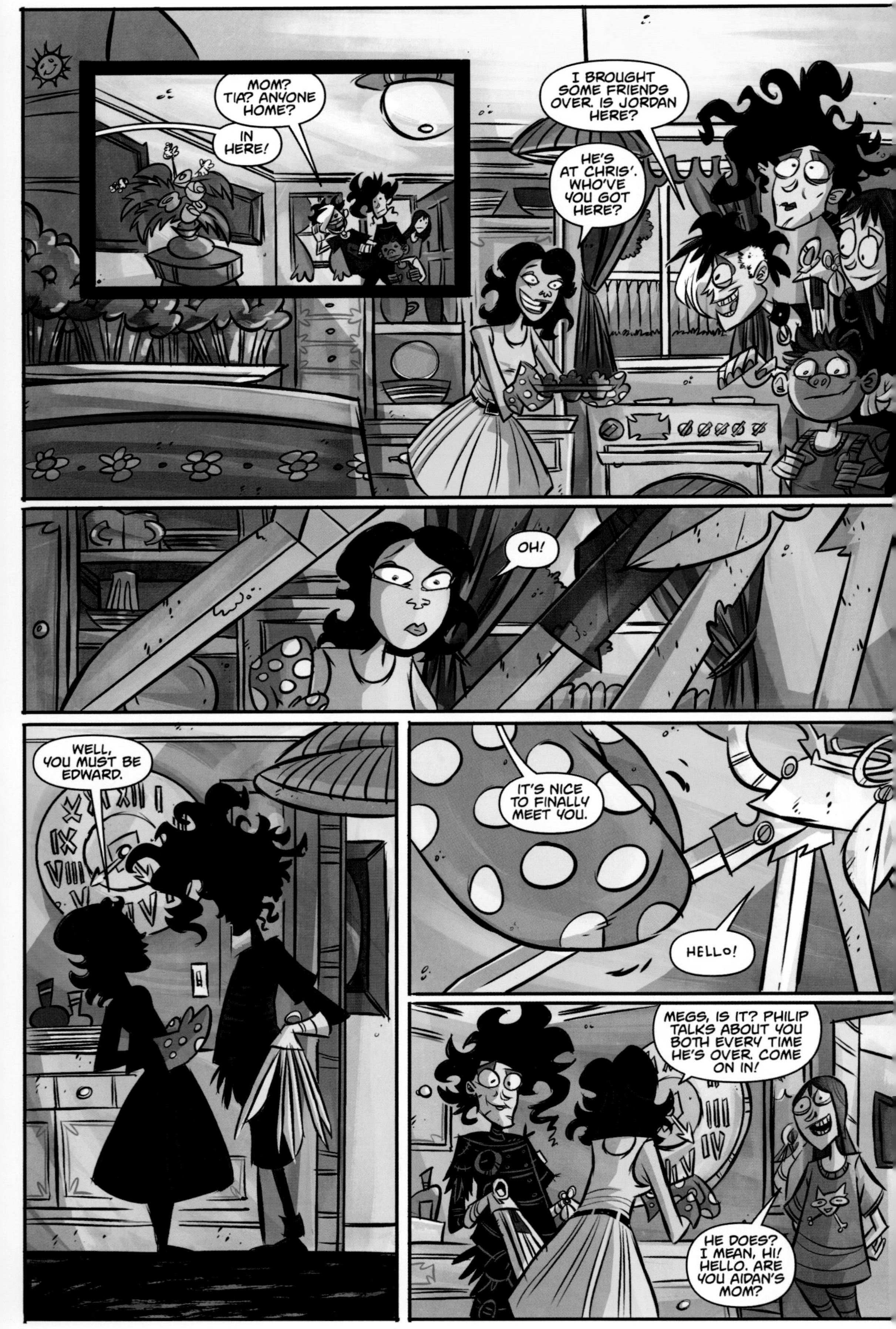
MOM? TIA? ANYONE HOME?
IN HERE!
I BROUGHT SOME FRIENDS OVER. IS JORDAN HERE?
HE'S AT CHRIS'. WHO'VE YOU GOT HERE?
OH!
WELL, YOU MUST BE EDWARD.
IT'S NICE TO FINALLY MEET YOU.
HELLO!
MEGS, IS IT? PHILIP TALKS ABOUT YOU BOTH EVERY TIME HE'S OVER. COME ON IN!
HE DOES? I MEAN, HI! HELLO. ARE YOU AIDAN'S MOM?

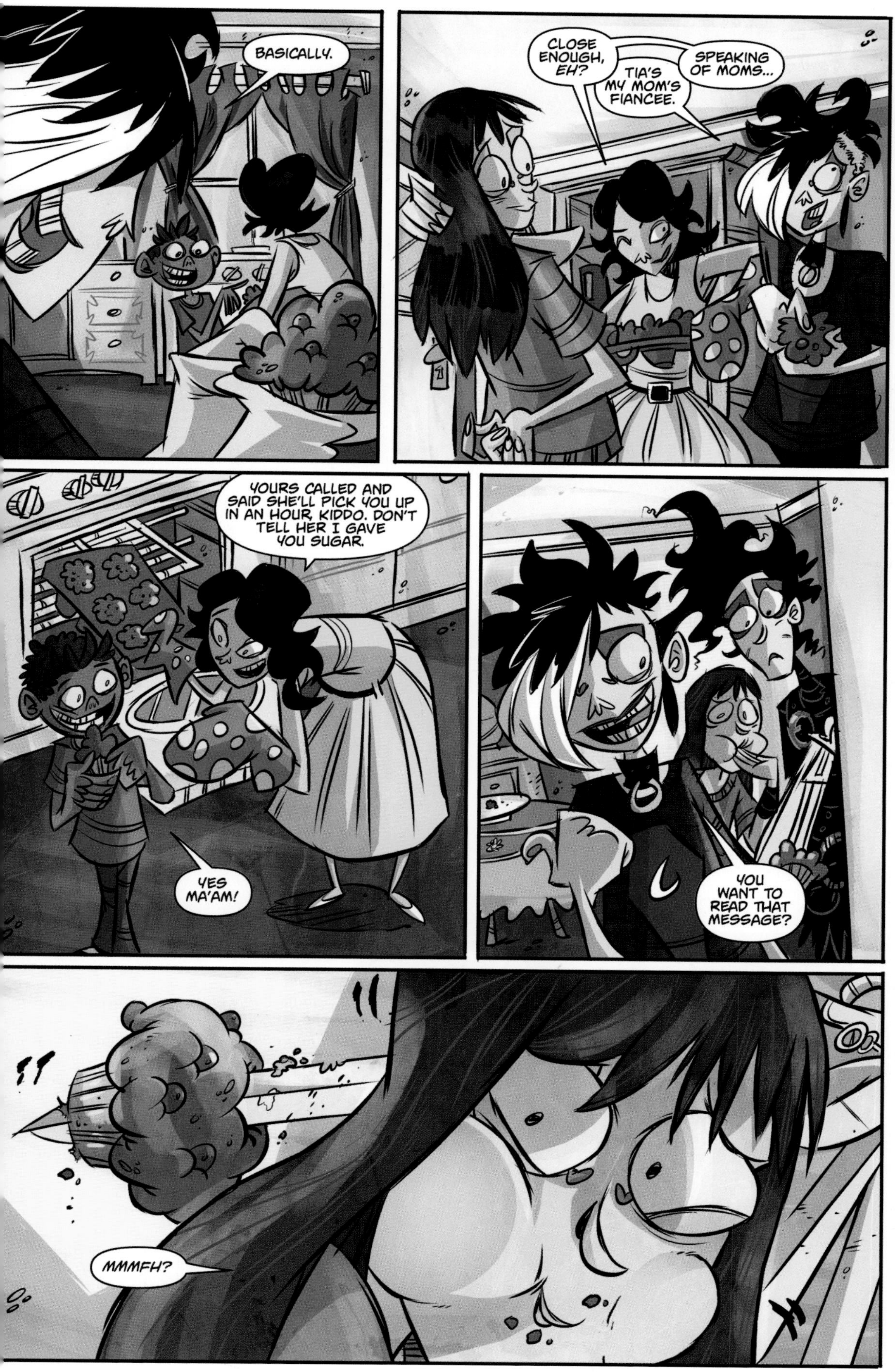
BASICALLY.
CLOSE ENOUGH, EH?
TIA'S MY MOM'S FIANCEE.
SPEAKING OF MOMS...
YOURS CALLED AND SAID SHE'LL PICK YOU UP IN AN HOUR, KIDDO. DON'T TELL HER I GAVE YOU SUGAR.
YES MA'AM!
YOU WANT TO READ THAT MESSAGE?
MMMFH?

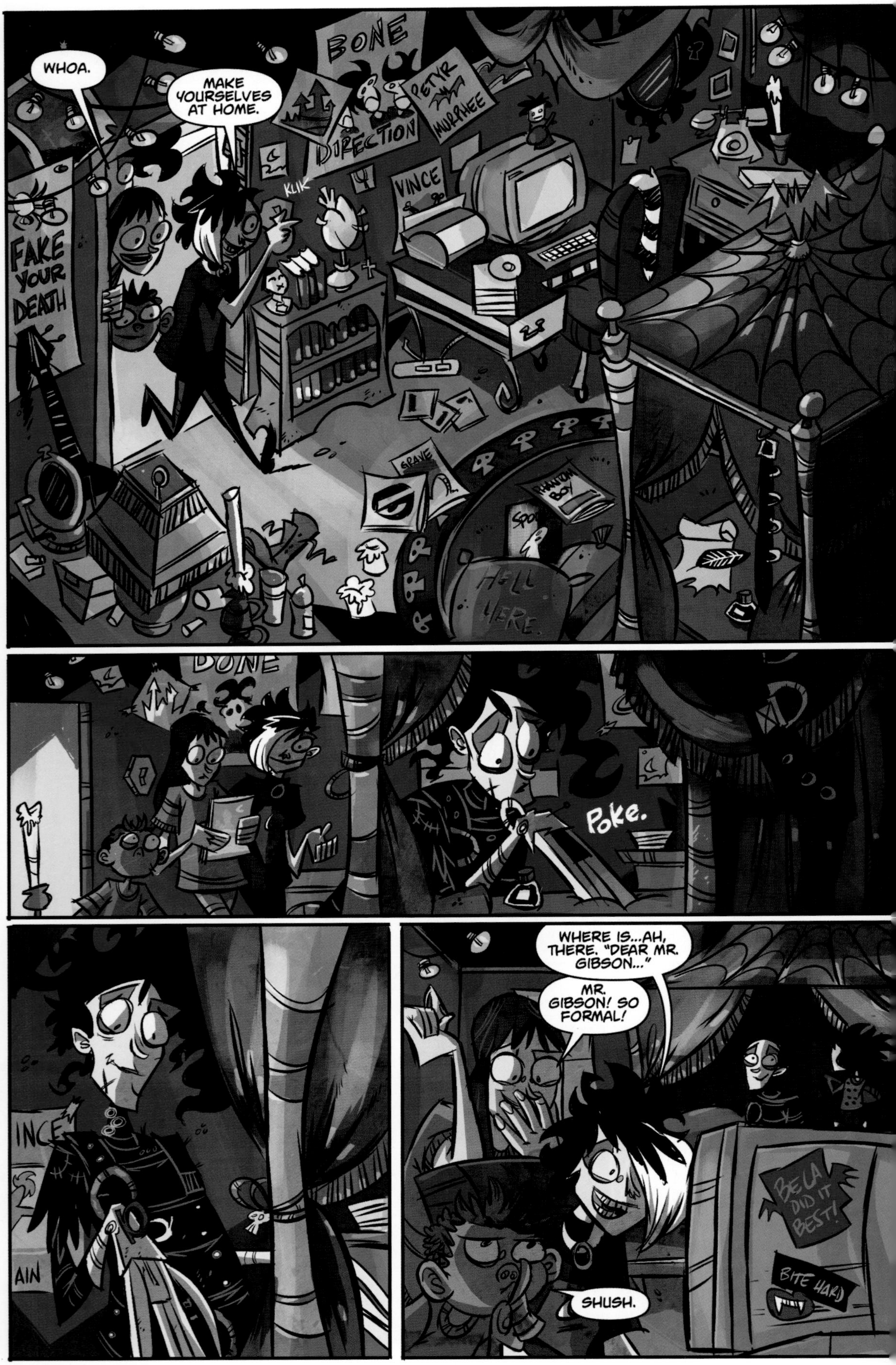
WHOA.
MAKE YOURSELVES AT HOME.
KLIK
BONE DIRECTION
PETYR MURPHEE
VINCE
FAKE YOUR DEATH
GRAVE
PHANTOM BOY
HELL HERE.
Poke.
WHERE IS...AH, THERE. "DEAR MR. GIBSON..."
MR. GIBSON! SO FORMAL!
BELA DID IT BEST!
BITE HARD
SHUSH.

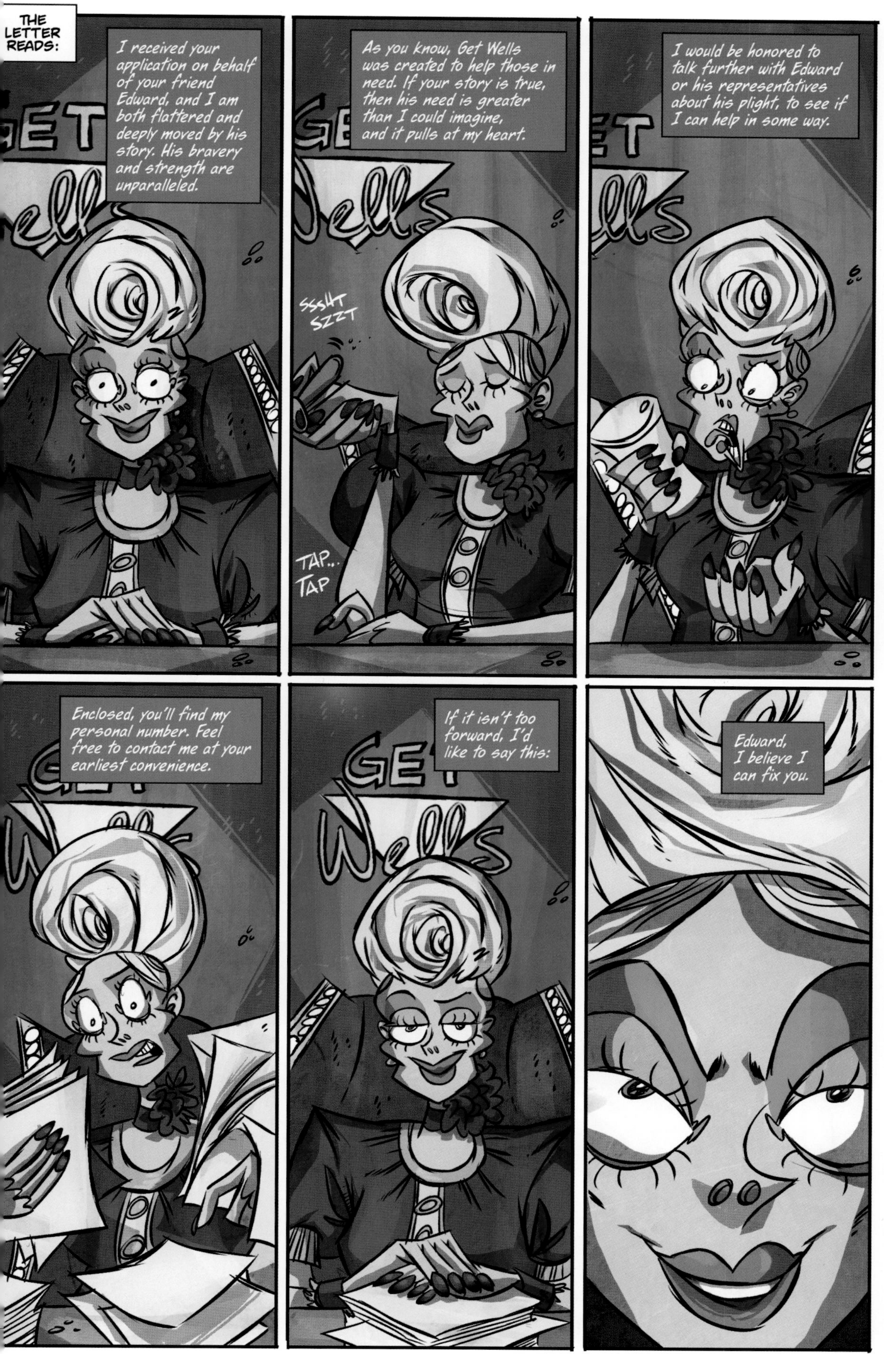
THE LETTER READS:
I received your application on behalf of your friend Edward, and I am both flattered and deeply moved by his story. His bravery and strength are unparalleled.
As you know, Get Wells was created to help those in need. If your story is true, then his need is greater than I could imagine, and it pulls at my heart.
SSSHT SZZT
TAP... TAP
I would be honored to talk further with Edward or his representatives about his plight, to see if I can help in some way.
Enclosed, you'll find my personal number. Feel free to contact me at your earliest convenience.
If it isn't too forward, I'd like to say this:
Edward, I believe I can fix you.

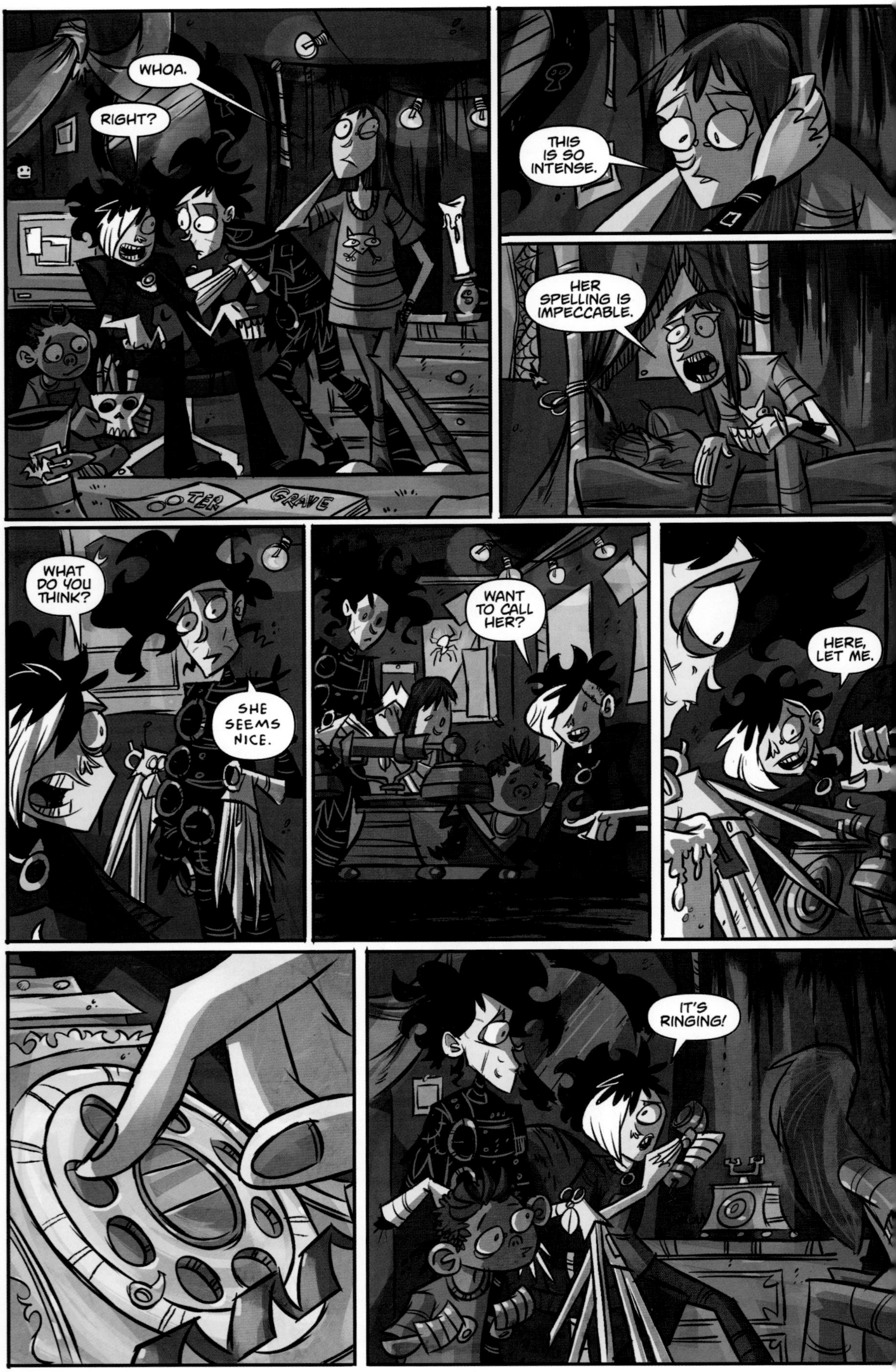
WHOA.
RIGHT?
OOTER
GRAVE
THIS IS SO INTENSE.
HER SPELLING IS IMPECCABLE.
WHAT DO YOU THINK?
SHE SEEMS NICE.
WANT TO CALL HER?
HERE, LET ME.
IT'S RINGING!

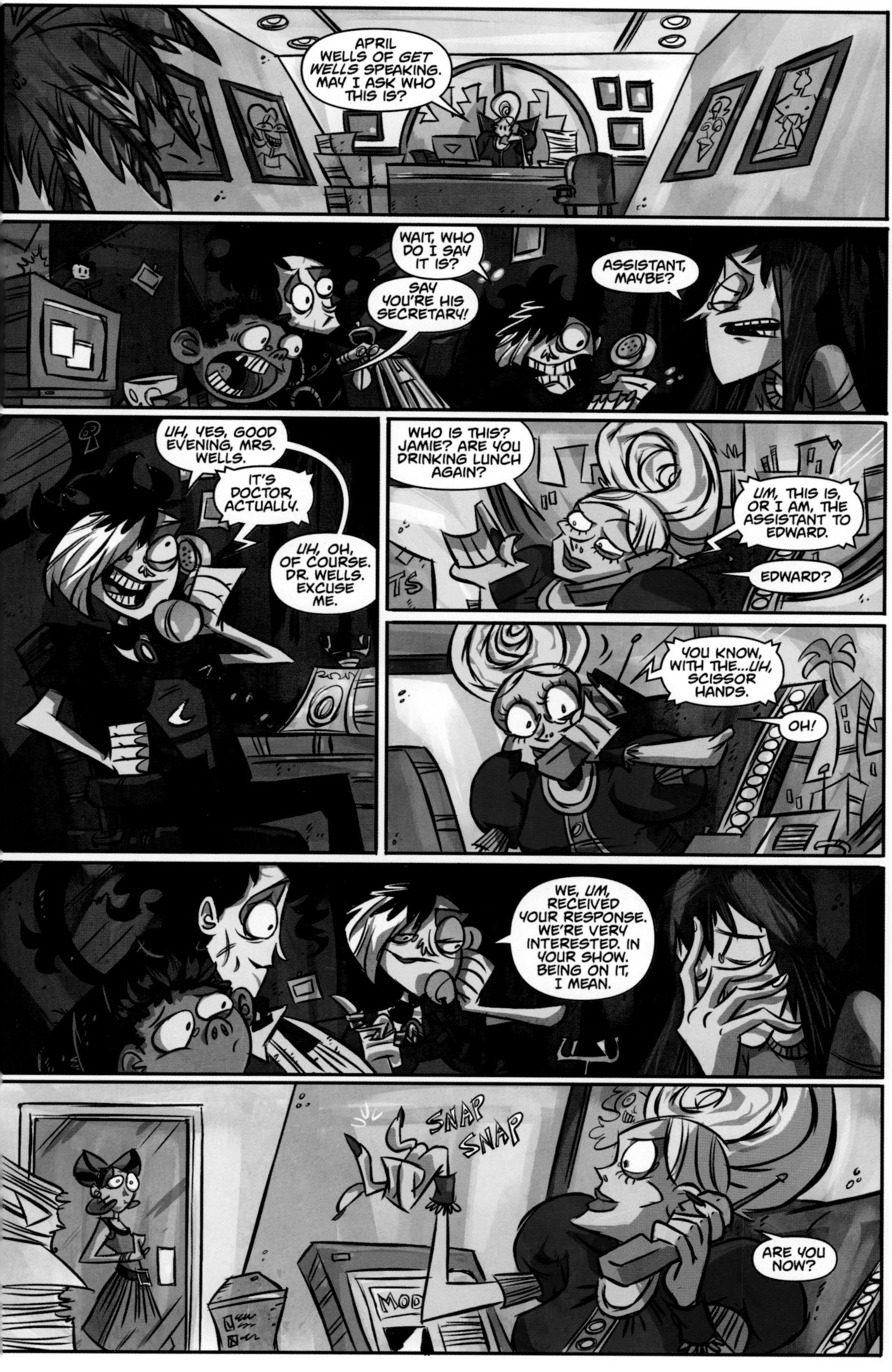

APRIL WELLS OF GET WELLS SPEAKING. MAY I ASK WHO THIS IS?
WAIT, WHO DO I SAY IT IS?
SAY YOU'RE HIS SECRETARY!
ASSISTANT, MAYBE?
UH, YES, GOOD EVENING, MRS. WELLS.
IT'S DOCTOR, ACTUALLY.
UH, OH, OF COURSE. DR. WELLS. EXCUSE ME.
WHO IS THIS? JAMIE? ARE YOU DRINKING LUNCH AGAIN?
UM, THIS IS, OR I AM, THE ASSISTANT TO EDWARD.
EDWARD?
YOU KNOW, WITH THE... UH, SCISSOR HANDS.
OH!
WE, UM, RECEIVED YOUR RESPONSE. WE'RE VERY INTERESTED. IN YOUR SHOW. BEING ON IT, I MEAN.
SNAP SNAP
ARE YOU NOW?

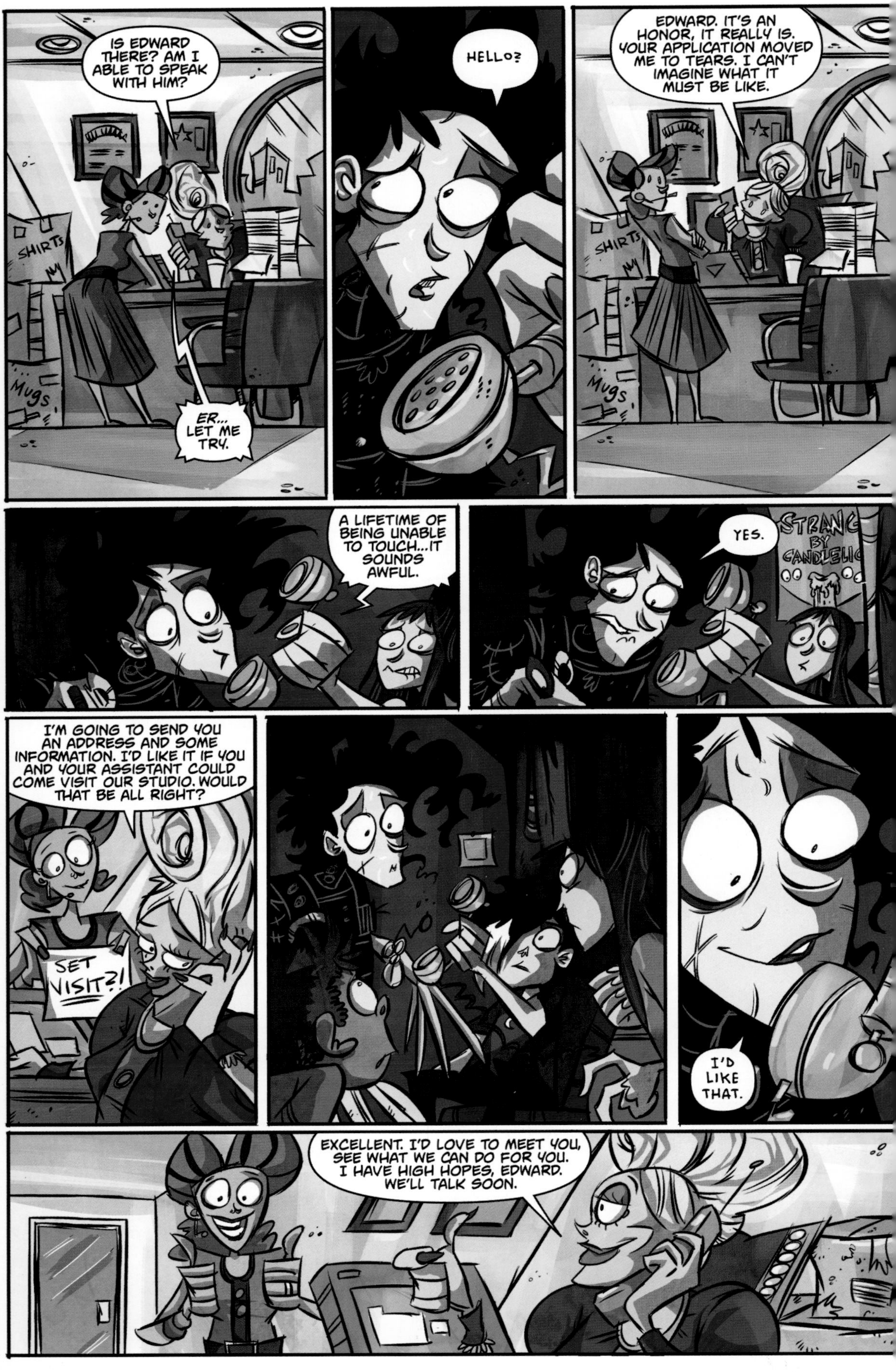
IS EDWARD THERE? AM I ABLE TO SPEAK WITH HIM?
SHIRTS
MUGS
ER... LET ME TRY.
HELLO?
EDWARD. IT'S AN HONOR, IT REALLY IS. YOUR APPLICATION MOVED ME TO TEARS. I CAN'T IMAGINE WHAT IT MUST BE LIKE.
SHIRTS
MUGS
A LIFETIME OF BEING UNABLE TO TOUCH...IT SOUNDS AWFUL.
YES.
STRANG BY CANDLELIG
I'M GOING TO SEND YOU AN ADDRESS AND SOME INFORMATION. I'D LIKE IT IF YOU AND YOUR ASSISTANT COULD COME VISIT OUR STUDIO. WOULD THAT BE ALL RIGHT?
SET VISIT?!
I'D LIKE THAT.
EXCELLENT. I'D LOVE TO MEET YOU, SEE WHAT WE CAN DO FOR YOU. I HAVE HIGH HOPES, EDWARD. WE'LL TALK SOON.

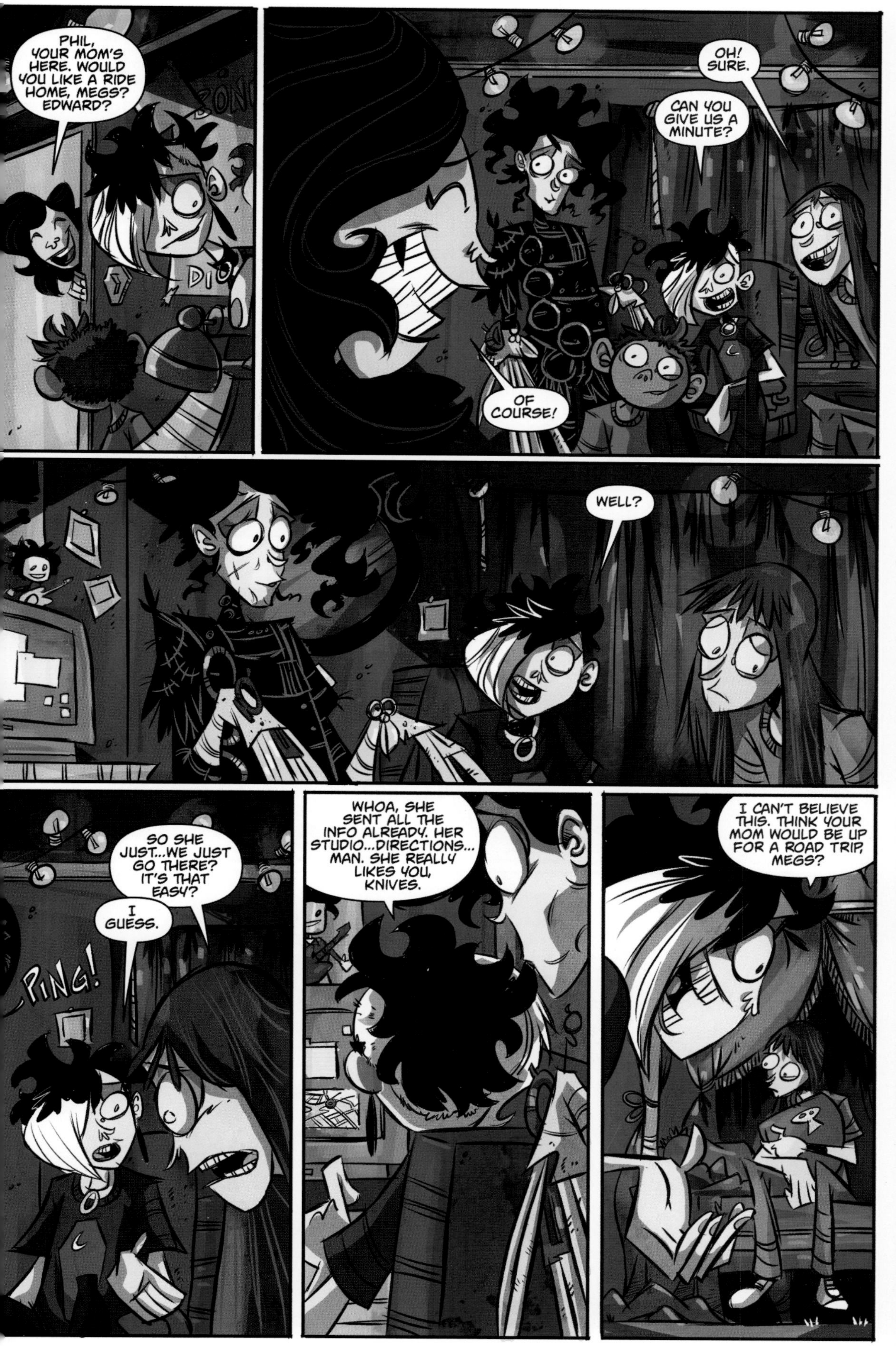
PHIL, YOUR MOM'S HERE. WOULD YOU LIKE A RIDE HOME, MEGS? EDWARD?
OH! SURE.
CAN YOU GIVE US A MINUTE?
OF COURSE!
WELL?
SO SHE JUST...WE JUST GO THERE? IT'S THAT EASY?
I GUESS.
PING!
WHOA, SHE SENT ALL THE INFO ALREADY. HER STUDIO...DIRECTIONS... MAN. SHE REALLY LIKES YOU, KNIVES.
I CAN'T BELIEVE THIS. THINK YOUR MOM WOULD BE UP FOR A ROAD TRIP, MEGS?

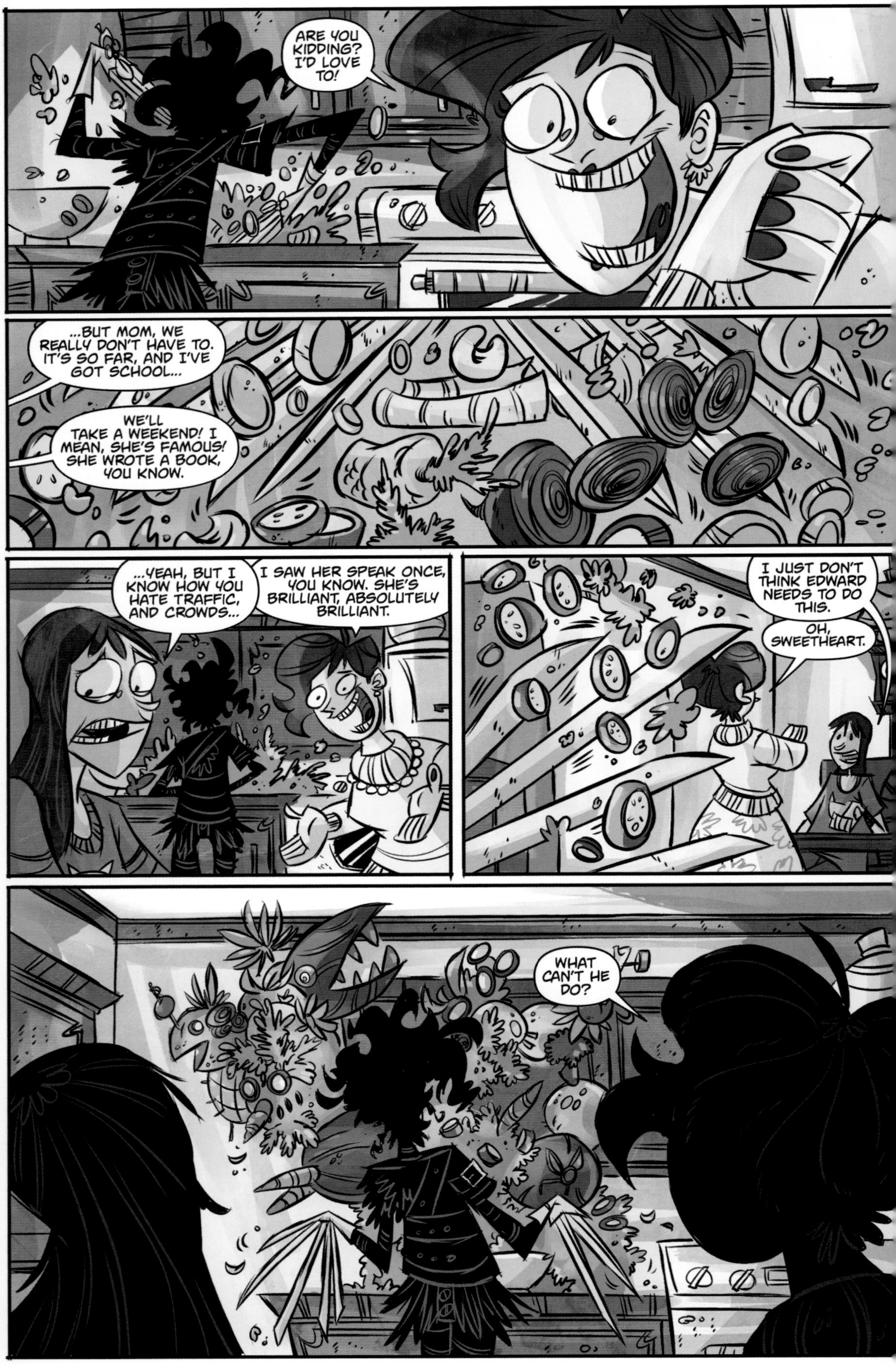
ARE YOU KIDDING? I'D LOVE TO!
...BUT MOM, WE REALLY DON'T HAVE TO. IT'S SO FAR, AND I'VE GOT SCHOOL...
WE'LL TAKE A WEEKEND! I MEAN, SHE'S FAMOUS! SHE WROTE A BOOK, YOU KNOW.
...YEAH, BUT I KNOW HOW YOU HATE TRAFFIC, AND CROWDS...
I SAW HER SPEAK ONCE, YOU KNOW. SHE'S BRILLIANT, ABSOLUTELY BRILLIANT.
I JUST DON'T THINK EDWARD NEEDS TO DO THIS.
OH, SWEETHEART.
WHAT CAN'T HE DO?

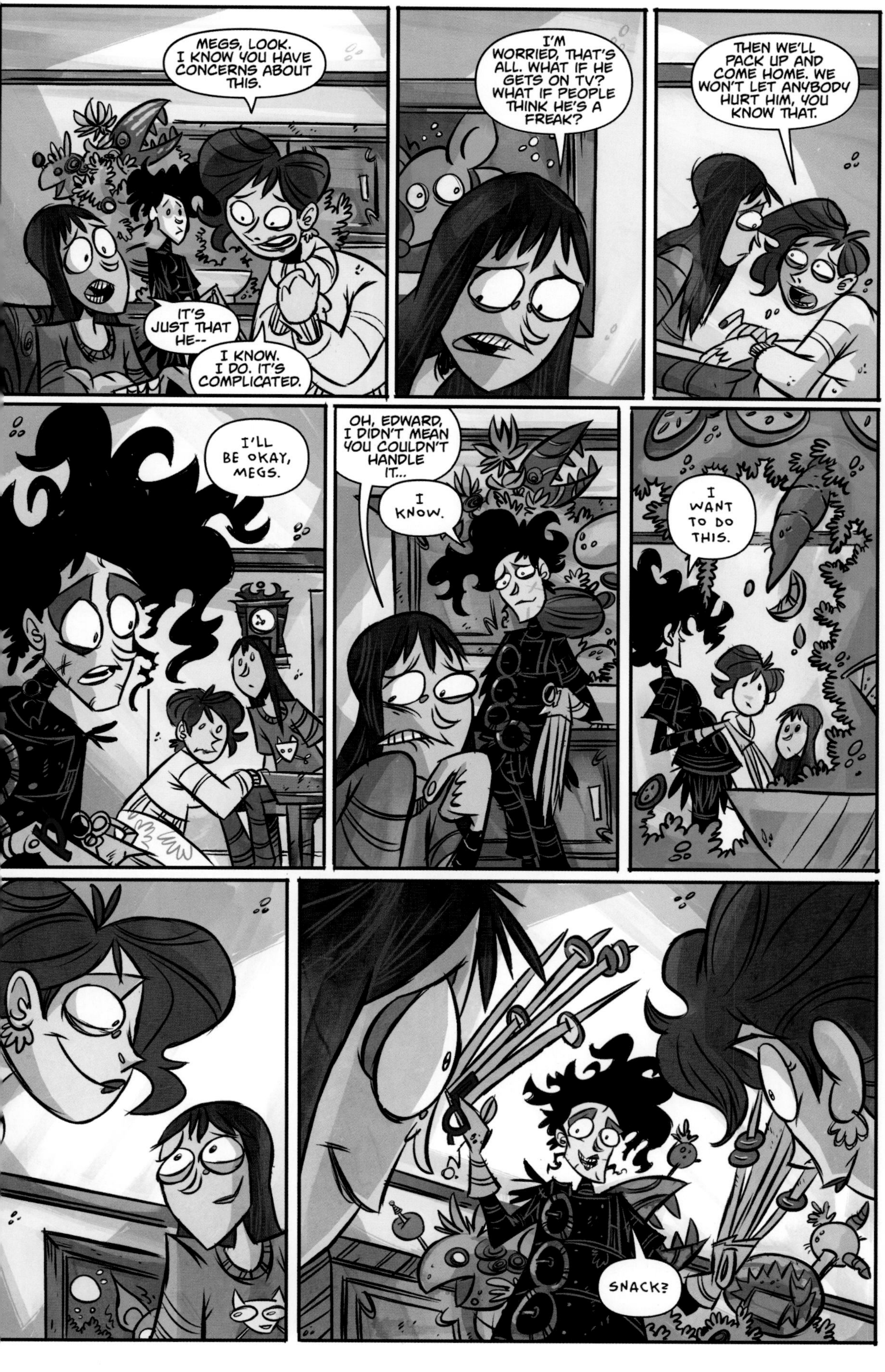
MEGS, LOOK. I KNOW YOU HAVE CONCERNS ABOUT THIS.
IT'S JUST THAT HE--
I KNOW. I DO. IT'S COMPLICATED.
I'M WORRIED, THAT'S ALL. WHAT IF HE GETS ON TV? WHAT IF PEOPLE THINK HE'S A FREAK?
THEN WE'LL PACK UP AND COME HOME. WE WON'T LET ANYBODY HURT HIM, YOU KNOW THAT.
I'LL BE OKAY, MEGS.
OH, EDWARD, I DIDN'T MEAN YOU COULDN'T HANDLE IT...
I KNOW.
I WANT TO DO THIS.
SNACK?

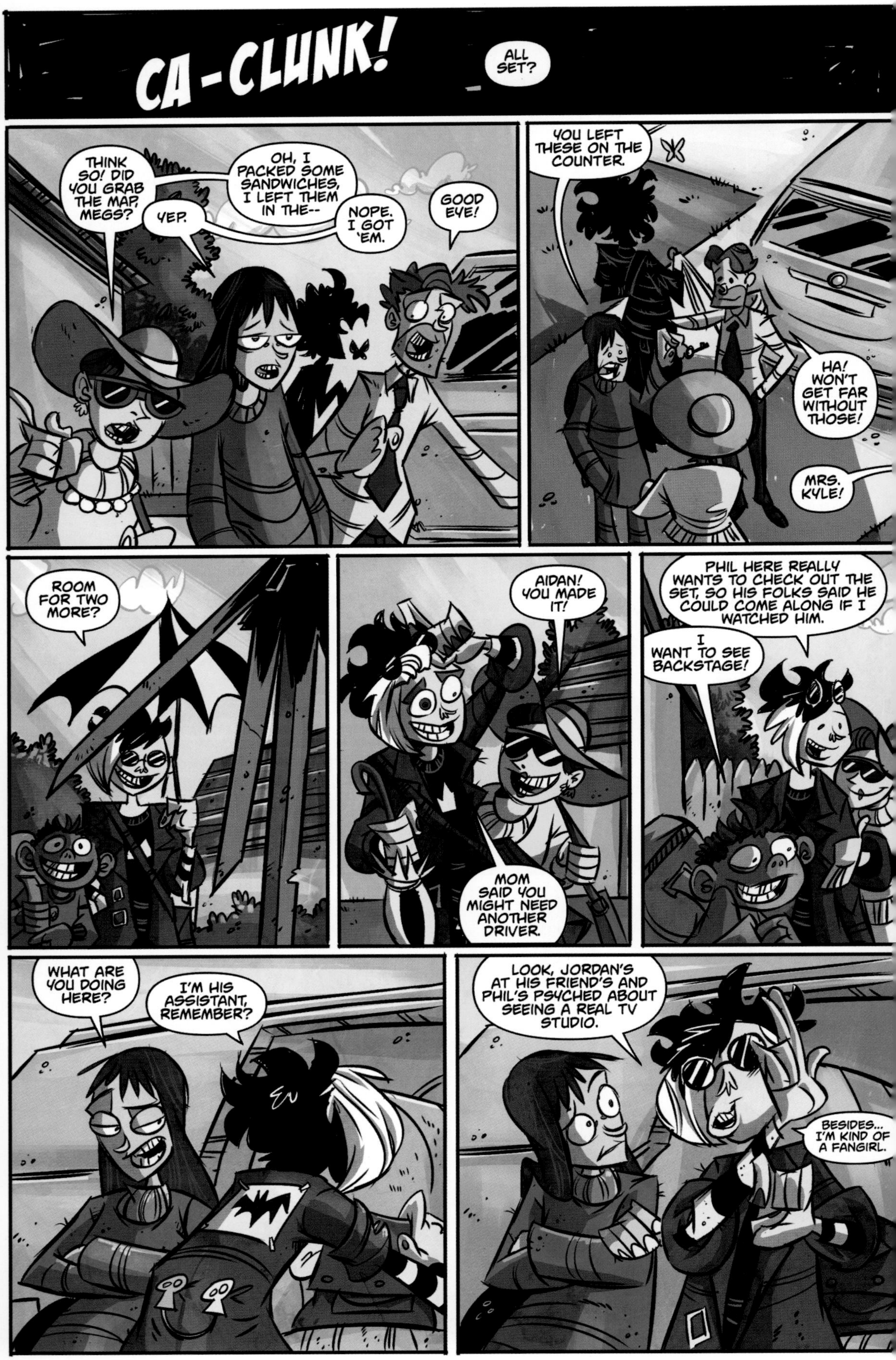
CA-CLUNK!
ALL SET?
THINK SO! DID YOU GRAB THE MAP, MEGS?
YEP.
OH, I PACKED SOME SANDWICHES, I LEFT THEM IN THE--
NOPE. I GOT 'EM.
GOOD EYE!
YOU LEFT THESE ON THE COUNTER.
HA! WON'T GET FAR WITHOUT THOSE!
MRS. KYLE!
ROOM FOR TWO MORE?
AIDAN! YOU MADE IT!
MOM SAID YOU MIGHT NEED ANOTHER DRIVER.
PHIL HERE REALLY WANTS TO CHECK OUT THE SET, SO HIS FOLKS SAID HE COULD COME ALONG IF I WATCHED HIM.
I WANT TO SEE BACKSTAGE!
WHAT ARE YOU DOING HERE?
I'M HIS ASSISTANT, REMEMBER?
LOOK, JORDAN'S AT HIS FRIEND'S AND PHIL'S PSYCHED ABOUT SEEING A REAL TV STUDIO.
BESIDES... I'M KIND OF A FANGIRL.

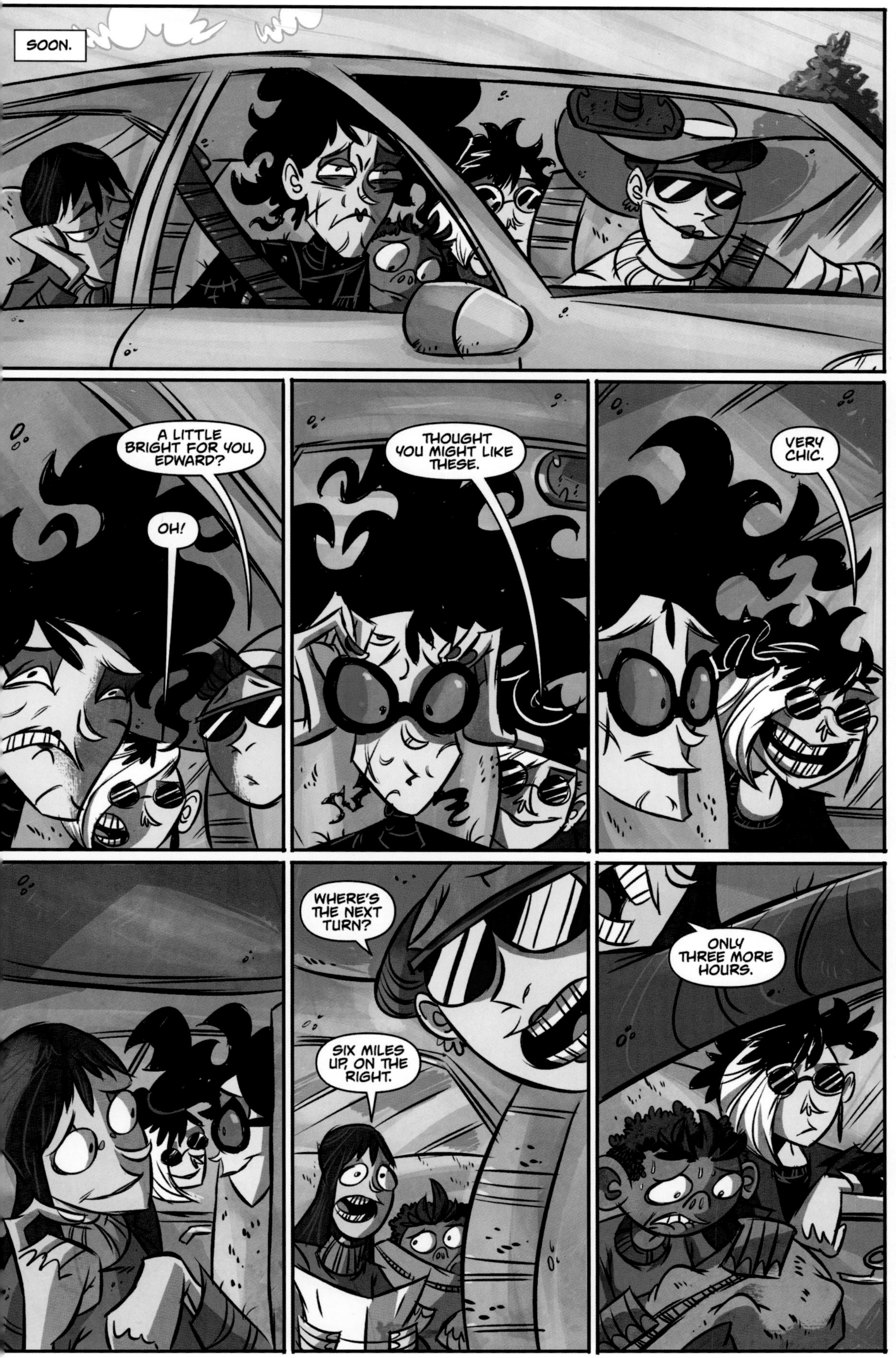
SOON.
A LITTLE BRIGHT FOR YOU, EDWARD?
OH!
THOUGHT YOU MIGHT LIKE THESE.
VERY CHIC.
WHERE'S THE NEXT TURN?
SIX MILES UP, ON THE RIGHT.
ONLY THREE MORE HOURS.

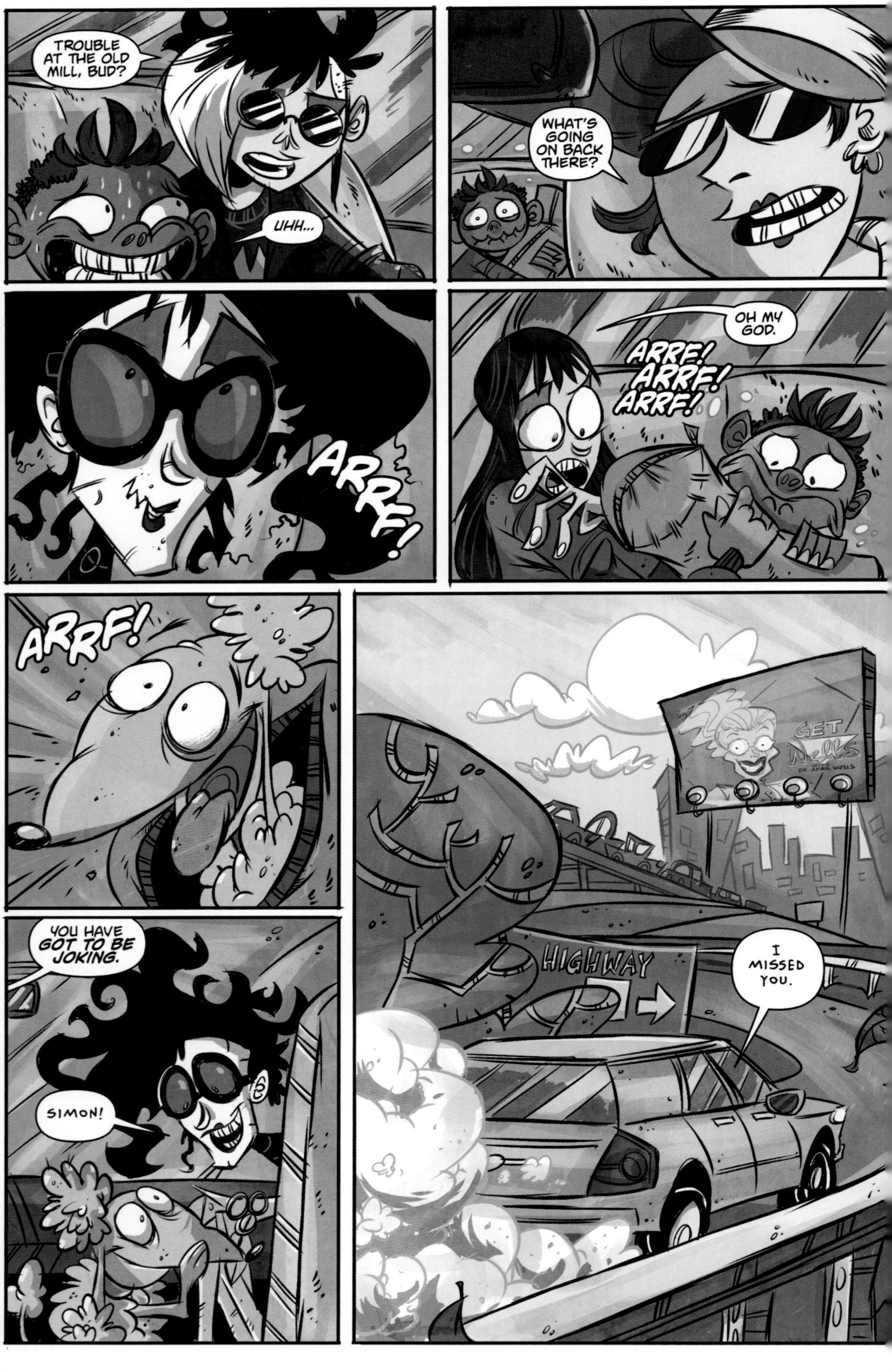

TROUBLE AT THE OLD MILL, BUD?
UHH...
WHAT'S GOING ON BACK THERE?
ARRF!
OH MY GOD.
ARRF! ARRF! ARRF!
ARRF!
YOU HAVE GOT TO BE JOKING.
SIMON!
GET Wells
WITH DR. APRIL WELLS
HIGHWAY
I MISSED YOU.

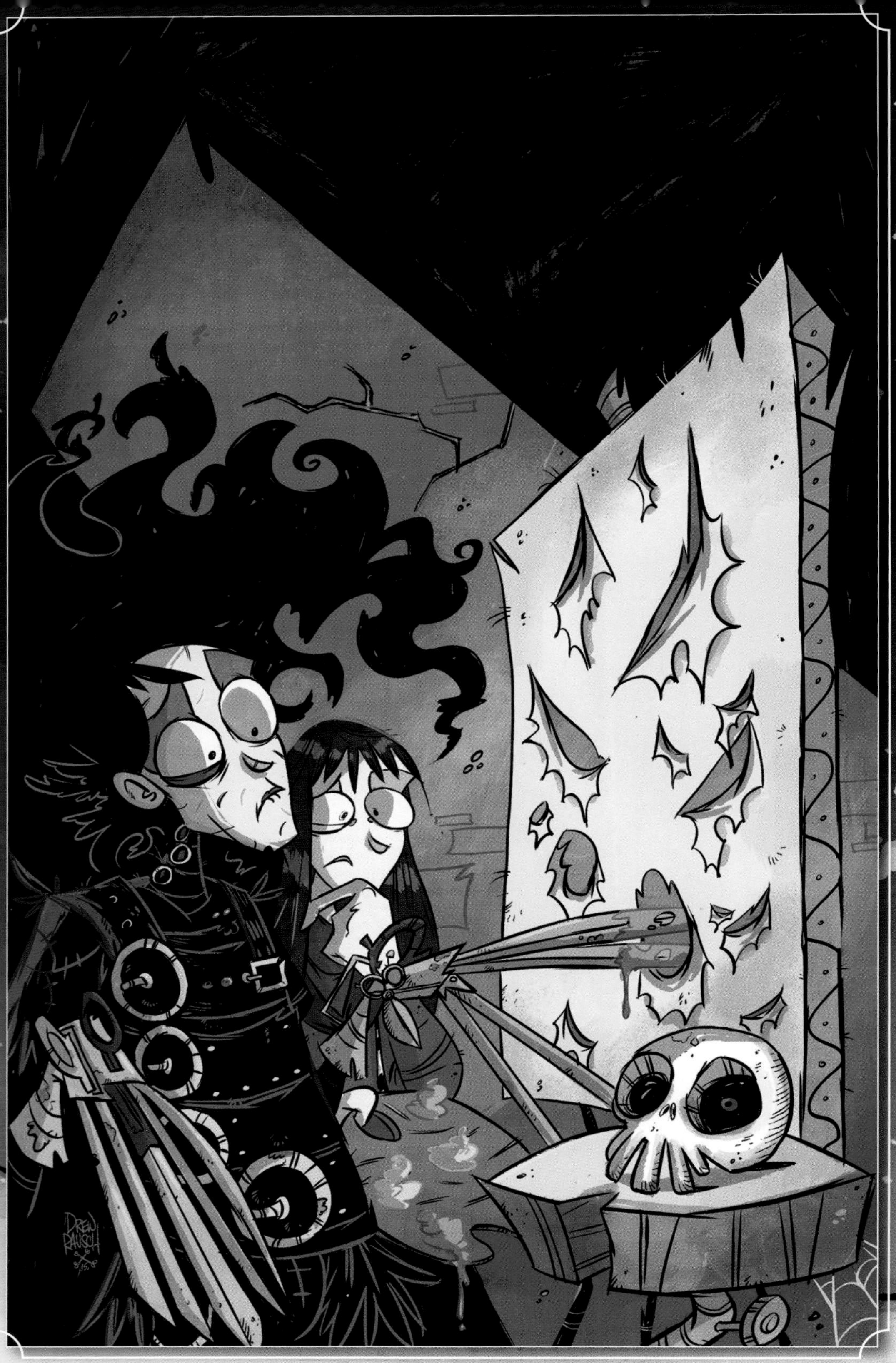
DREW RAUSCH

ART BY
DREW RAUSCH

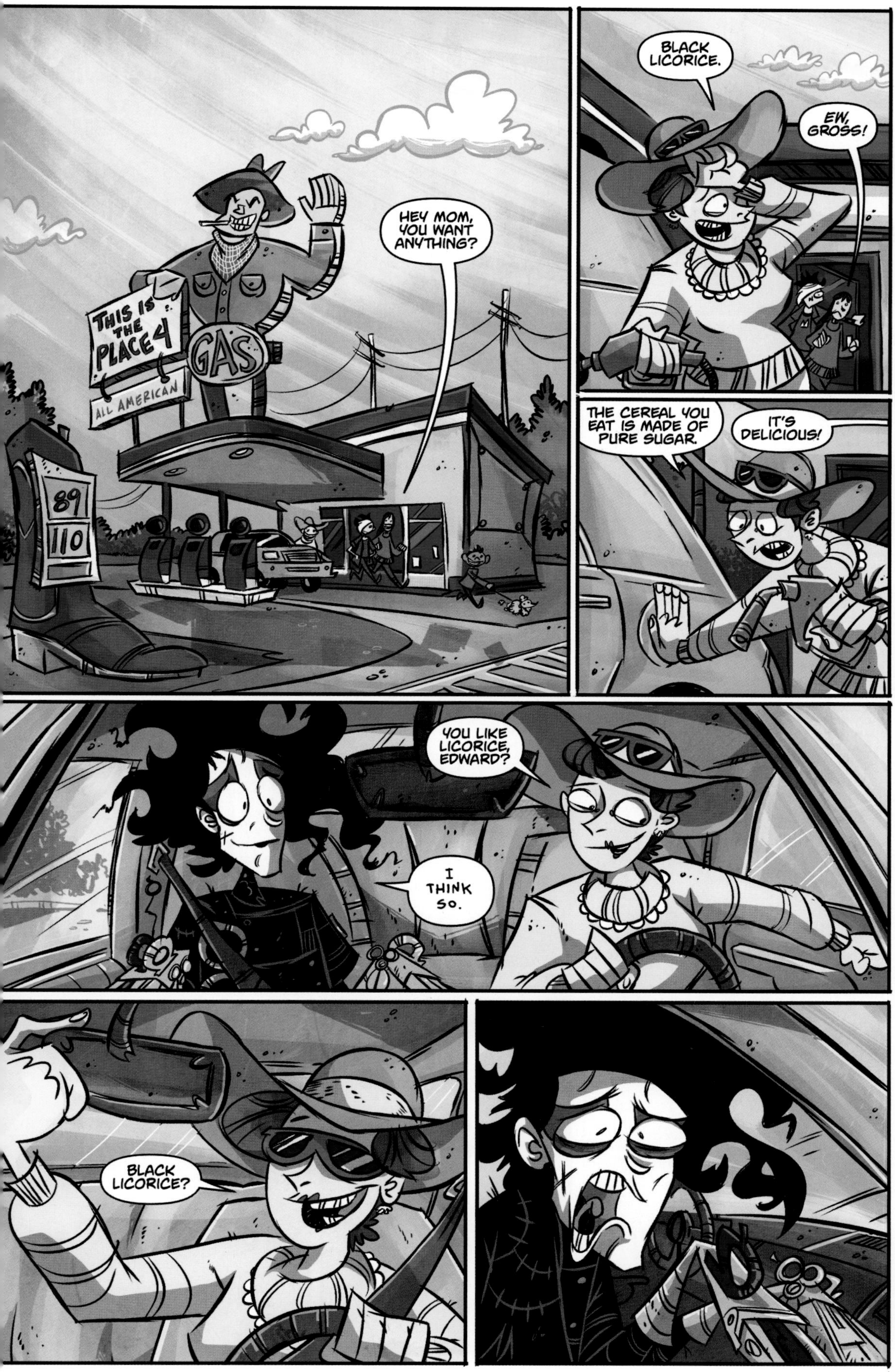
THIS IS THE PLACE 4
GAS
ALL AMERICAN
89
110
HEY MOM, YOU WANT ANYTHING?
BLACK LICORICE.
EW, GROSS!
THE CEREAL YOU EAT IS MADE OF PURE SUGAR.
IT'S DELICIOUS!
YOU LIKE LICORICE, EDWARD?
I THINK SO.
BLACK LICORICE?

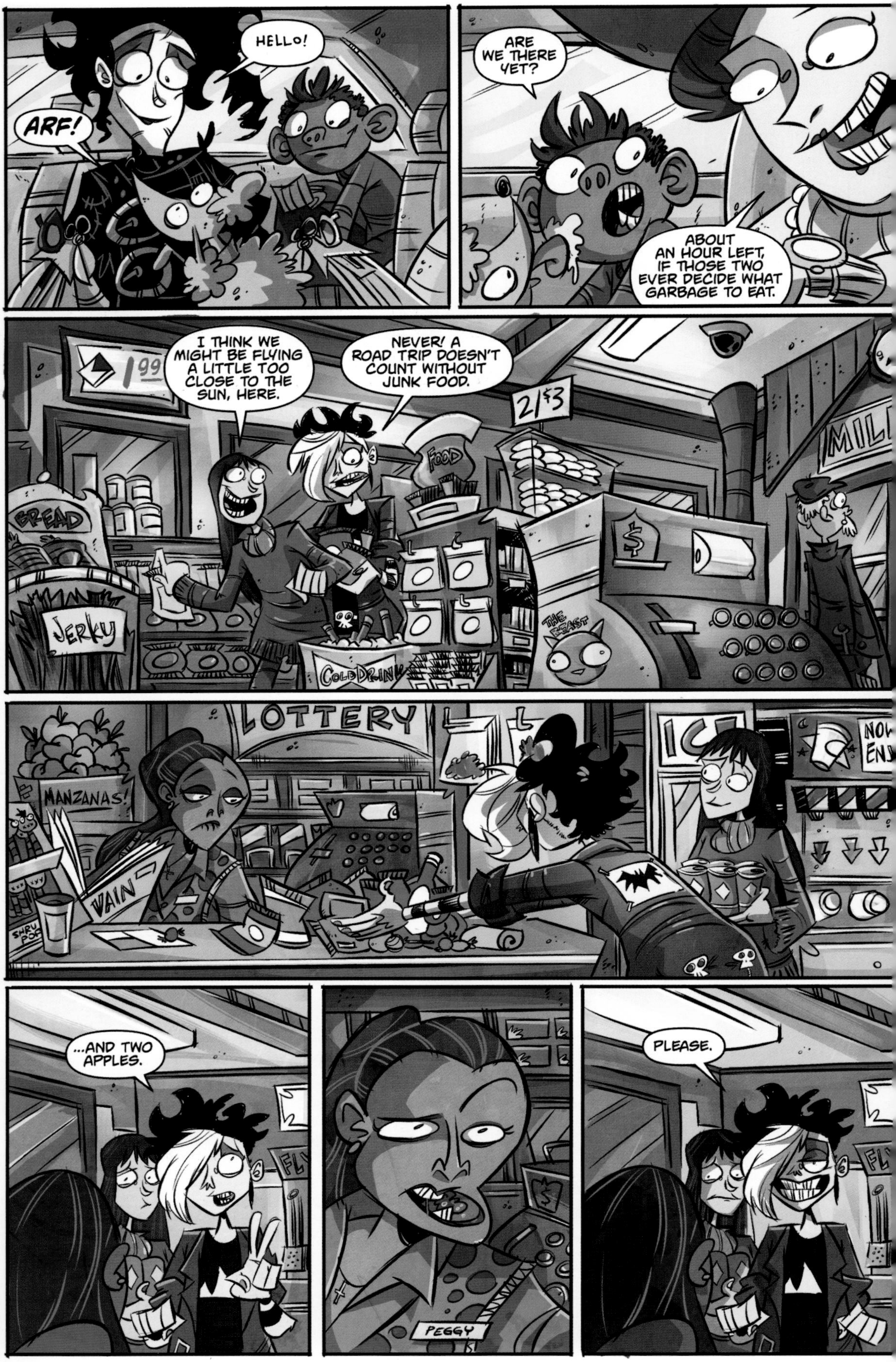
HELLO!
ARF!
ARE WE THERE YET?
ABOUT AN HOUR LEFT, IF THOSE TWO EVER DECIDE WHAT GARBAGE TO EAT.
I THINK WE MIGHT BE FLYING A LITTLE TOO CLOSE TO THE SUN, HERE.
NEVER! A ROAD TRIP DOESN'T COUNT WITHOUT JUNK FOOD.
1.99
2/$3
BREAD
FOOD
JERKY
COLD DRINK
THE BEAST
LOTTERY
MANZANAS!
VAIN
...AND TWO APPLES.
PEGGY
PLEASE.

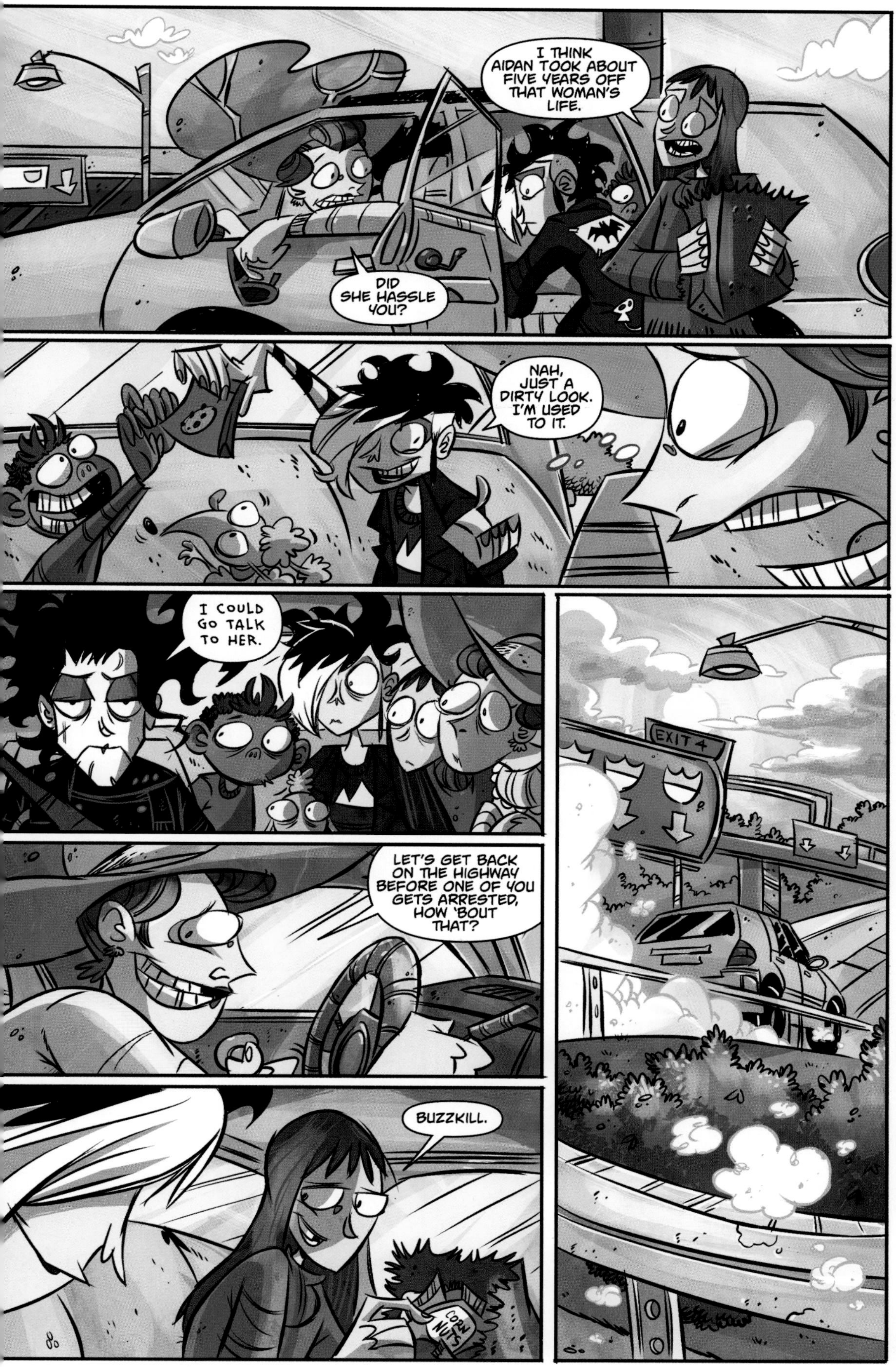
I THINK AIDAN TOOK ABOUT FIVE YEARS OFF THAT WOMAN'S LIFE.
DID SHE HASSLE YOU?
NAH, JUST A DIRTY LOOK. I'M USED TO IT.
I COULD GO TALK TO HER.
LET'S GET BACK ON THE HIGHWAY BEFORE ONE OF YOU GETS ARRESTED, HOW 'BOUT THAT?
BUZZKILL.
CORN NUTS
EXIT 4

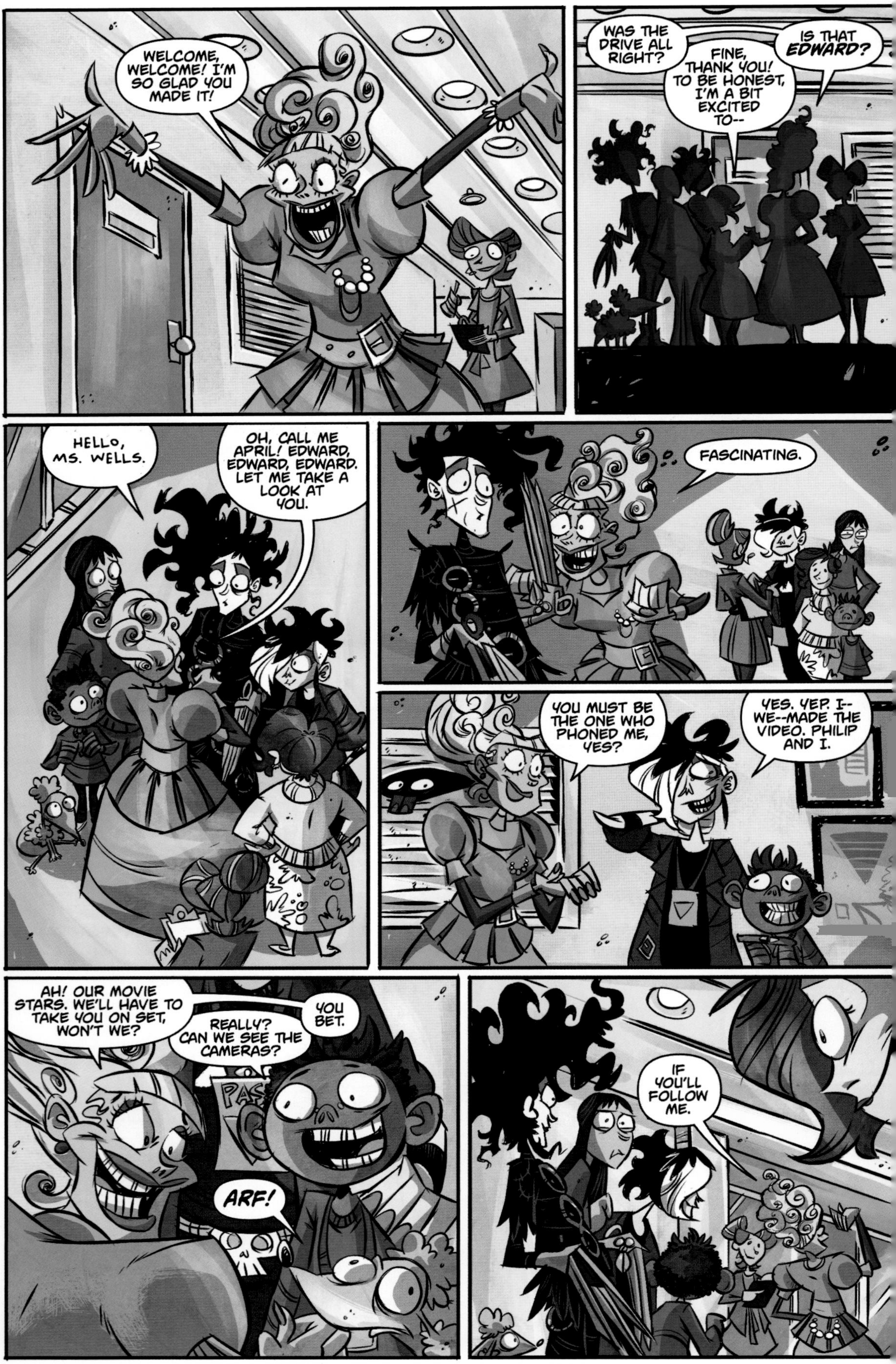
WELCOME, WELCOME! I'M SO GLAD YOU MADE IT!
WAS THE DRIVE ALL RIGHT?
FINE, THANK YOU! TO BE HONEST, I'M A BIT EXCITED TO--
IS THAT EDWARD?
HELLO, MS. WELLS.
OH, CALL ME APRIL! EDWARD, EDWARD, EDWARD. LET ME TAKE A LOOK AT YOU.
FASCINATING.
YOU MUST BE THE ONE WHO PHONED ME, YES?
YES. YEP. I-- WE--MADE THE VIDEO. PHILIP AND I.
AH! OUR MOVIE STARS. WE'LL HAVE TO TAKE YOU ON SET, WON'T WE?
REALLY? CAN WE SEE THE CAMERAS?
YOU BET.
ARF!
IF YOU'LL FOLLOW ME.

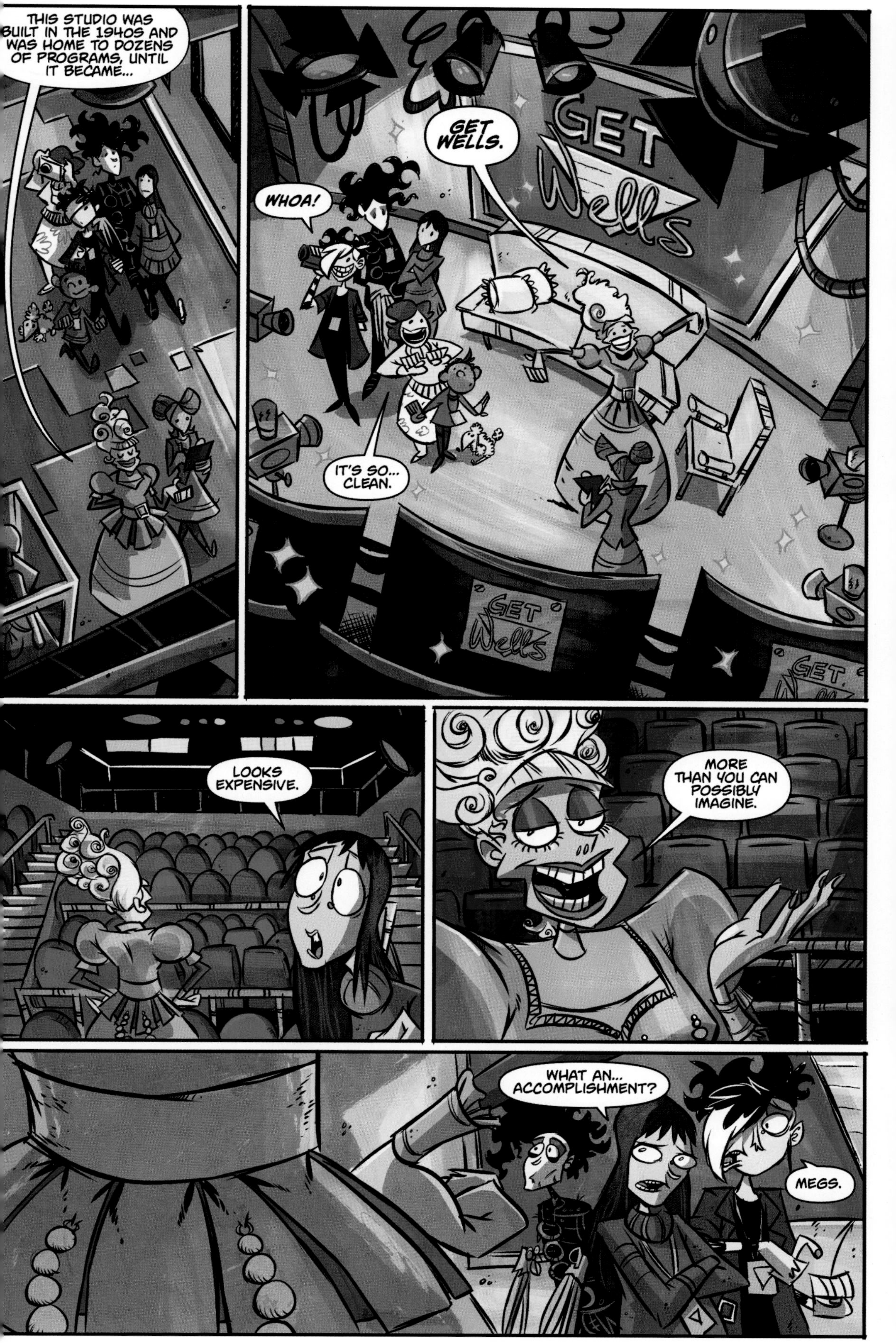
THIS STUDIO WAS BUILT IN THE 1940S AND WAS HOME TO DOZENS OF PROGRAMS, UNTIL IT BECAME...
GET WELLS.
WHOA!
GET Wells
IT'S SO... CLEAN.
GET Wells
LOOKS EXPENSIVE.
MORE THAN YOU CAN POSSIBLY IMAGINE.
WHAT AN... ACCOMPLISHMENT?
MEGS.

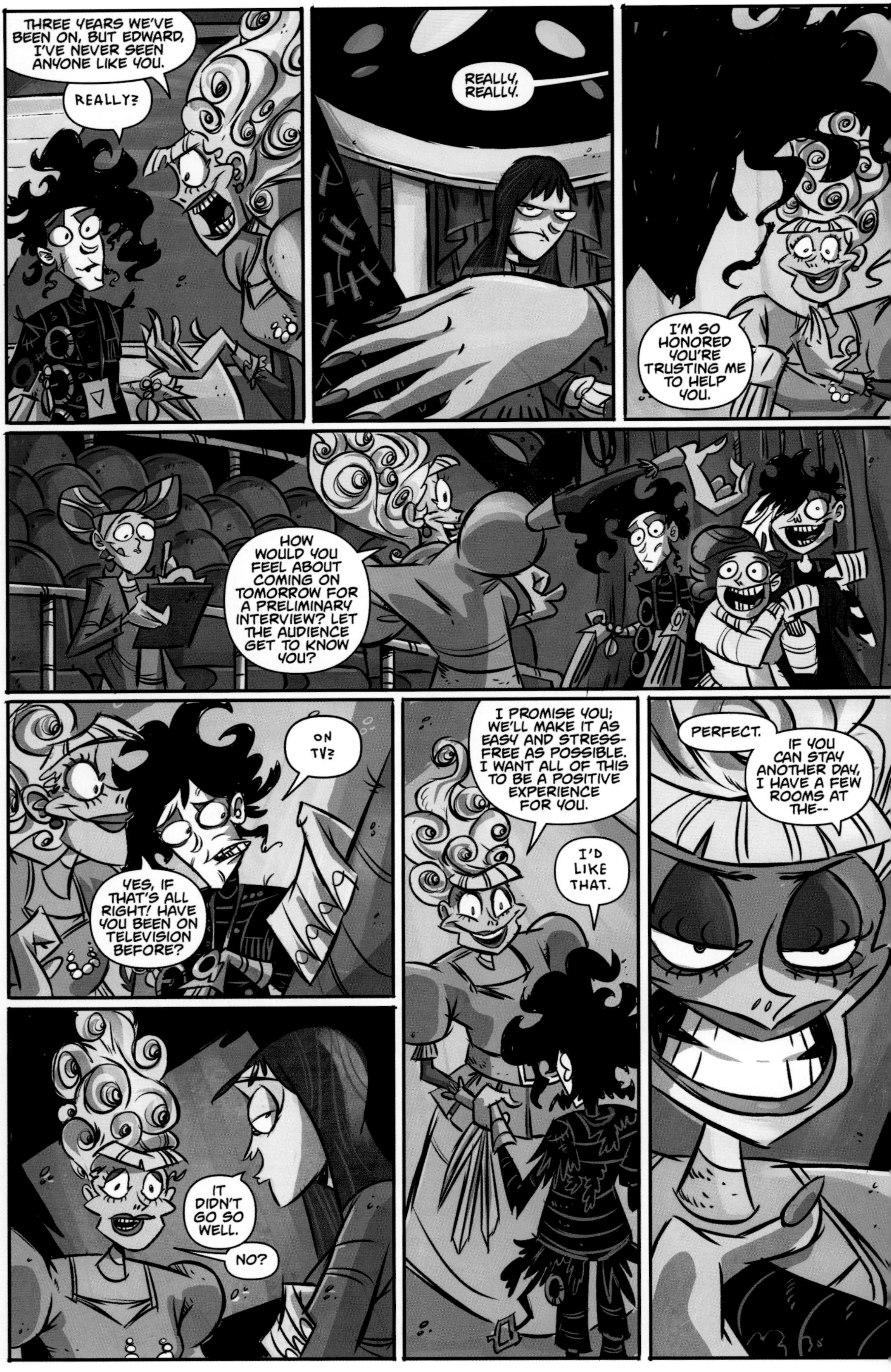
THREE YEARS WE'VE BEEN ON, BUT EDWARD, I'VE NEVER SEEN ANYONE LIKE YOU.
REALLY?
REALLY, REALLY.
I'M SO HONORED YOU'RE TRUSTING ME TO HELP YOU.
HOW WOULD YOU FEEL ABOUT COMING ON TOMORROW FOR A PRELIMINARY INTERVIEW? LET THE AUDIENCE GET TO KNOW YOU?
ON TV?
YES, IF THAT'S ALL RIGHT! HAVE YOU BEEN ON TELEVISION BEFORE?
IT DIDN'T GO SO WELL.
NO?
I PROMISE YOU; WE'LL MAKE IT AS EASY AND STRESS-FREE AS POSSIBLE. I WANT ALL OF THIS TO BE A POSITIVE EXPERIENCE FOR YOU.
I'D LIKE THAT.
PERFECT.
IF YOU CAN STAY ANOTHER DAY, I HAVE A FEW ROOMS AT THE--

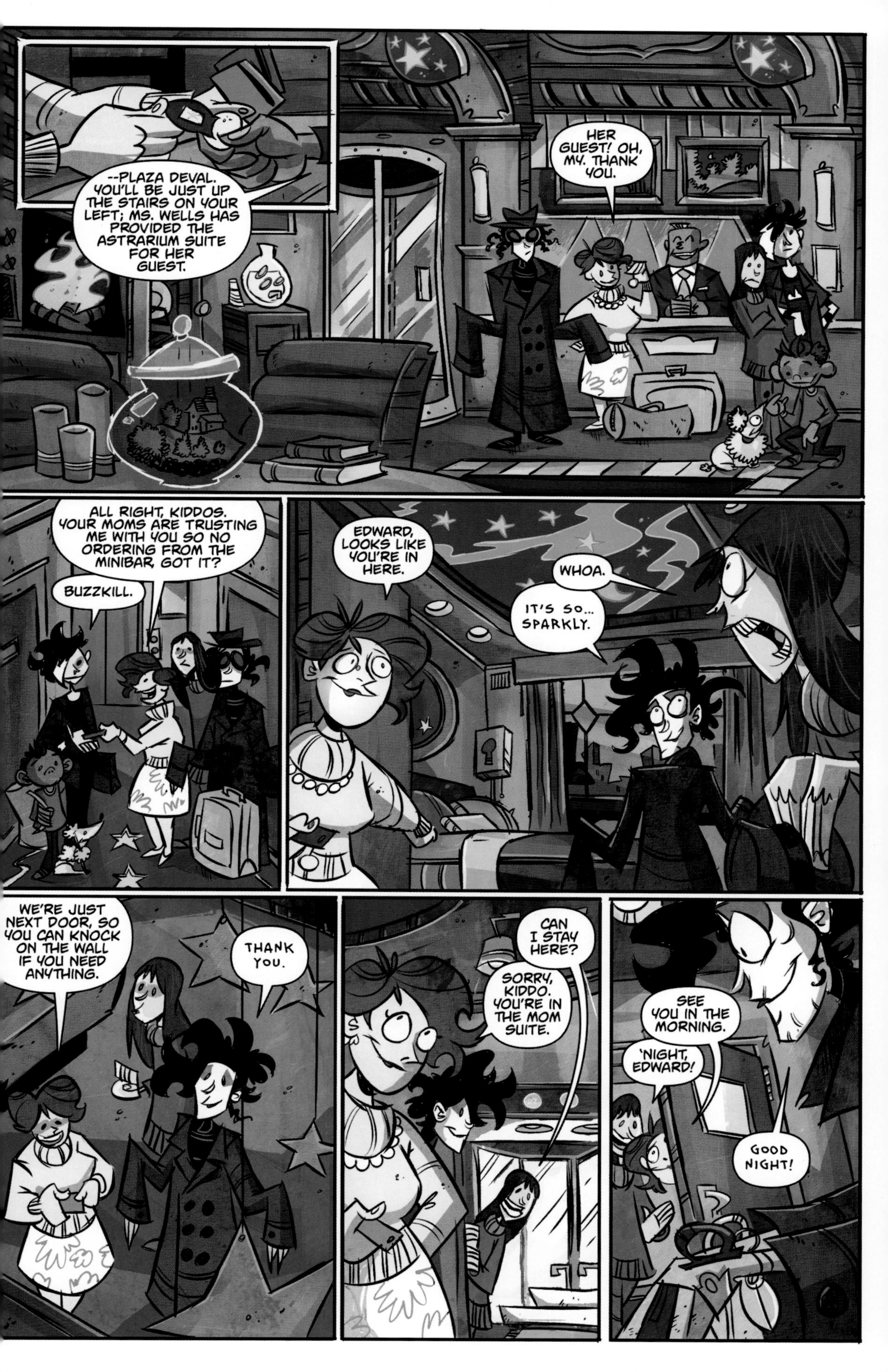
--PLAZA DEVAL. YOU'LL BE JUST UP THE STAIRS ON YOUR LEFT; MS. WELLS HAS PROVIDED THE ASTRARIUM SUITE FOR HER GUEST.
HER GUEST! OH, MY. THANK YOU.
ALL RIGHT, KIDDOS. YOUR MOMS ARE TRUSTING ME WITH YOU SO NO ORDERING FROM THE MINIBAR, GOT IT?
BUZZKILL.
EDWARD, LOOKS LIKE YOU'RE IN HERE.
WHOA.
IT'S SO... SPARKLY.
WE'RE JUST NEXT DOOR, SO YOU CAN KNOCK ON THE WALL IF YOU NEED ANYTHING.
THANK YOU.
CAN I STAY HERE?
SORRY, KIDDO. YOU'RE IN THE MOM SUITE.
SEE YOU IN THE MORNING.
'NIGHT, EDWARD!
GOOD NIGHT!

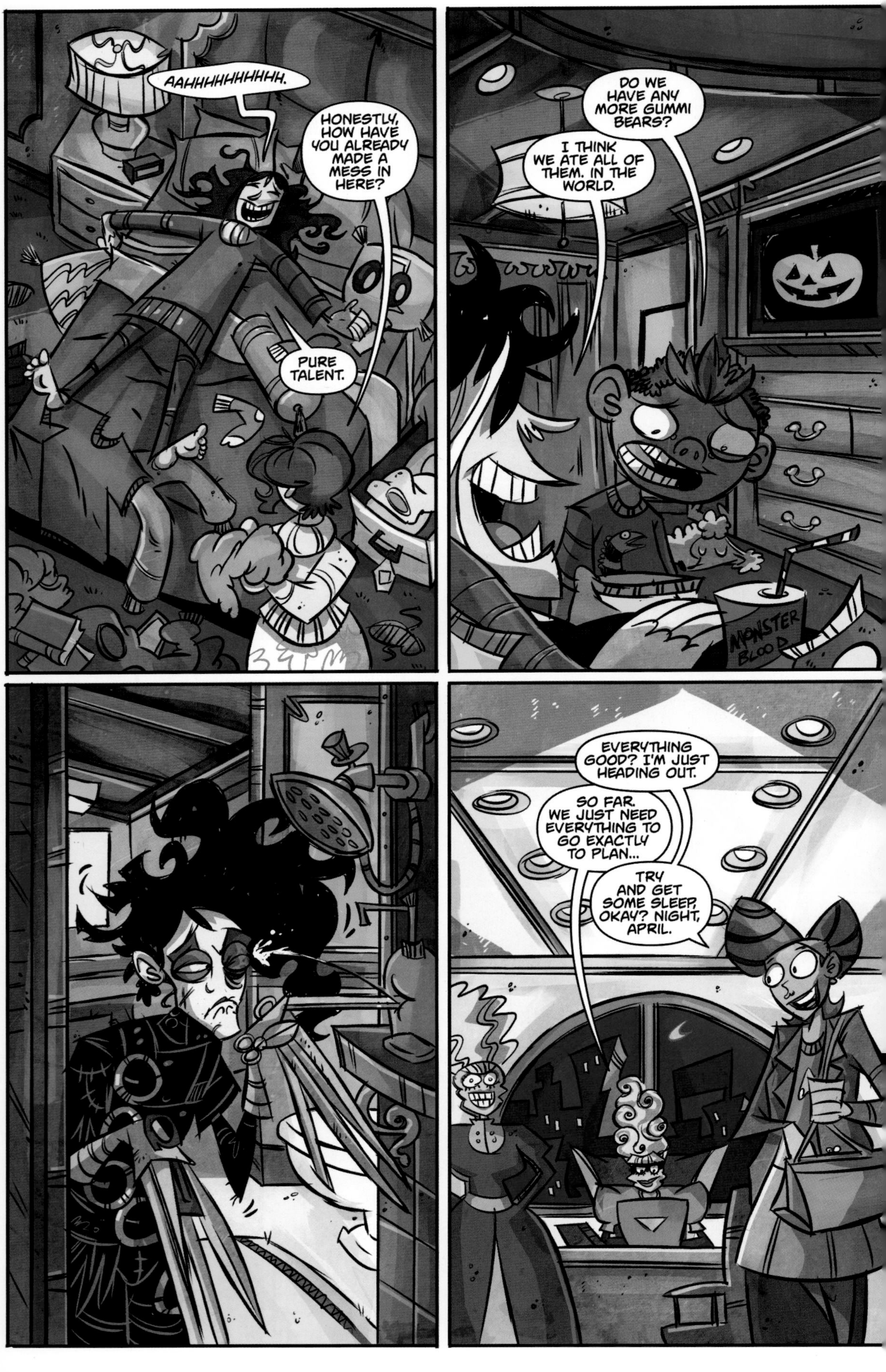
AAHHHHHHHHHH.
HONESTLY, HOW HAVE YOU ALREADY MADE A MESS IN HERE?
PURE TALENT.
DO WE HAVE ANY MORE GUMMI BEARS?
I THINK WE ATE ALL OF THEM. IN THE WORLD.
MONSTER BLOOD
EVERYTHING GOOD? I'M JUST HEADING OUT.
SO FAR. WE JUST NEED EVERYTHING TO GO EXACTLY TO PLAN...
TRY AND GET SOME SLEEP, OKAY? NIGHT, APRIL.

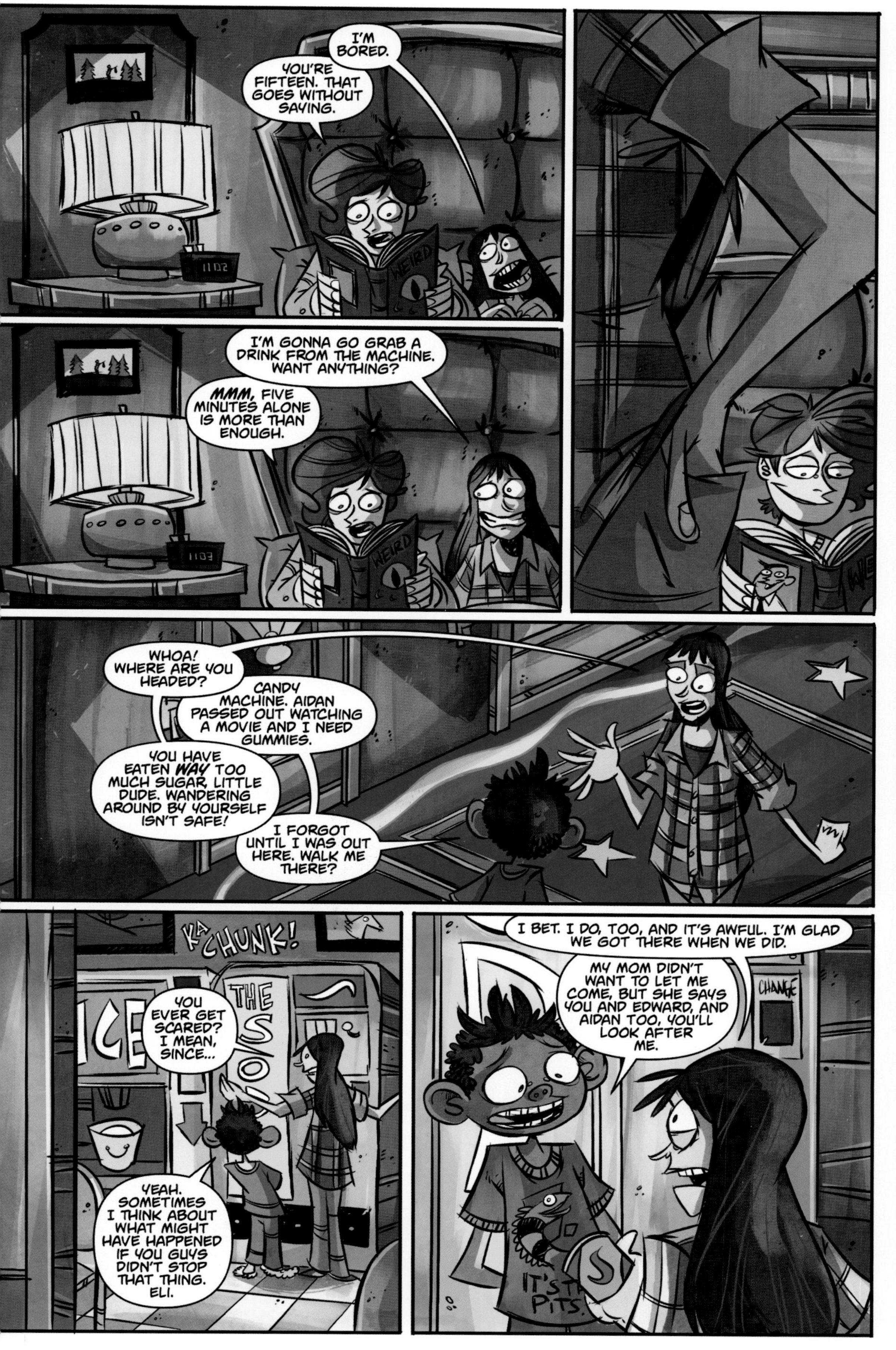
I'M BORED.
YOU'RE FIFTEEN. THAT GOES WITHOUT SAYING.
WEIRD
1102
I'M GONNA GO GRAB A DRINK FROM THE MACHINE. WANT ANYTHING?
MMM, FIVE MINUTES ALONE IS MORE THAN ENOUGH.
WEIRD
1103
WHOA! WHERE ARE YOU HEADED?
CANDY MACHINE. AIDAN PASSED OUT WATCHING A MOVIE AND I NEED GUMMIES.
YOU HAVE EATEN WAY TOO MUCH SUGAR, LITTLE DUDE. WANDERING AROUND BY YOURSELF ISN'T SAFE!
I FORGOT UNTIL I WAS OUT HERE. WALK ME THERE?
KACHUNK!
ICE
YOU EVER GET SCARED? I MEAN, SINCE...
YEAH. SOMETIMES I THINK ABOUT WHAT MIGHT HAVE HAPPENED IF YOU GUYS DIDN'T STOP THAT THING. ELI.
I BET. I DO, TOO, AND IT'S AWFUL. I'M GLAD WE GOT THERE WHEN WE DID.
MY MOM DIDN'T WANT TO LET ME COME, BUT SHE SAYS YOU AND EDWARD, AND AIDAN TOO, YOU'LL LOOK AFTER ME.
CHANGE

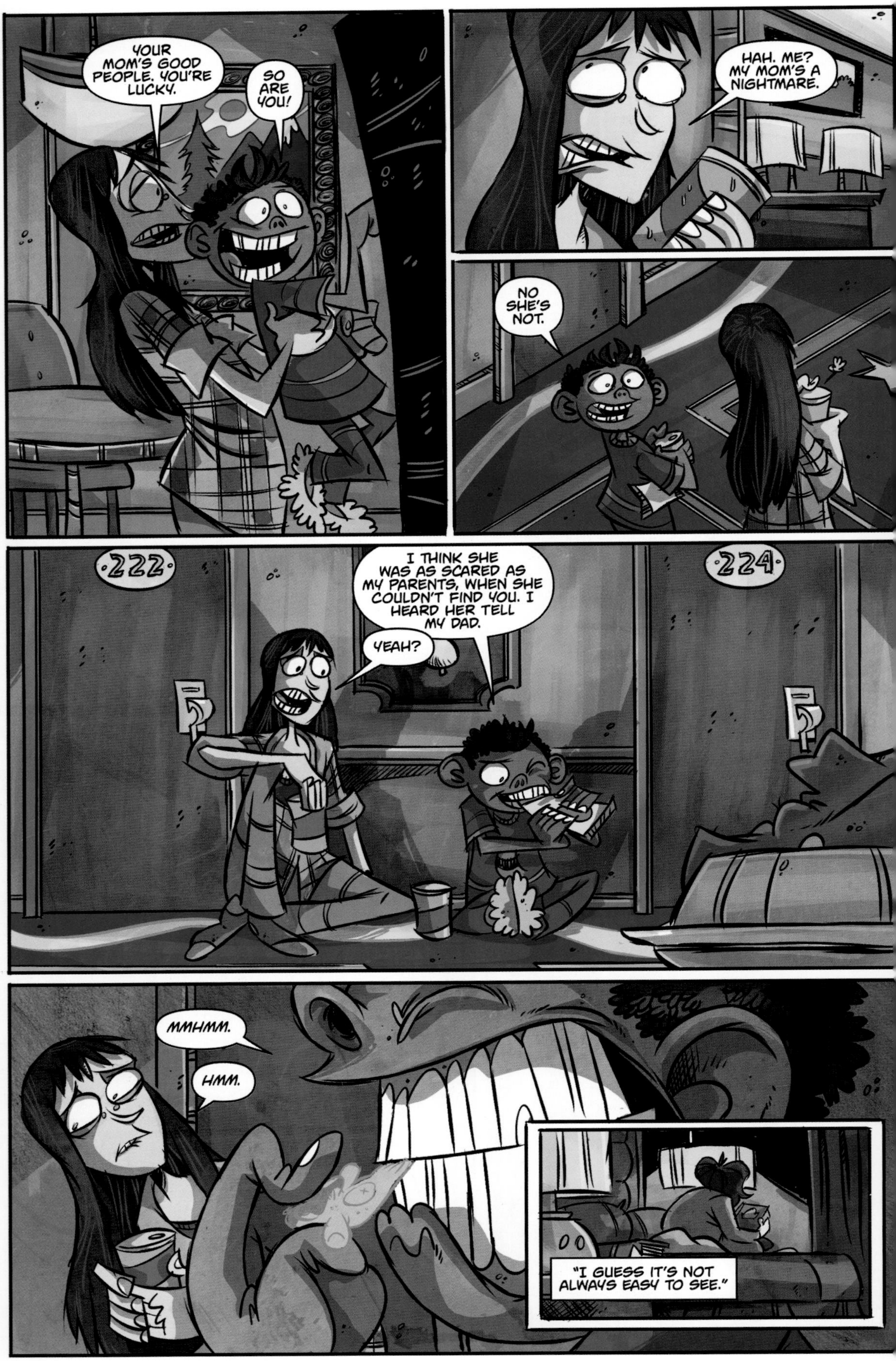
YOUR MOM'S GOOD PEOPLE. YOU'RE LUCKY.
SO ARE YOU!
HAH. ME? MY MOM'S A NIGHTMARE.
NO SHE'S NOT.
222
224
I THINK SHE WAS AS SCARED AS MY PARENTS, WHEN SHE COULDN'T FIND YOU. I HEARD HER TELL MY DAD.
YEAH?
MMHMM.
HMM.
"I GUESS IT'S NOT ALWAYS EASY TO SEE."

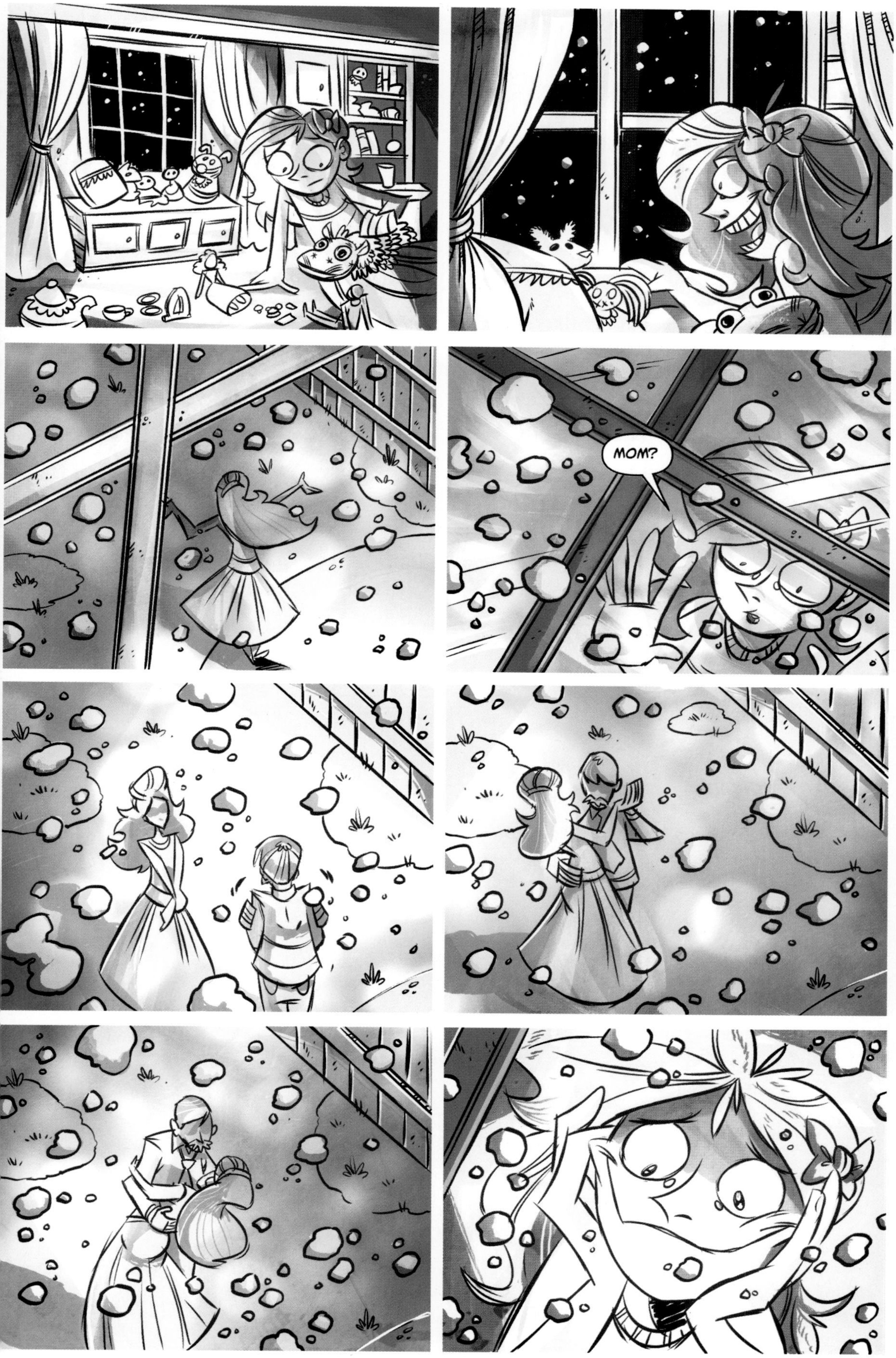
MOM?

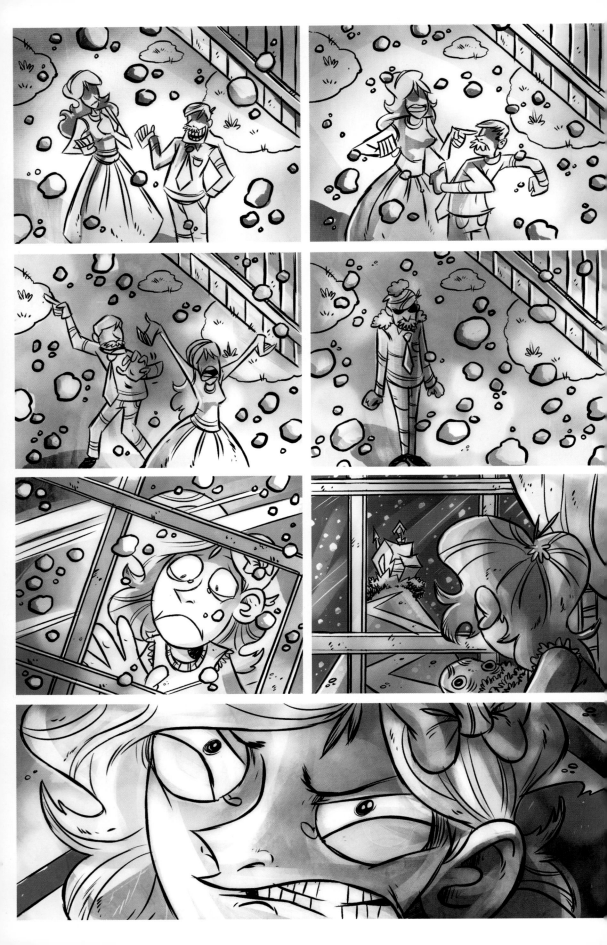

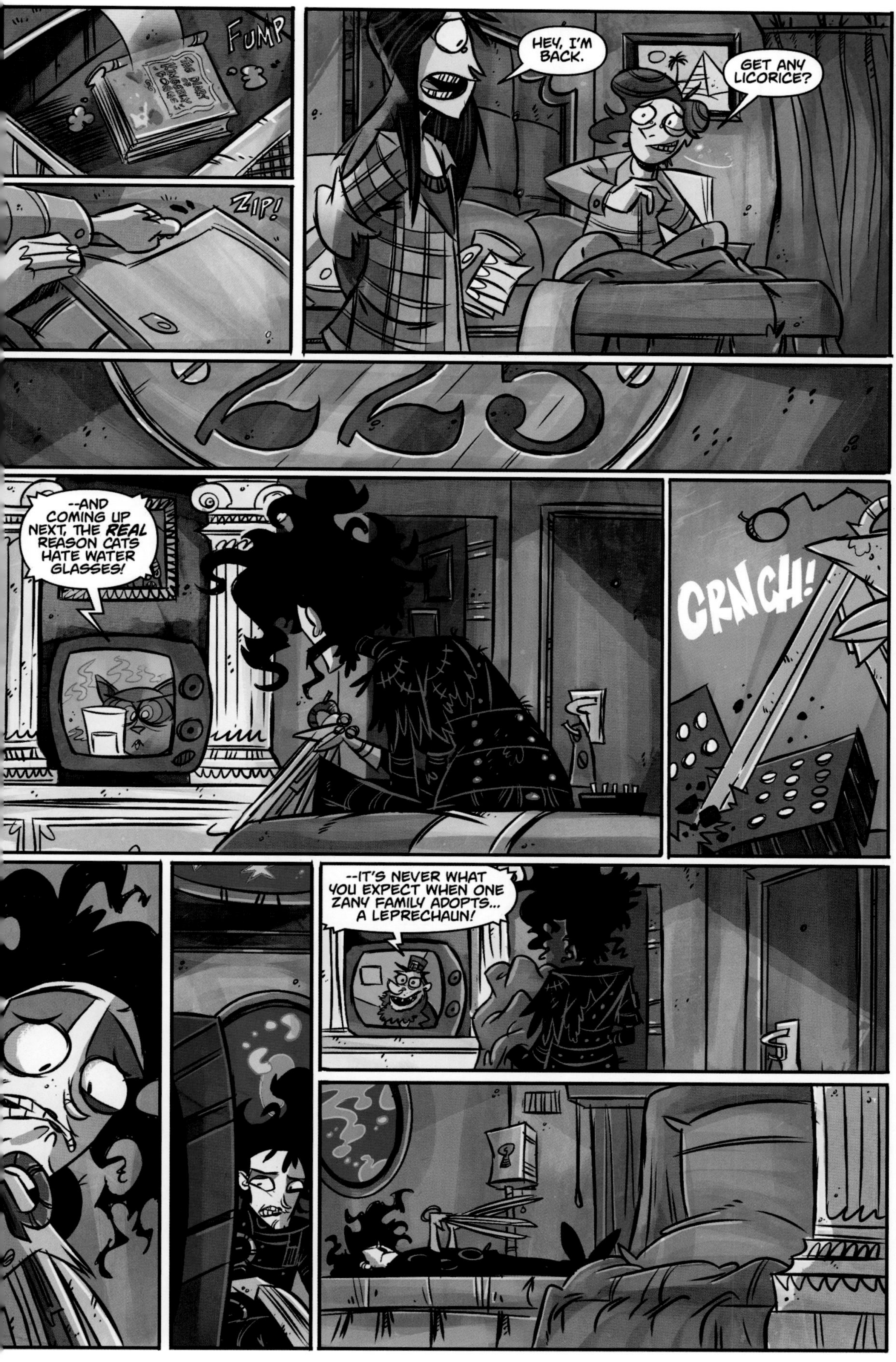
FUMP
THE DIARY OF KIMBERLY BOGGS
ZIP!
HEY, I'M BACK.
GET ANY LICORICE?
--AND COMING UP NEXT, THE REAL REASON CATS HATE WATER GLASSES!
GRNCH!
--IT'S NEVER WHAT YOU EXPECT WHEN ONE ZANY FAMILY ADOPTS... A LEPRECHAUN!

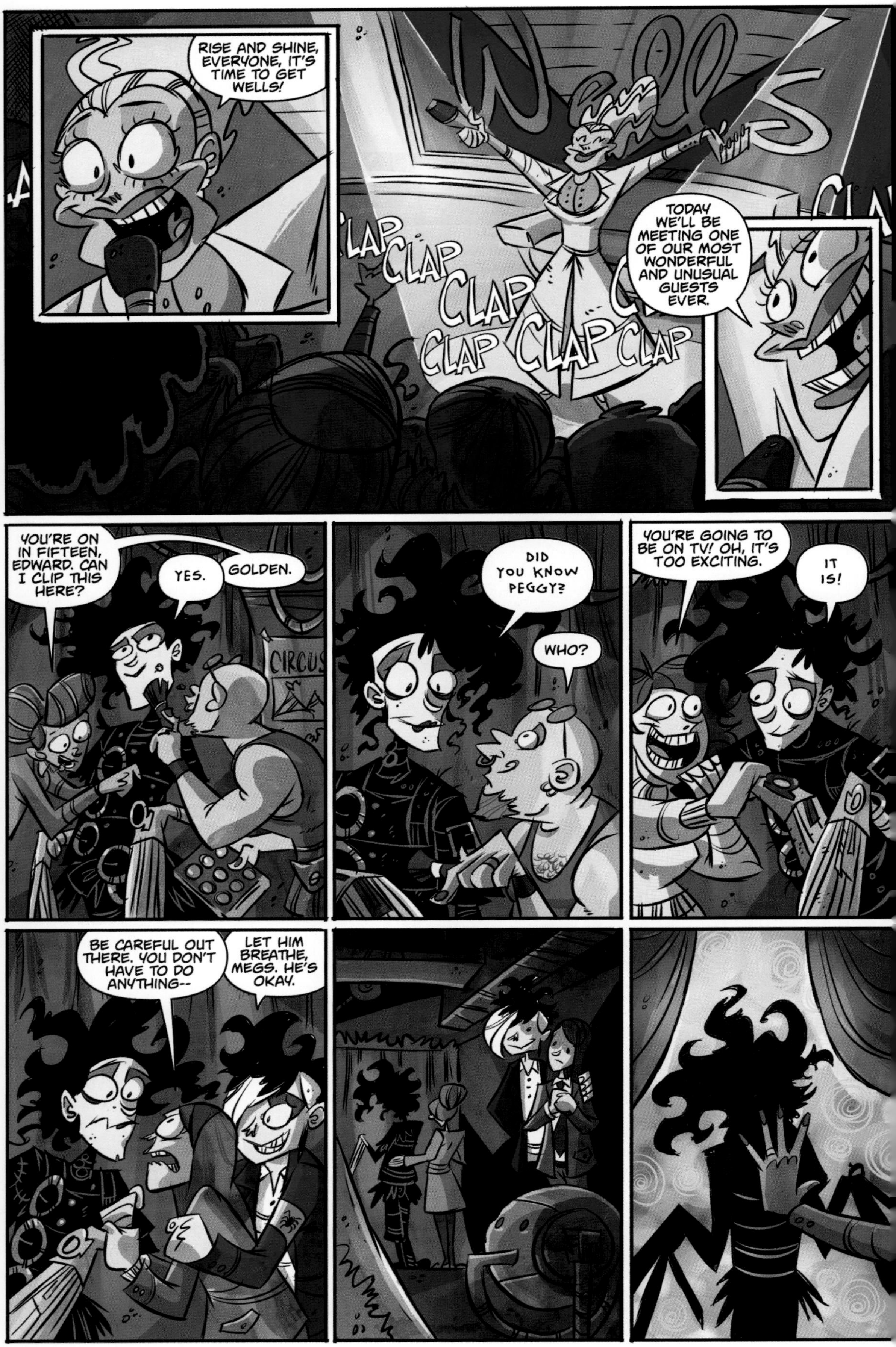
RISE AND SHINE, EVERYONE, IT'S TIME TO GET WELLS!
WELLS
CLAP CLAP CLAP CLAP CLAP CLAP
TODAY WE'LL BE MEETING ONE OF OUR MOST WONDERFUL AND UNUSUAL GUESTS EVER.
YOU'RE ON IN FIFTEEN, EDWARD. CAN I CLIP THIS HERE?
YES.
GOLDEN.
CIRCUS
DID YOU KNOW PEGGY?
WHO?
YOU'RE GOING TO BE ON TV! OH, IT'S TOO EXCITING.
IT IS!
BE CAREFUL OUT THERE. YOU DON'T HAVE TO DO ANYTHING--
LET HIM BREATHE, MEGS. HE'S OKAY.

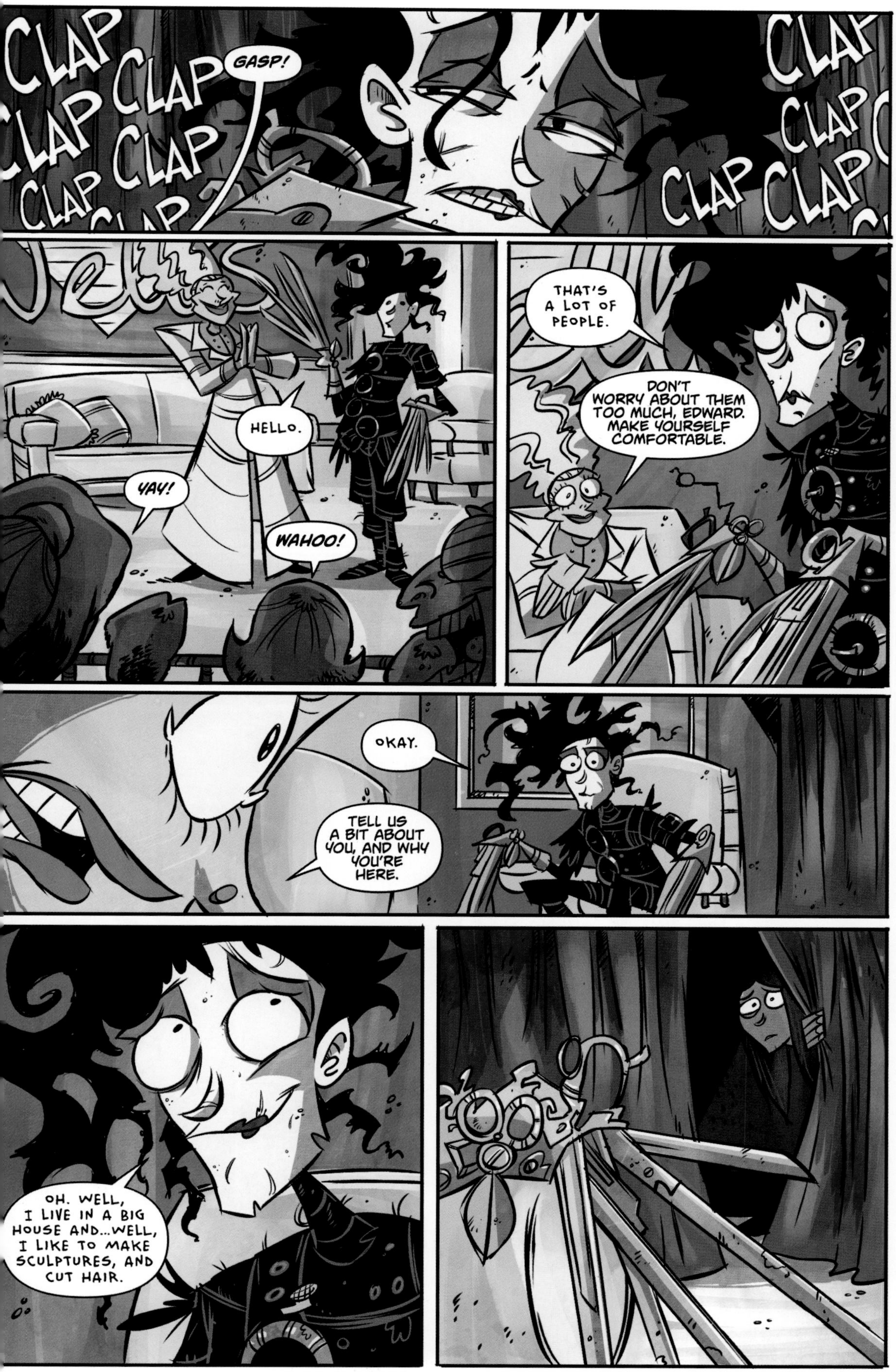
CLAP CLAP CLAP CLAP CLAP CLAP
GASP!
CLAP CLAP CLAP CLAP
HELLO.
YAY!
WAHOO!
THAT'S A LOT OF PEOPLE.
DON'T WORRY ABOUT THEM TOO MUCH, EDWARD. MAKE YOURSELF COMFORTABLE.
OKAY.
TELL US A BIT ABOUT YOU, AND WHY YOU'RE HERE.
OH. WELL, I LIVE IN A BIG HOUSE AND...WELL, I LIKE TO MAKE SCULPTURES, AND CUT HAIR.

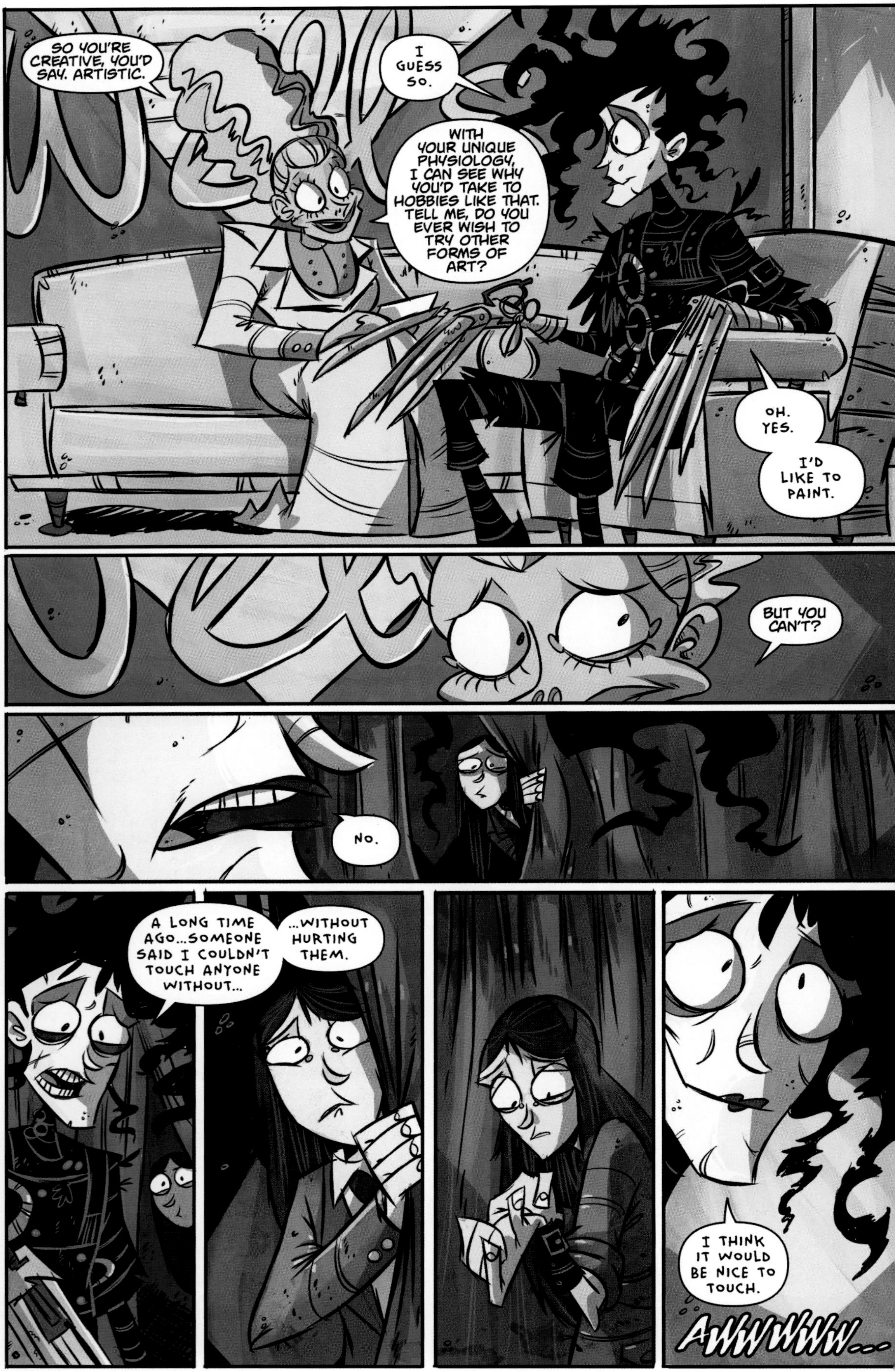
SO YOU'RE CREATIVE, YOU'D SAY. ARTISTIC.
I GUESS SO.
WITH YOUR UNIQUE PHYSIOLOGY, I CAN SEE WHY YOU'D TAKE TO HOBBIES LIKE THAT. TELL ME, DO YOU EVER WISH TO TRY OTHER FORMS OF ART?
OH. YES.
I'D LIKE TO PAINT.
BUT YOU CAN'T?
NO.
A LONG TIME AGO...SOMEONE SAID I COULDN'T TOUCH ANYONE WITHOUT...
...WITHOUT HURTING THEM.
I THINK IT WOULD BE NICE TO TOUCH.
AWWWWW...

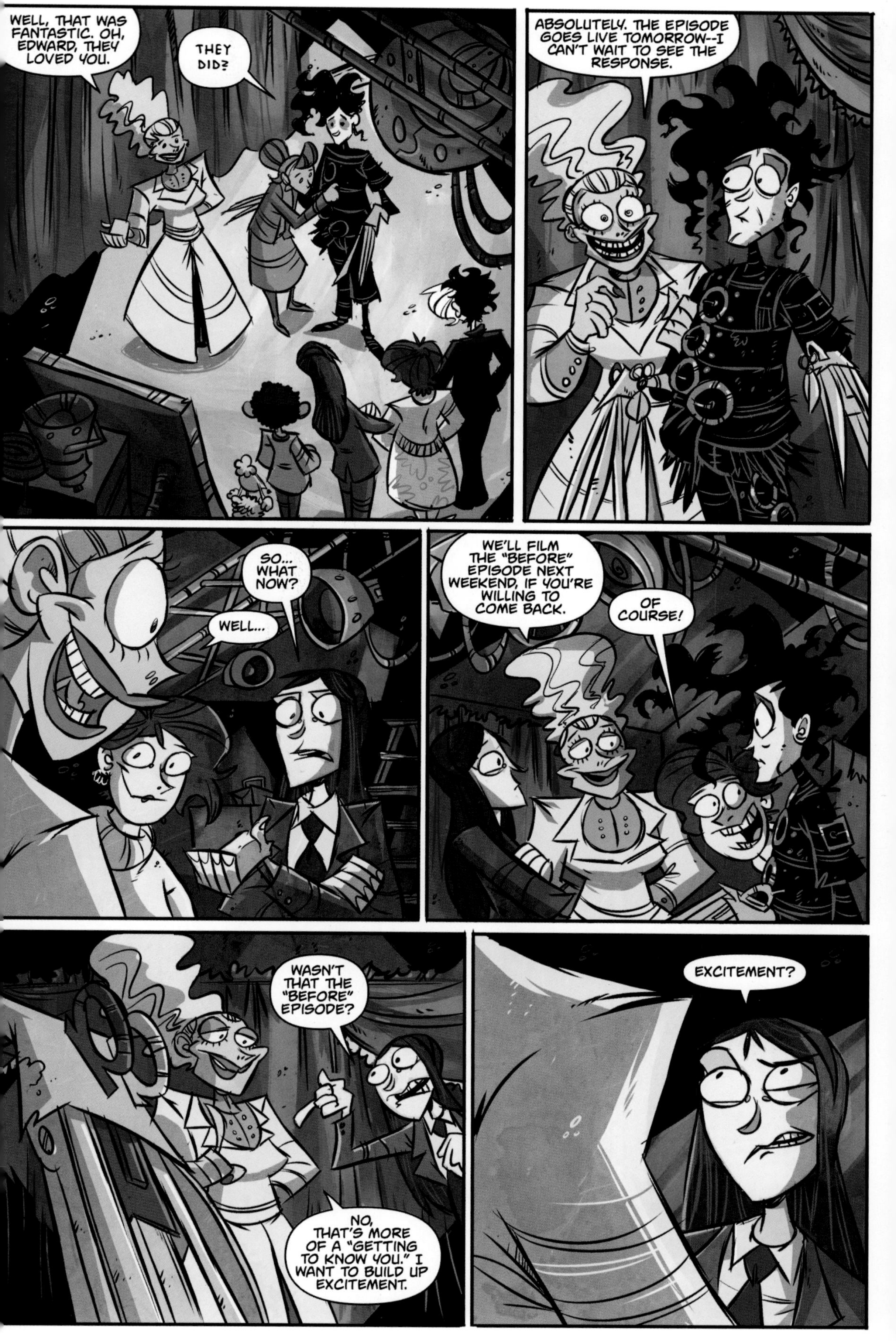
WELL, THAT WAS FANTASTIC. OH, EDWARD, THEY LOVED YOU.
THEY DID?
ABSOLUTELY. THE EPISODE GOES LIVE TOMORROW--I CAN'T WAIT TO SEE THE RESPONSE.
SO... WHAT NOW?
WELL...
WE'LL FILM THE "BEFORE" EPISODE NEXT WEEKEND, IF YOU'RE WILLING TO COME BACK.
OF COURSE!
WASN'T THAT THE "BEFORE" EPISODE?
NO, THAT'S MORE OF A "GETTING TO KNOW YOU." I WANT TO BUILD UP EXCITEMENT.
EXCITEMENT?

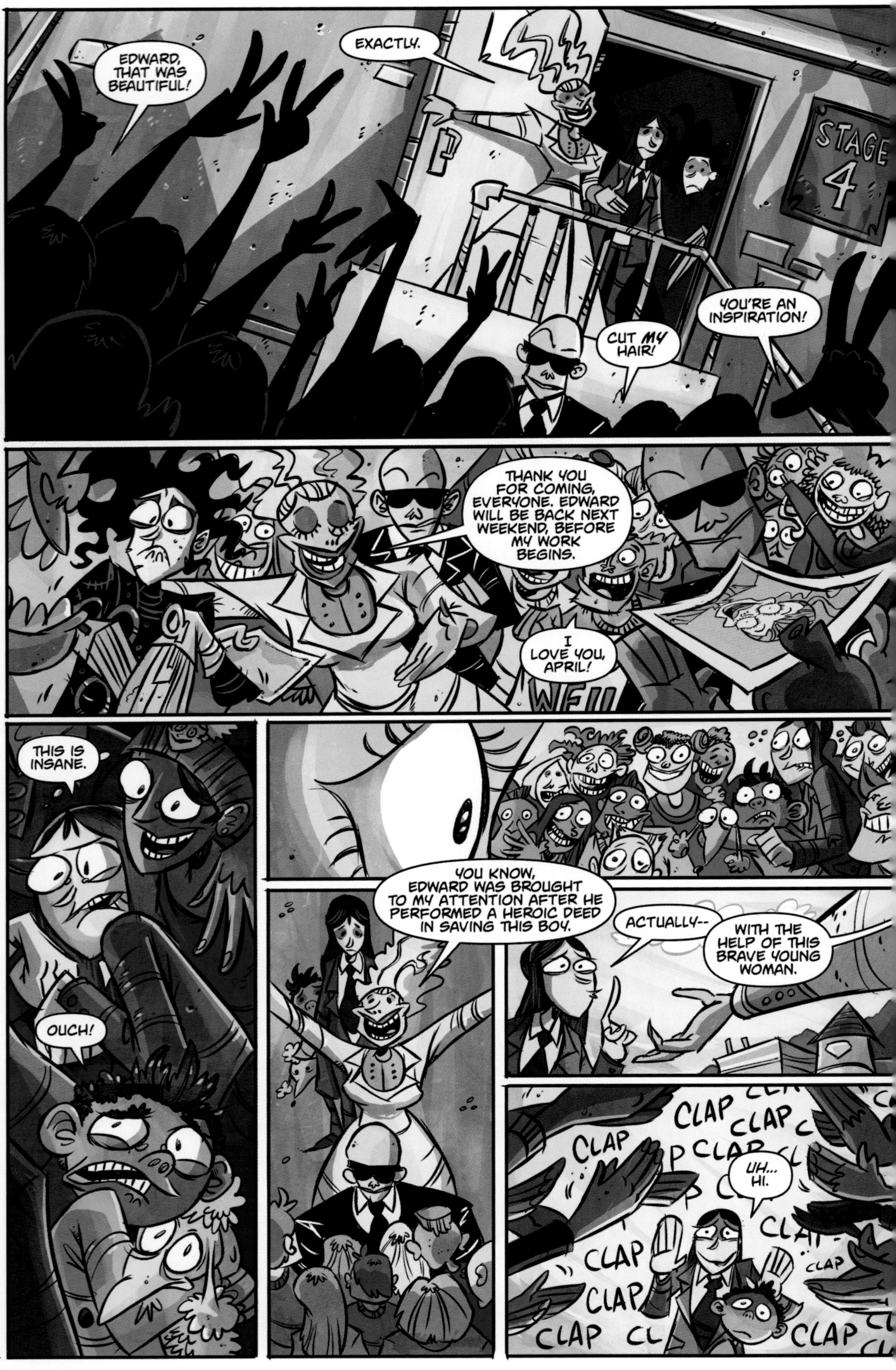
EDWARD, THAT WAS BEAUTIFUL!
EXACTLY.
STAGE 4
CUT MY HAIR!
YOU'RE AN INSPIRATION!
THANK YOU FOR COMING, EVERYONE. EDWARD WILL BE BACK NEXT WEEKEND, BEFORE MY WORK BEGINS.
I LOVE YOU, APRIL!
THIS IS INSANE.
OUCH!
YOU KNOW, EDWARD WAS BROUGHT TO MY ATTENTION AFTER HE PERFORMED A HEROIC DEED IN SAVING THIS BOY.
ACTUALLY--
WITH THE HELP OF THIS BRAVE YOUNG WOMAN.
CLAP CLAP CLAP CLAP CLAP
UH... HI.
CLAP CLAP CLAP CLAP CLAP

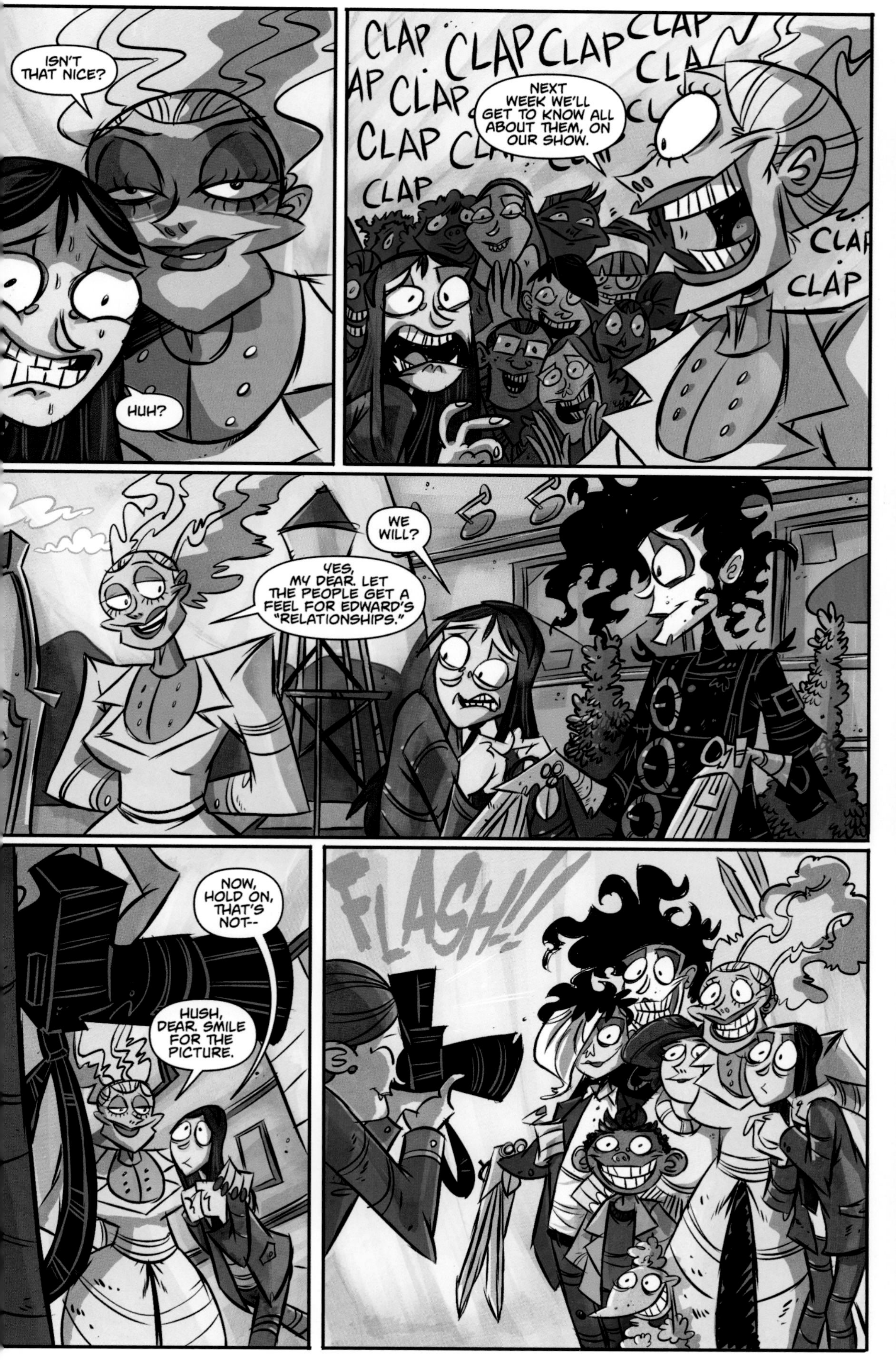
ISN'T THAT NICE?
HUH?
CLAP CLAP CLAP CLAP CLAP CLAP CLAP CLAP CLAP CLAP CLAP CLAP
NEXT WEEK WE'LL GET TO KNOW ALL ABOUT THEM, ON OUR SHOW.
WE WILL?
YES, MY DEAR. LET THE PEOPLE GET A FEEL FOR EDWARD'S "RELATIONSHIPS."
NOW, HOLD ON, THAT'S NOT--
HUSH, DEAR. SMILE FOR THE PICTURE.
FLASH!!

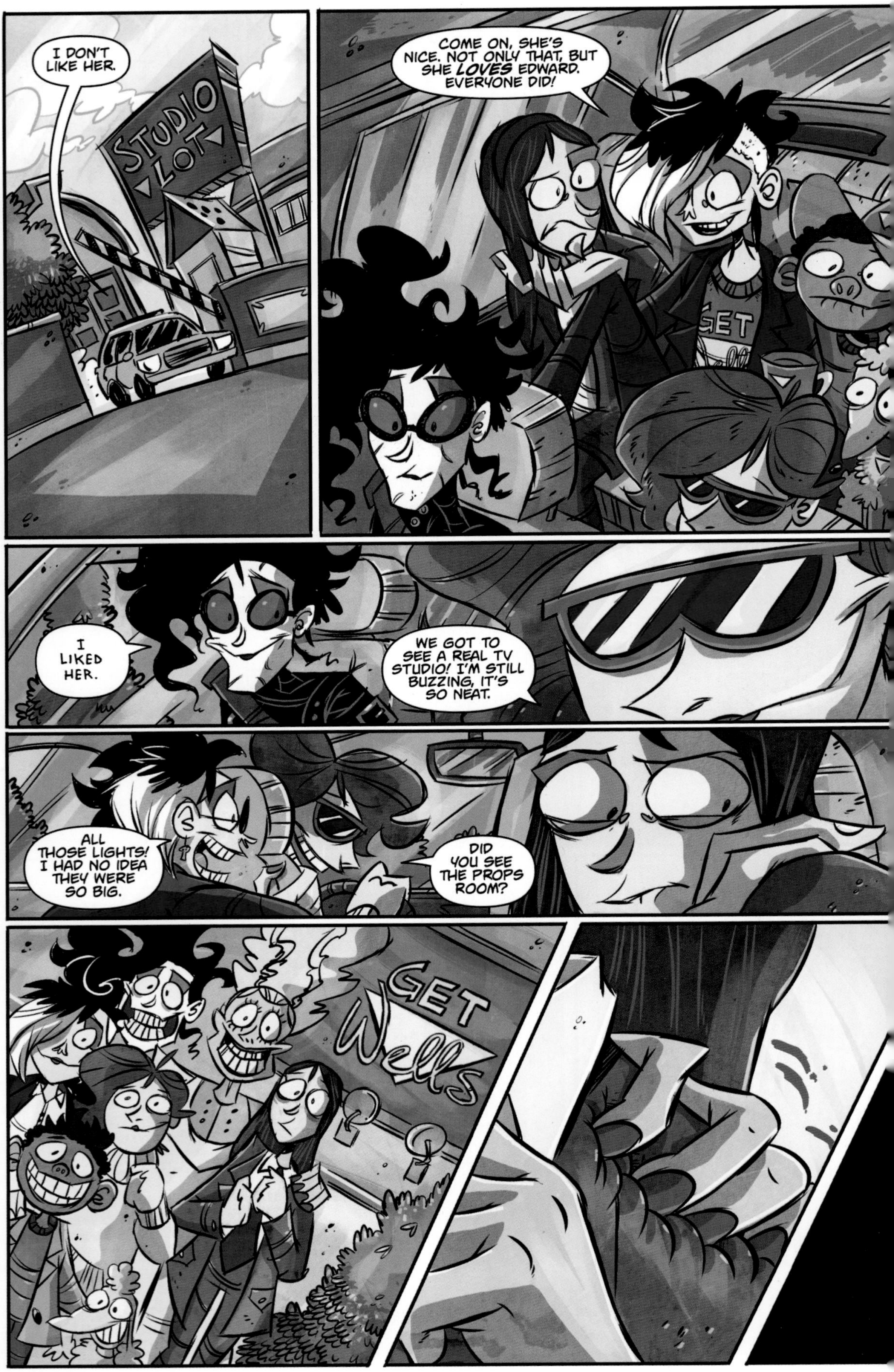
STUDIO LOT
I DON'T LIKE HER.
COME ON, SHE'S NICE. NOT ONLY THAT, BUT SHE *LOVES* EDWARD. EVERYONE DID!
GET
I LIKED HER.
WE GOT TO SEE A REAL TV STUDIO! I'M STILL BUZZING, IT'S SO NEAT.
ALL THOSE LIGHTS! I HAD NO IDEA THEY WERE SO BIG.
DID YOU SEE THE PROPS ROOM?
GET Wells

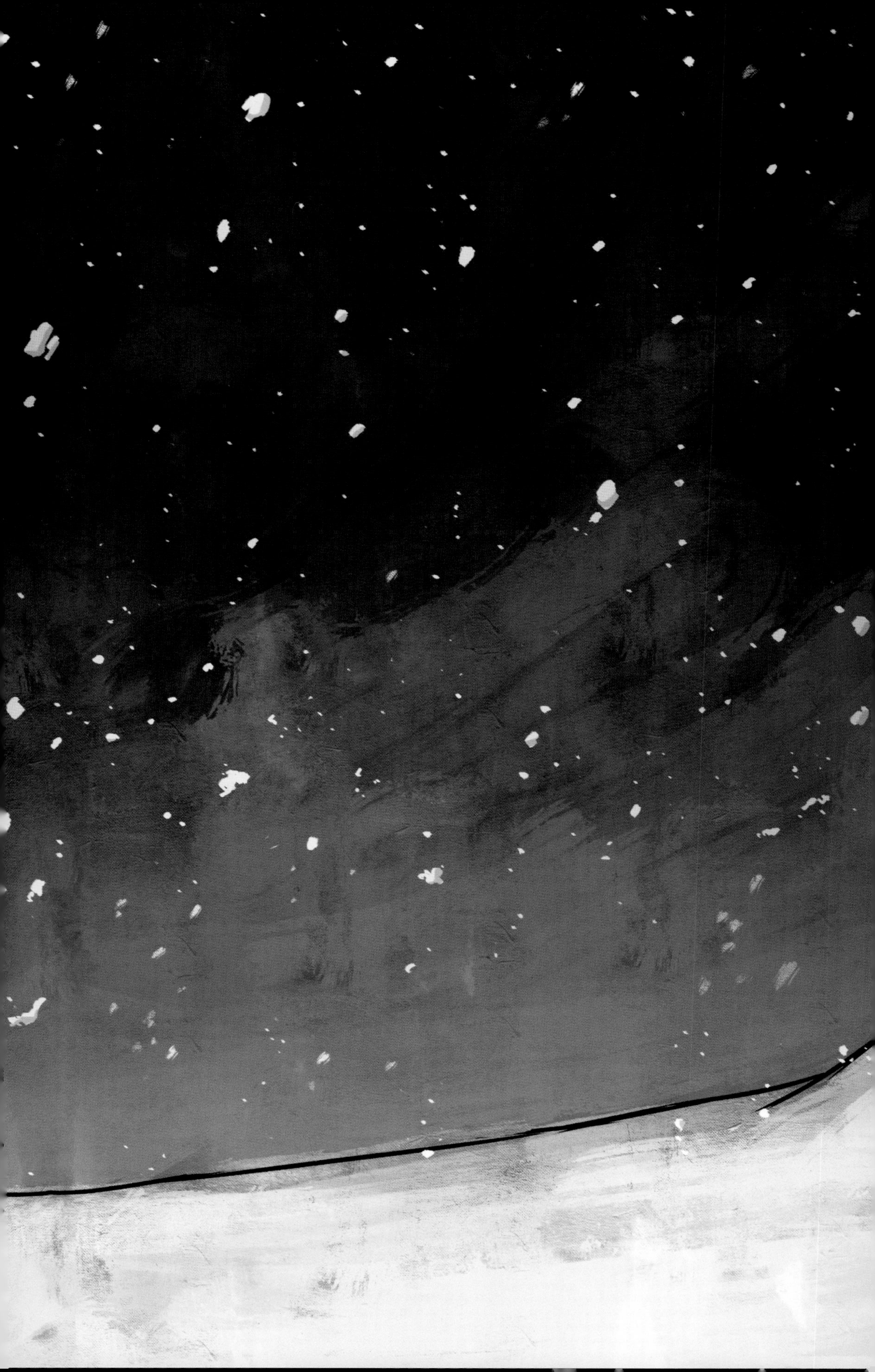

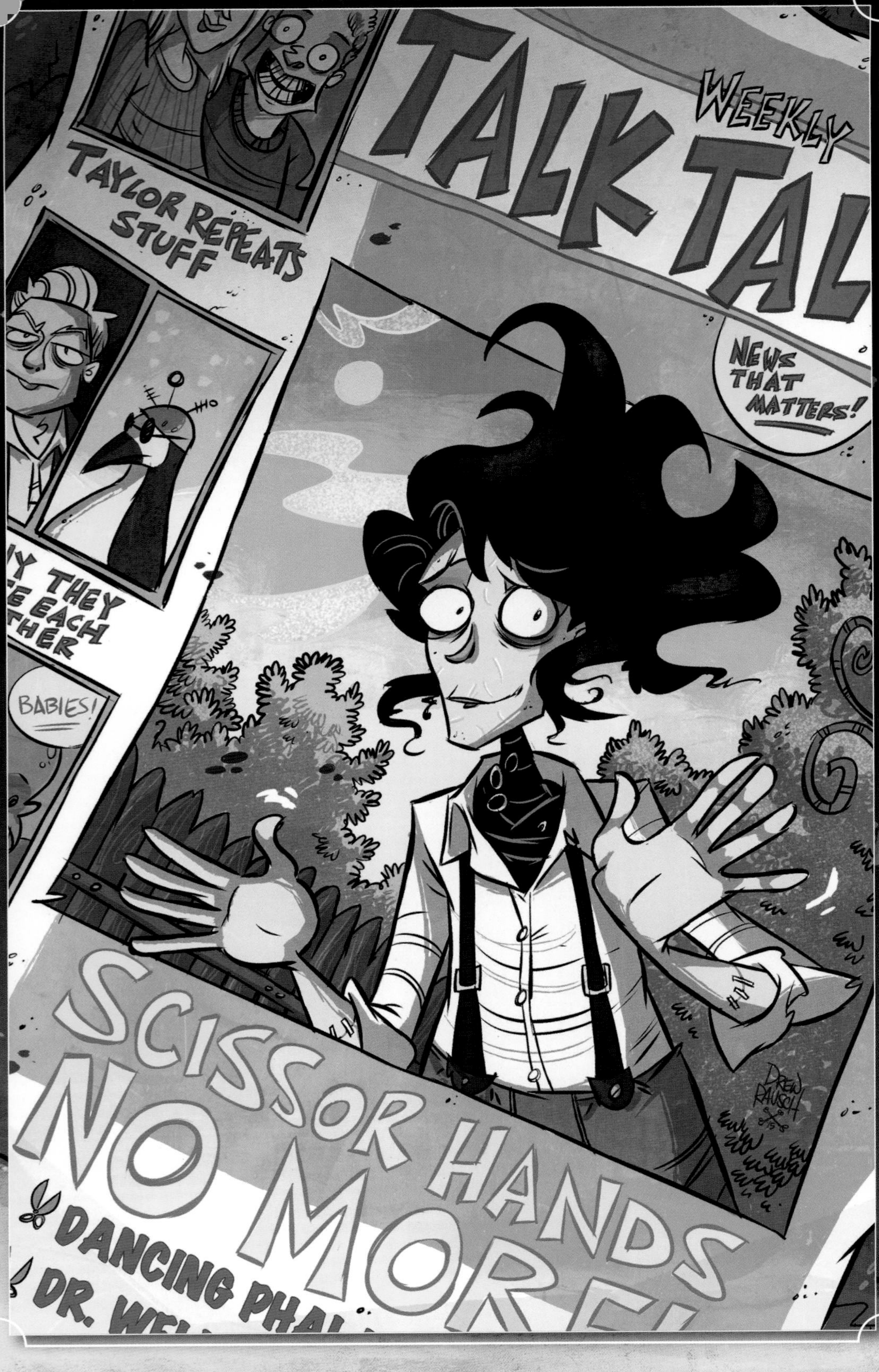
WEEKLY
TAYLOR REPEATS STUFF
NEWS THAT MATTERS!
BABIES!
SCISSOR HANDS
DREW RAUSCH

ART BY
DREW RAUSCH

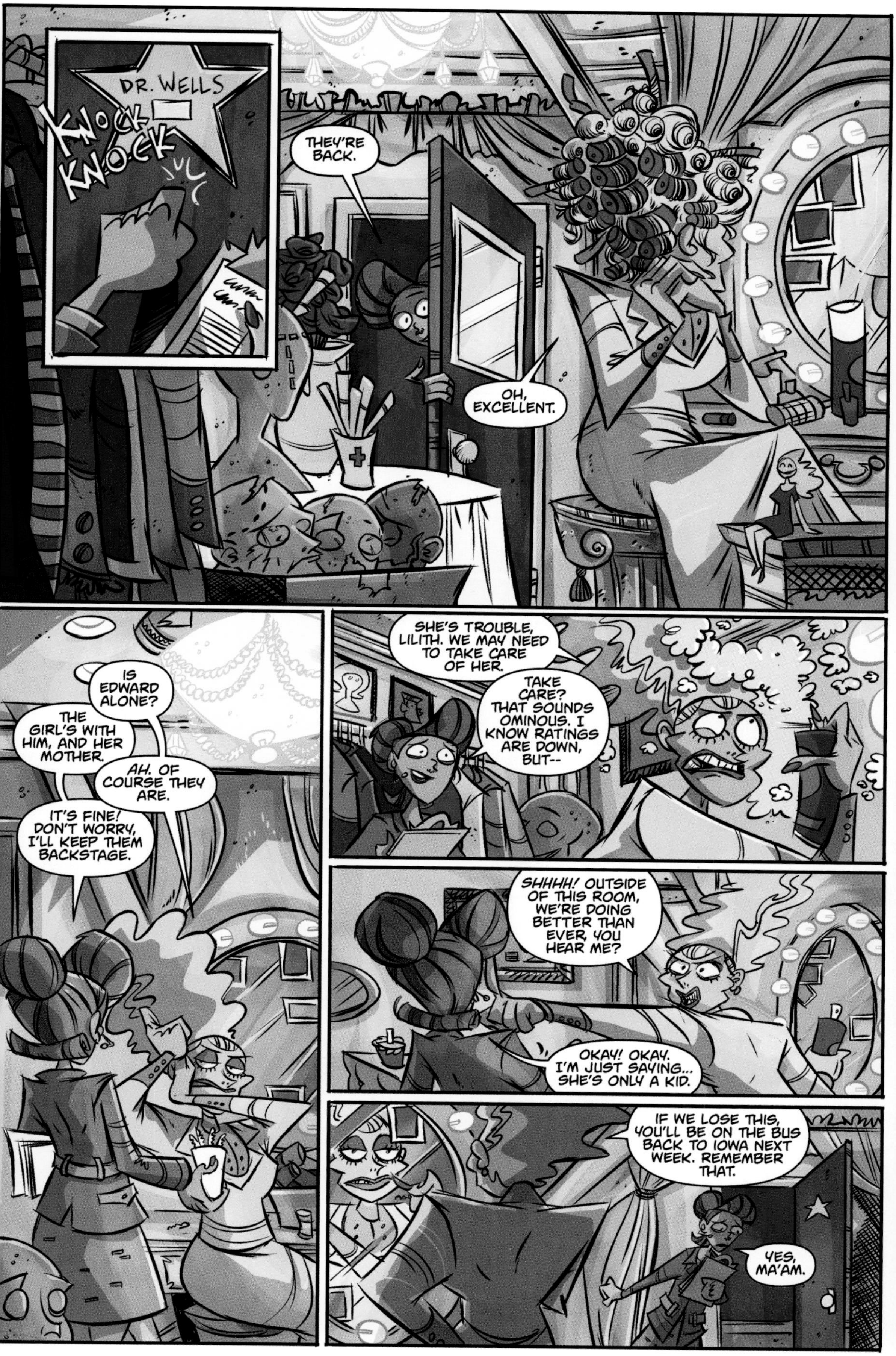
DR. WELLS
KNOCK KNOCK
THEY'RE BACK.
OH, EXCELLENT.
IS EDWARD ALONE?
THE GIRL'S WITH HIM, AND HER MOTHER.
AH. OF COURSE THEY ARE.
IT'S FINE! DON'T WORRY, I'LL KEEP THEM BACKSTAGE.
SHE'S TROUBLE, LILITH. WE MAY NEED TO TAKE CARE OF HER.
TAKE CARE? THAT SOUNDS OMINOUS. I KNOW RATINGS ARE DOWN, BUT--
SHHHH! OUTSIDE OF THIS ROOM, WE'RE DOING BETTER THAN EVER, YOU HEAR ME?
OKAY! OKAY. I'M JUST SAYING... SHE'S ONLY A KID.
IF WE LOSE THIS, YOU'LL BE ON THE BUS BACK TO IOWA NEXT WEEK. REMEMBER THAT.
YES, MA'AM.

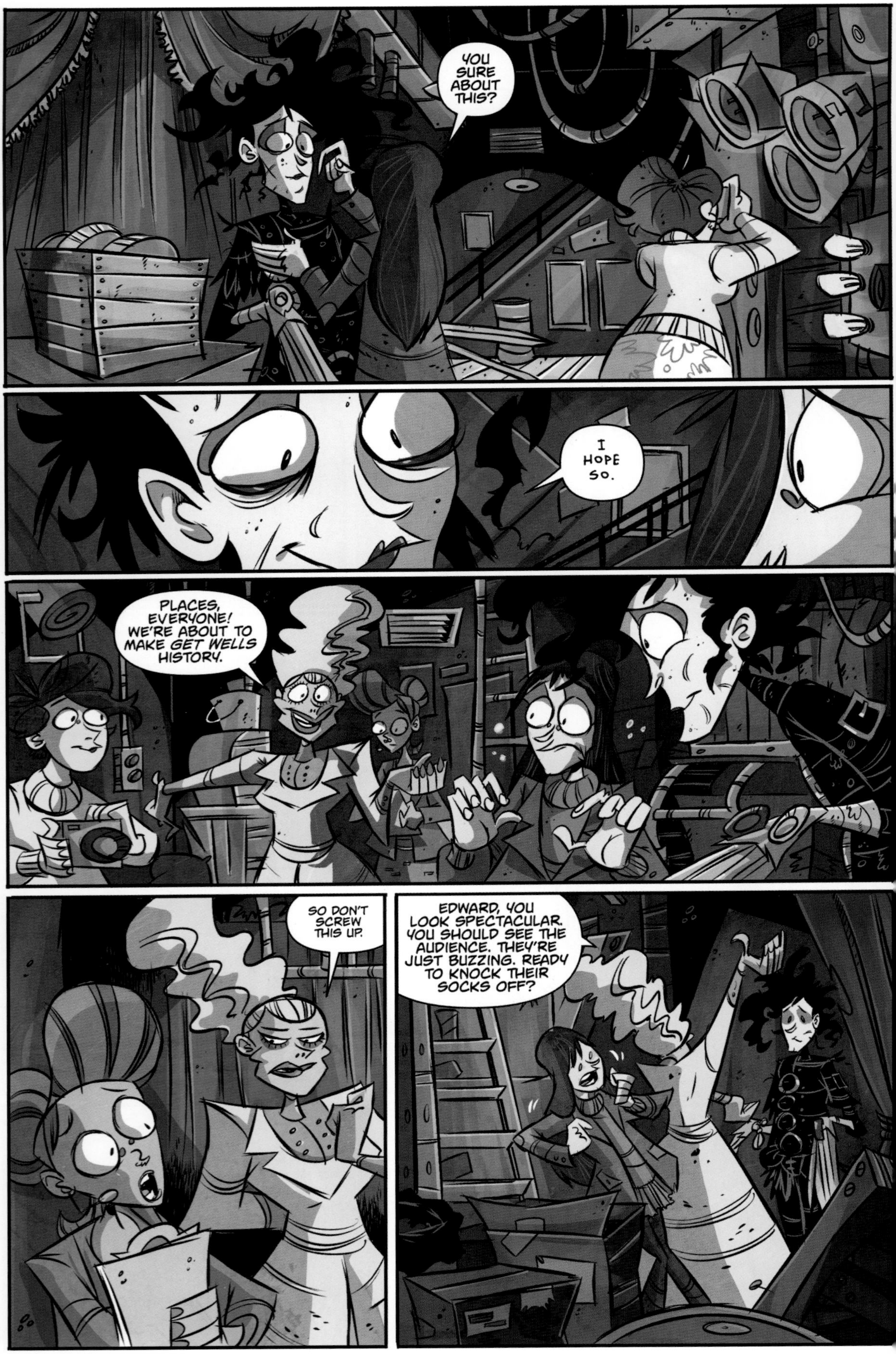

YOU SURE ABOUT THIS?
I HOPE SO.
PLACES, EVERYONE! WE'RE ABOUT TO MAKE GET WELLS HISTORY.
SO DON'T SCREW THIS UP.
EDWARD, YOU LOOK SPECTACULAR. YOU SHOULD SEE THE AUDIENCE. THEY'RE JUST BUZZING. READY TO KNOCK THEIR SOCKS OFF?

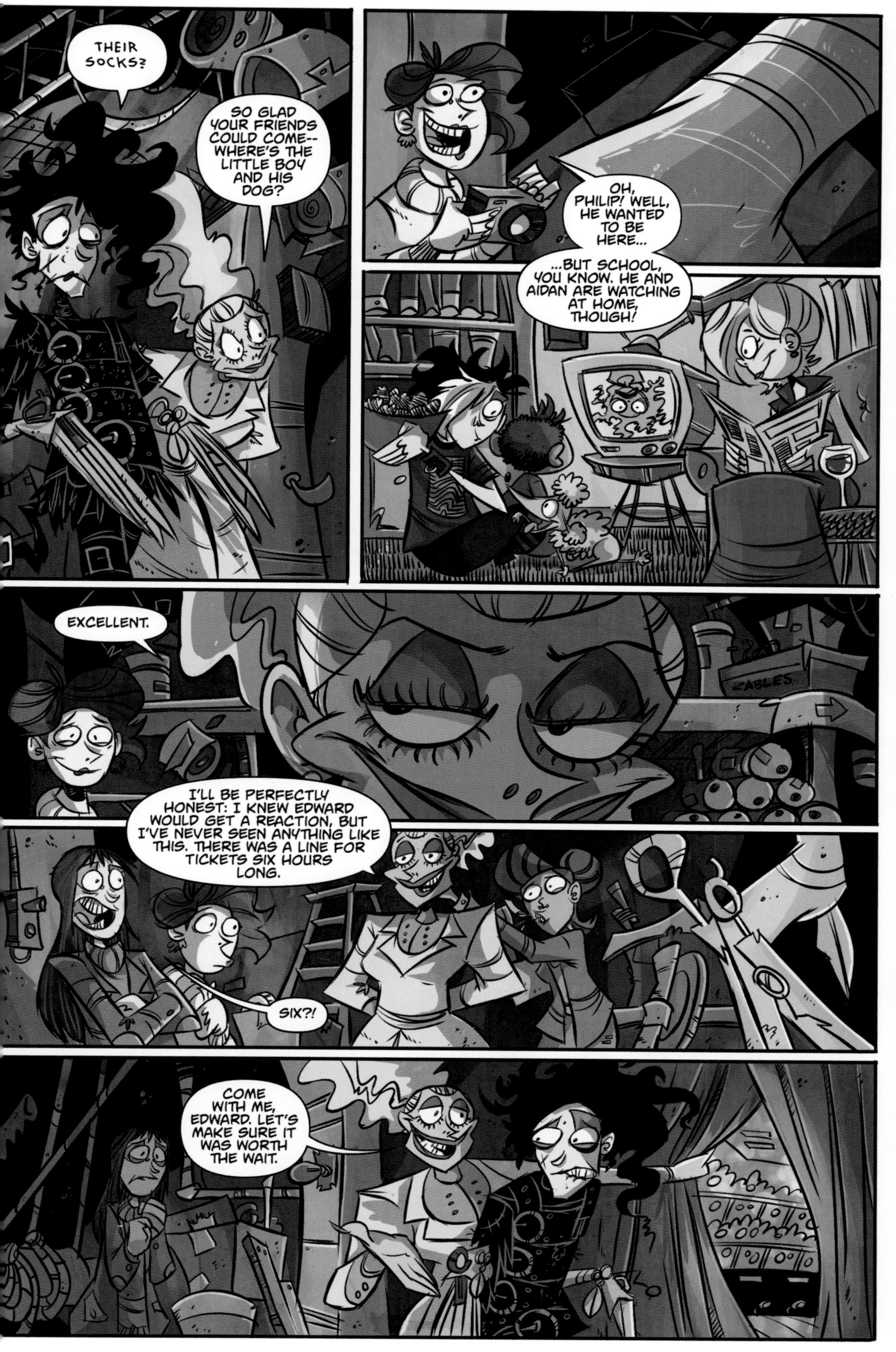
THEIR SOCKS?
SO GLAD YOUR FRIENDS COULD COME-- WHERE'S THE LITTLE BOY AND HIS DOG?
OH, PHILIP! WELL, HE WANTED TO BE HERE...
...BUT SCHOOL, YOU KNOW. HE AND AIDAN ARE WATCHING AT HOME, THOUGH!
EXCELLENT.
CABLES
I'LL BE PERFECTLY HONEST: I KNEW EDWARD WOULD GET A REACTION, BUT I'VE NEVER SEEN ANYTHING LIKE THIS. THERE WAS A LINE FOR TICKETS SIX HOURS LONG.
SIX?!
COME WITH ME, EDWARD. LET'S MAKE SURE IT WAS WORTH THE WAIT.

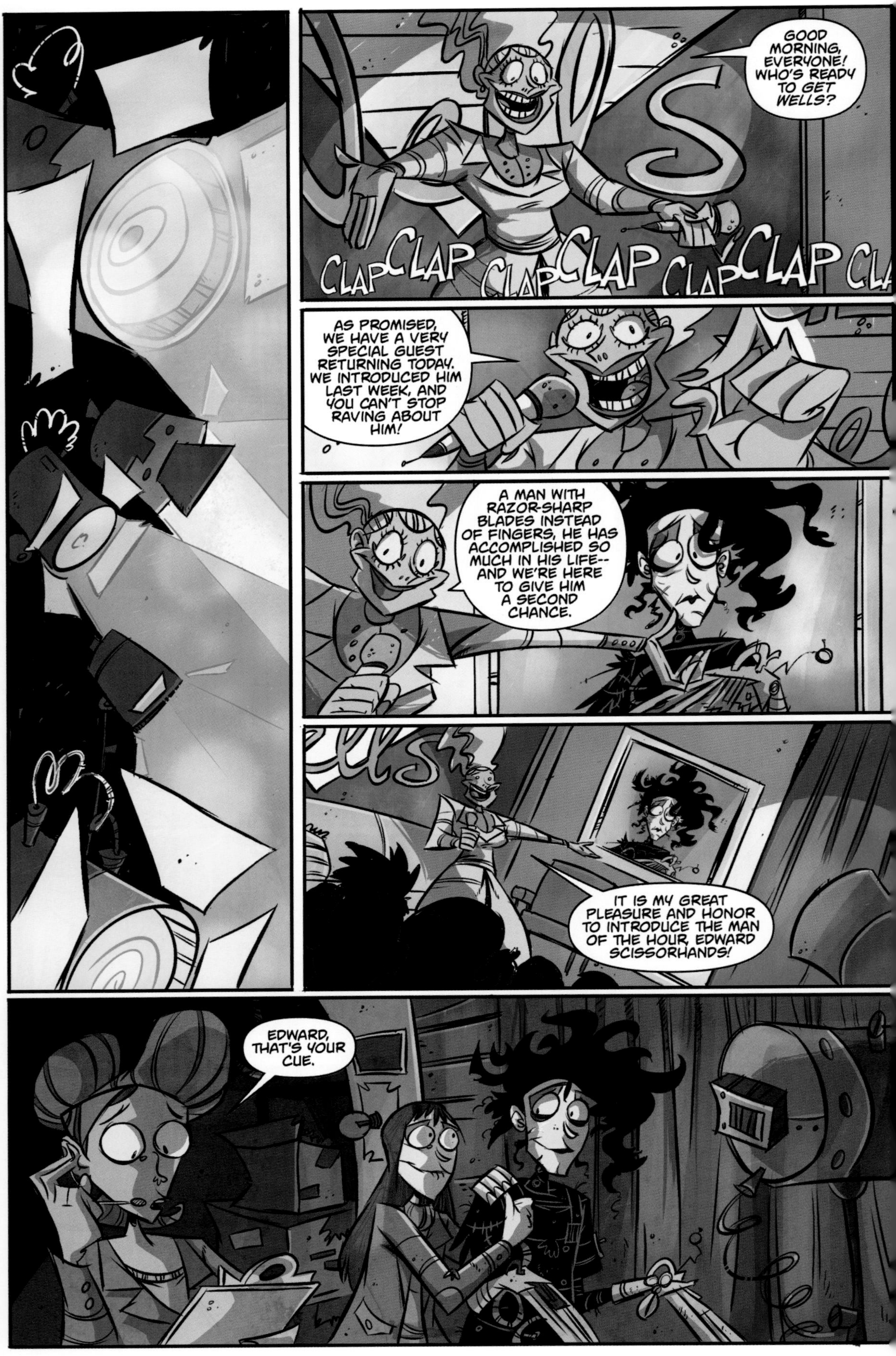
GOOD MORNING, EVERYONE! WHO'S READY TO GET WELLS?
CLAP CLAP CLAP CLAP CLAP CLAP
AS PROMISED, WE HAVE A VERY SPECIAL GUEST RETURNING TODAY. WE INTRODUCED HIM LAST WEEK, AND YOU CAN'T STOP RAVING ABOUT HIM!
A MAN WITH RAZOR-SHARP BLADES INSTEAD OF FINGERS, HE HAS ACCOMPLISHED SO MUCH IN HIS LIFE-- AND WE'RE HERE TO GIVE HIM A SECOND CHANCE.
IT IS MY GREAT PLEASURE AND HONOR TO INTRODUCE THE MAN OF THE HOUR, EDWARD SCISSORHANDS!
EDWARD, THAT'S YOUR CUE.

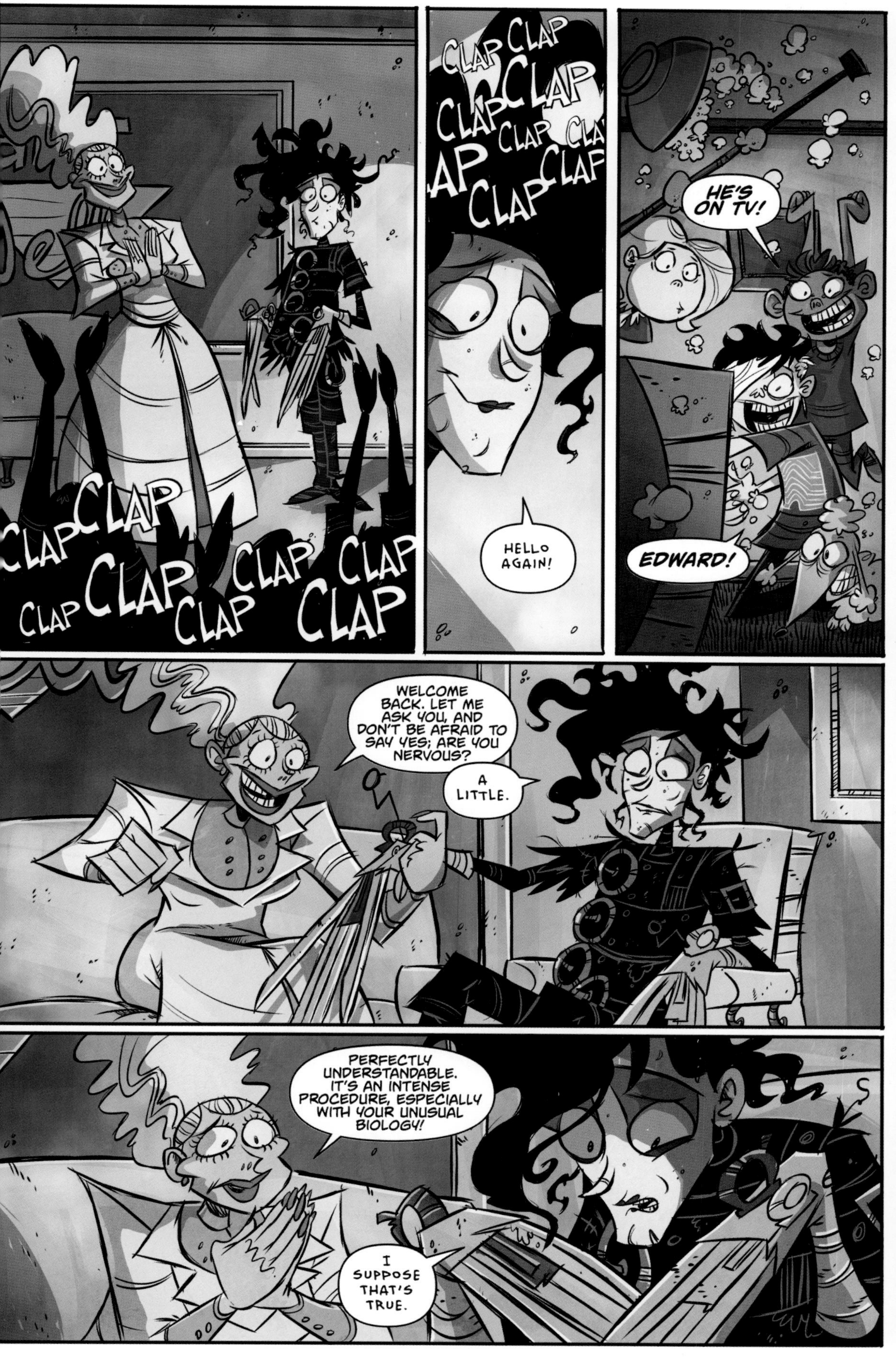
CLAP CLAP
CLAP CLAP CLAP CLAP CLAP CLAP
CLAP CLAP CLAP CLAP CLAP CLAP CLAP CLAP
HELLO AGAIN!
HE'S ON TV!
EDWARD!
WELCOME BACK. LET ME ASK YOU, AND DON'T BE AFRAID TO SAY YES; ARE YOU NERVOUS?
A LITTLE.
PERFECTLY UNDERSTANDABLE. IT'S AN INTENSE PROCEDURE, ESPECIALLY WITH YOUR UNUSUAL BIOLOGY!
I SUPPOSE THAT'S TRUE.

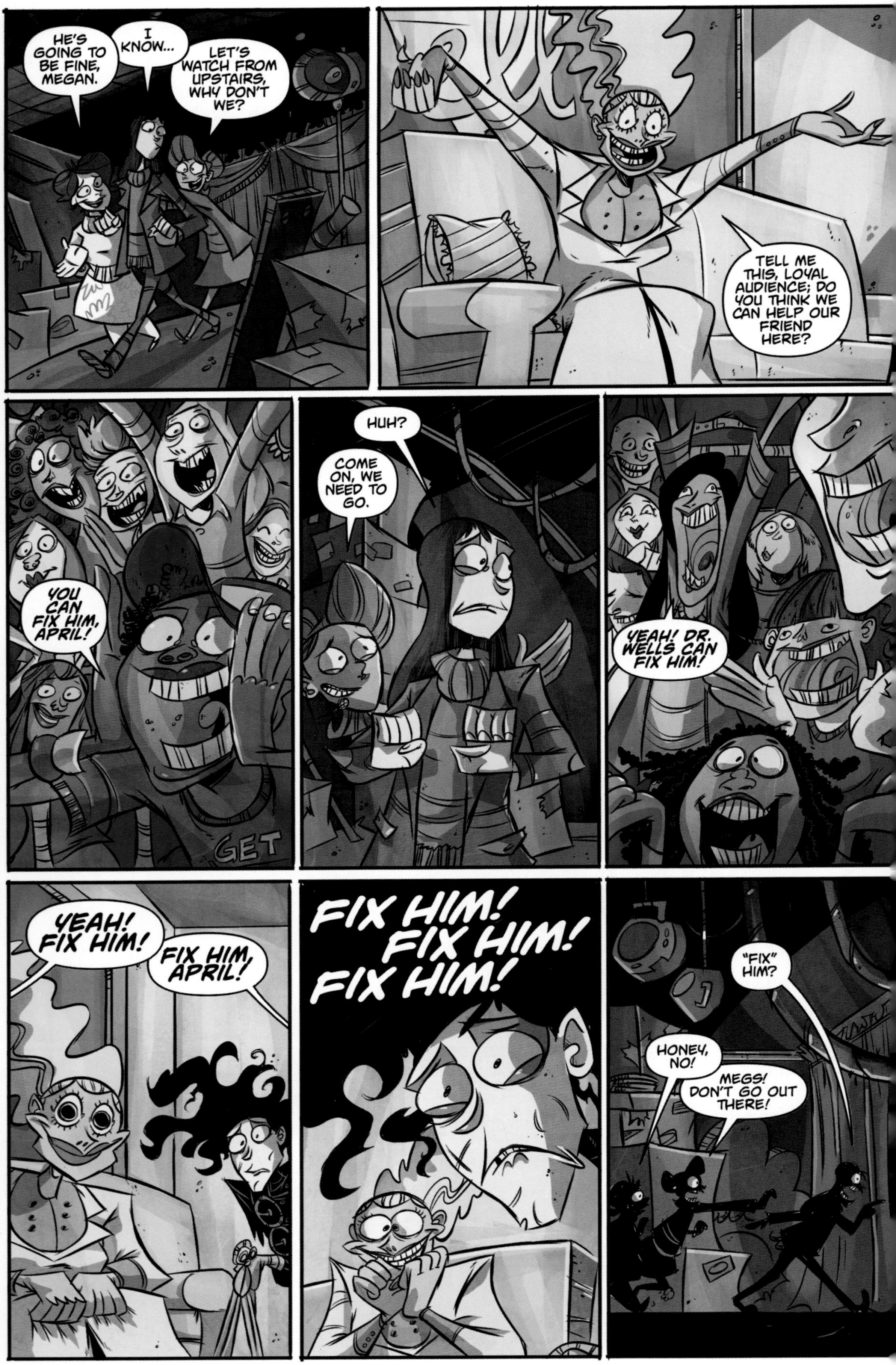

HE'S GOING TO BE FINE, MEGAN.
I KNOW...
LET'S WATCH FROM UPSTAIRS, WHY DON'T WE?
TELL ME THIS, LOYAL AUDIENCE; DO YOU THINK WE CAN HELP OUR FRIEND HERE?
YOU CAN FIX HIM, APRIL!
GET
HUH?
COME ON, WE NEED TO GO.
YEAH! DR. WELLS CAN FIX HIM!
YEAH! FIX HIM!
FIX HIM, APRIL!
FIX HIM! FIX HIM! FIX HIM!
"FIX" HIM?
HONEY, NO!
MEGS! DON'T GO OUT THERE!

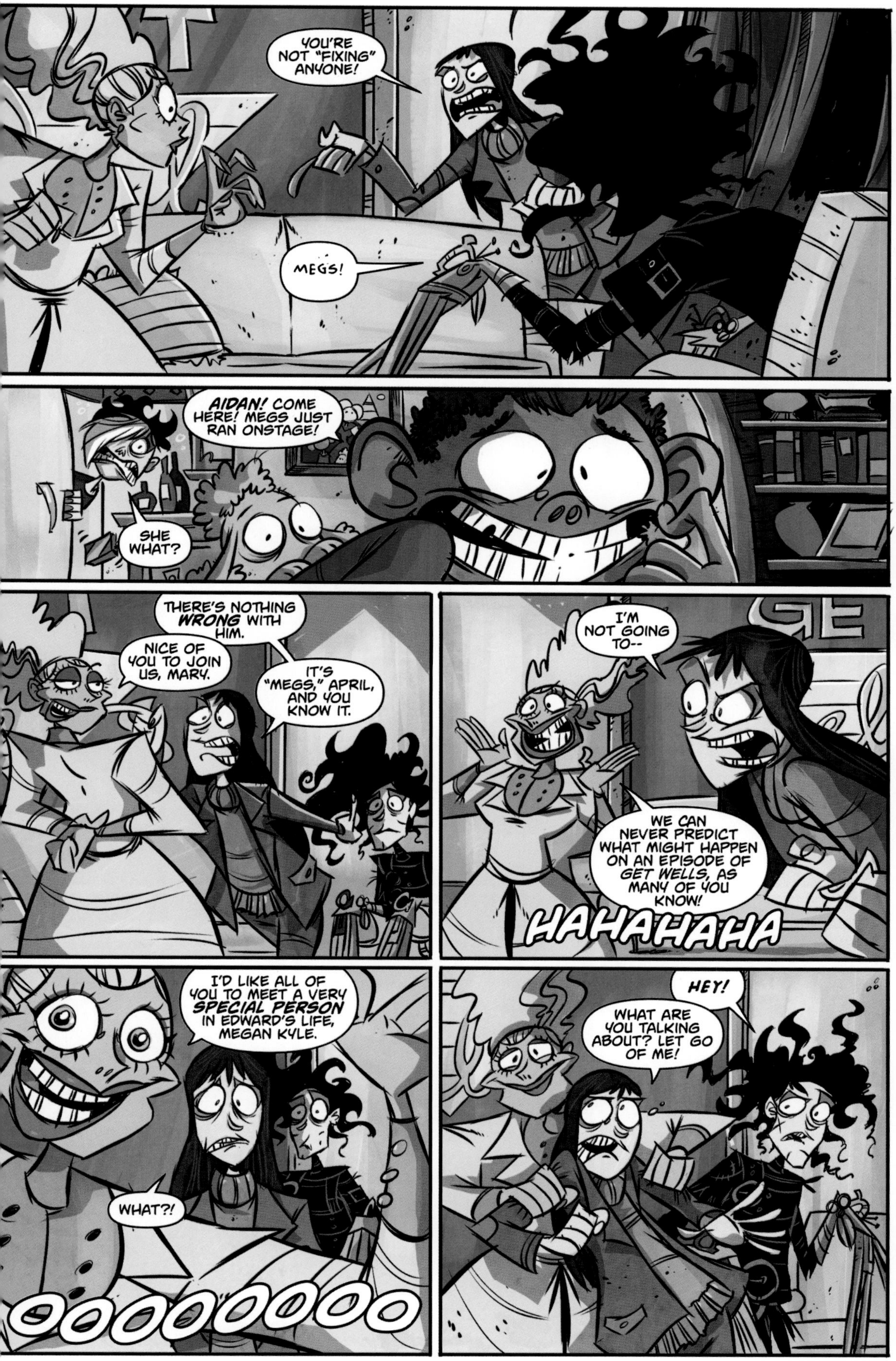
YOU'RE NOT "FIXING" ANYONE!
MEGS!
AIDAN! COME HERE! MEGS JUST RAN ONSTAGE!
SHE WHAT?
THERE'S NOTHING WRONG WITH HIM.
NICE OF YOU TO JOIN US, MARY.
IT'S "MEGS," APRIL, AND YOU KNOW IT.
I'M NOT GOING TO--
WE CAN NEVER PREDICT WHAT MIGHT HAPPEN ON AN EPISODE OF GET WELLS, AS MANY OF YOU KNOW!
HAHAHAHA
I'D LIKE ALL OF YOU TO MEET A VERY SPECIAL PERSON IN EDWARD'S LIFE, MEGAN KYLE.
WHAT?!
OOOOOOOO
HEY!
WHAT ARE YOU TALKING ABOUT? LET GO OF ME!

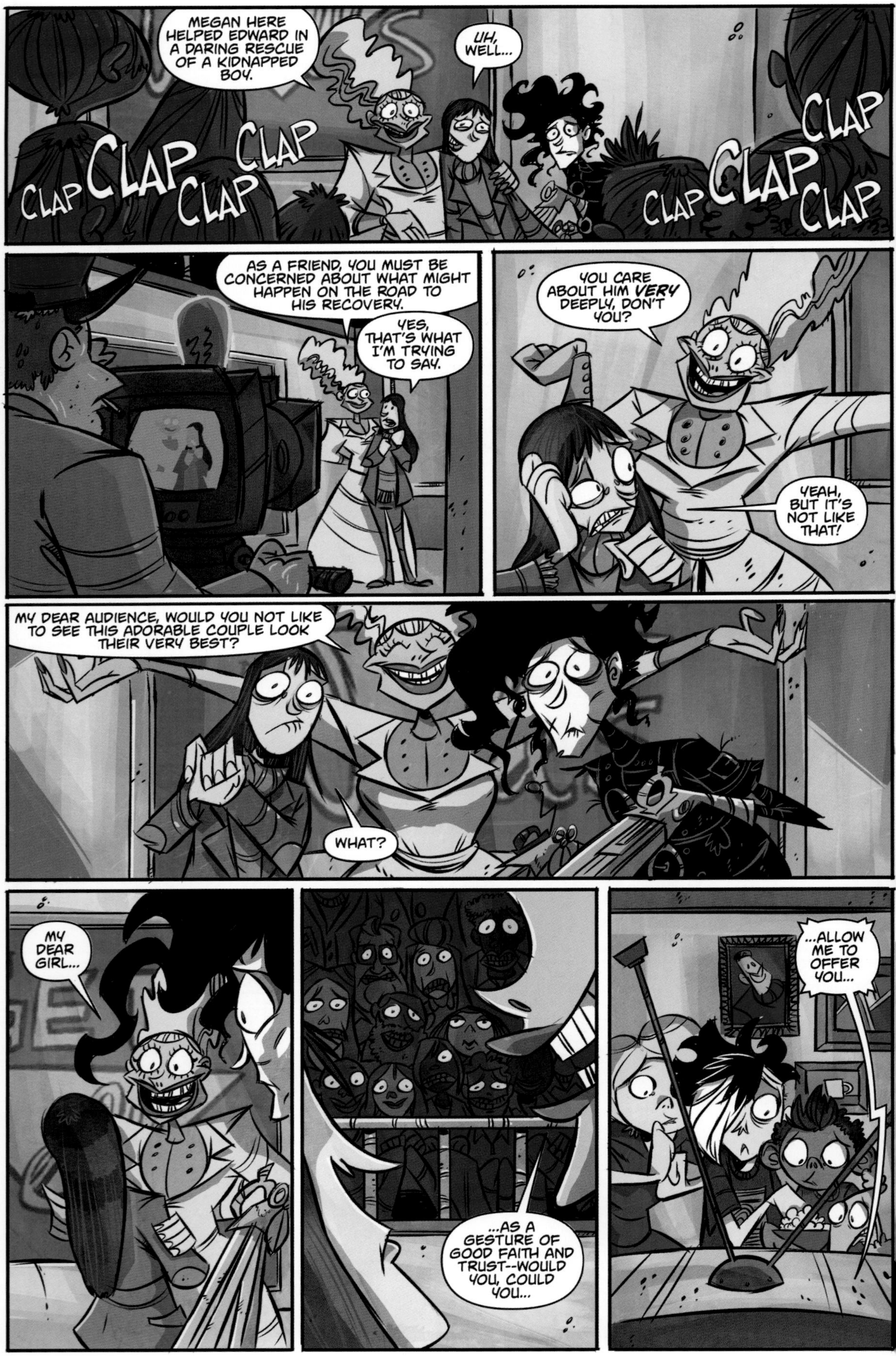

MEGAN HERE HELPED EDWARD IN A DARING RESCUE OF A KIDNAPPED BOY.
UH, WELL...
CLAP CLAP CLAP CLAP
CLAP CLAP CLAP CLAP
AS A FRIEND, YOU MUST BE CONCERNED ABOUT WHAT MIGHT HAPPEN ON THE ROAD TO HIS RECOVERY.
YES, THAT'S WHAT I'M TRYING TO SAY.
YOU CARE ABOUT HIM VERY DEEPLY, DON'T YOU?
YEAH, BUT IT'S NOT LIKE THAT!
MY DEAR AUDIENCE, WOULD YOU NOT LIKE TO SEE THIS ADORABLE COUPLE LOOK THEIR VERY BEST?
WHAT?
MY DEAR GIRL...
...AS A GESTURE OF GOOD FAITH AND TRUST--WOULD YOU, COULD YOU...
...ALLOW ME TO OFFER YOU...

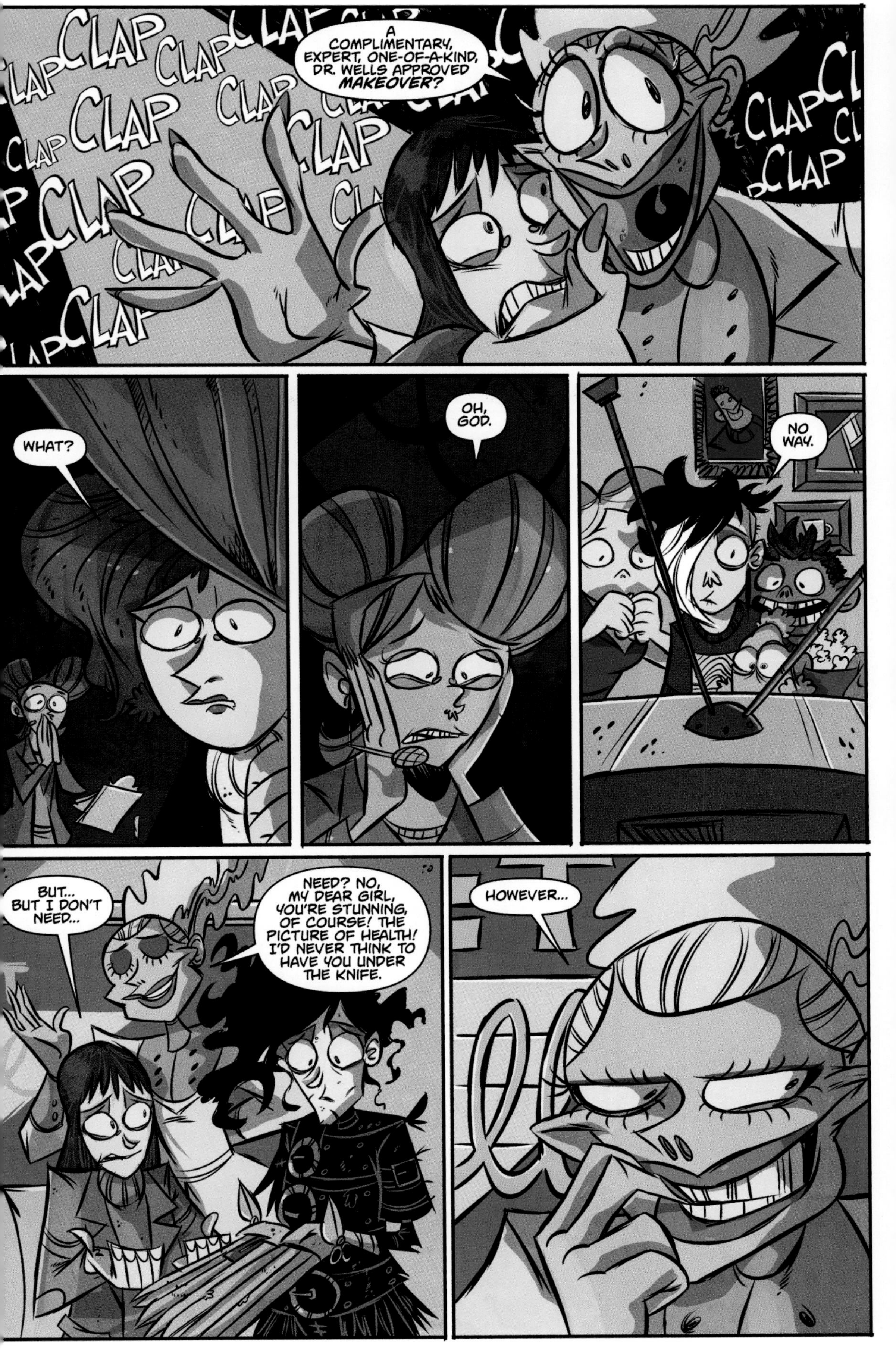
CLAP CLAP CLAP CLAP CLAP CLAP CLAP CLAP CLAP CLAP CLAP
A COMPLIMENTARY, EXPERT, ONE-OF-A-KIND, DR. WELLS APPROVED *MAKEOVER?*
CLAP CLAP CLAP
WHAT?
OH, GOD.
NO WAY.
BUT... BUT I DON'T NEED...
NEED? NO, MY DEAR GIRL, YOU'RE STUNNING, OF COURSE! THE PICTURE OF HEALTH! I'D NEVER THINK TO HAVE YOU UNDER THE KNIFE.
HOWEVER...

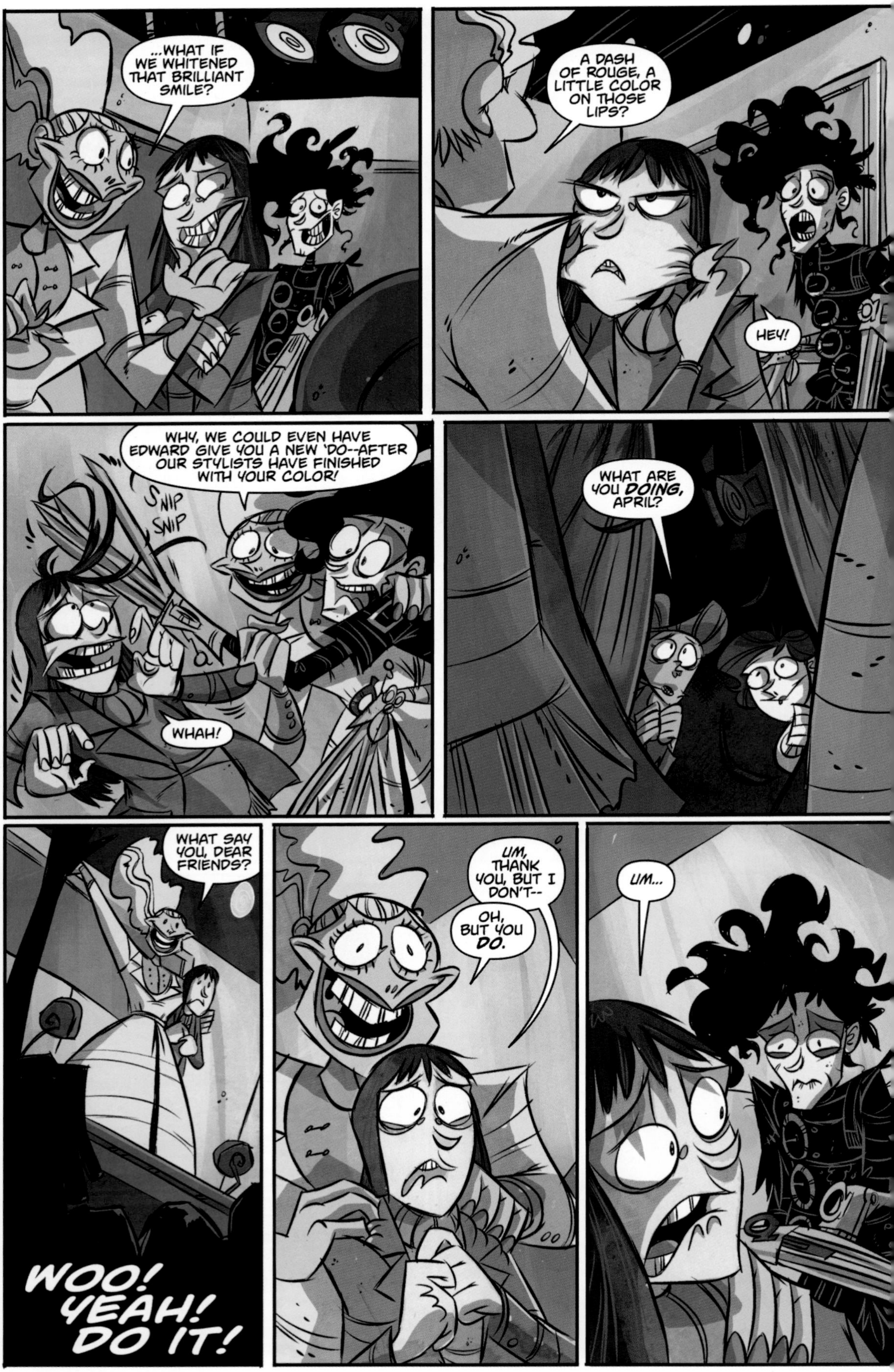
...WHAT IF WE WHITENED THAT BRILLIANT SMILE?
A DASH OF ROUGE, A LITTLE COLOR ON THOSE LIPS?
HEY!
WHY, WE COULD EVEN HAVE EDWARD GIVE YOU A NEW 'DO--AFTER OUR STYLISTS HAVE FINISHED WITH YOUR COLOR!
SNIP SNIP
WHAH!
WHAT ARE YOU DOING, APRIL?
WHAT SAY YOU, DEAR FRIENDS?
WOO! YEAH! DO IT!
UM, THANK YOU, BUT I DON'T--
OH, BUT YOU DO.
UM...

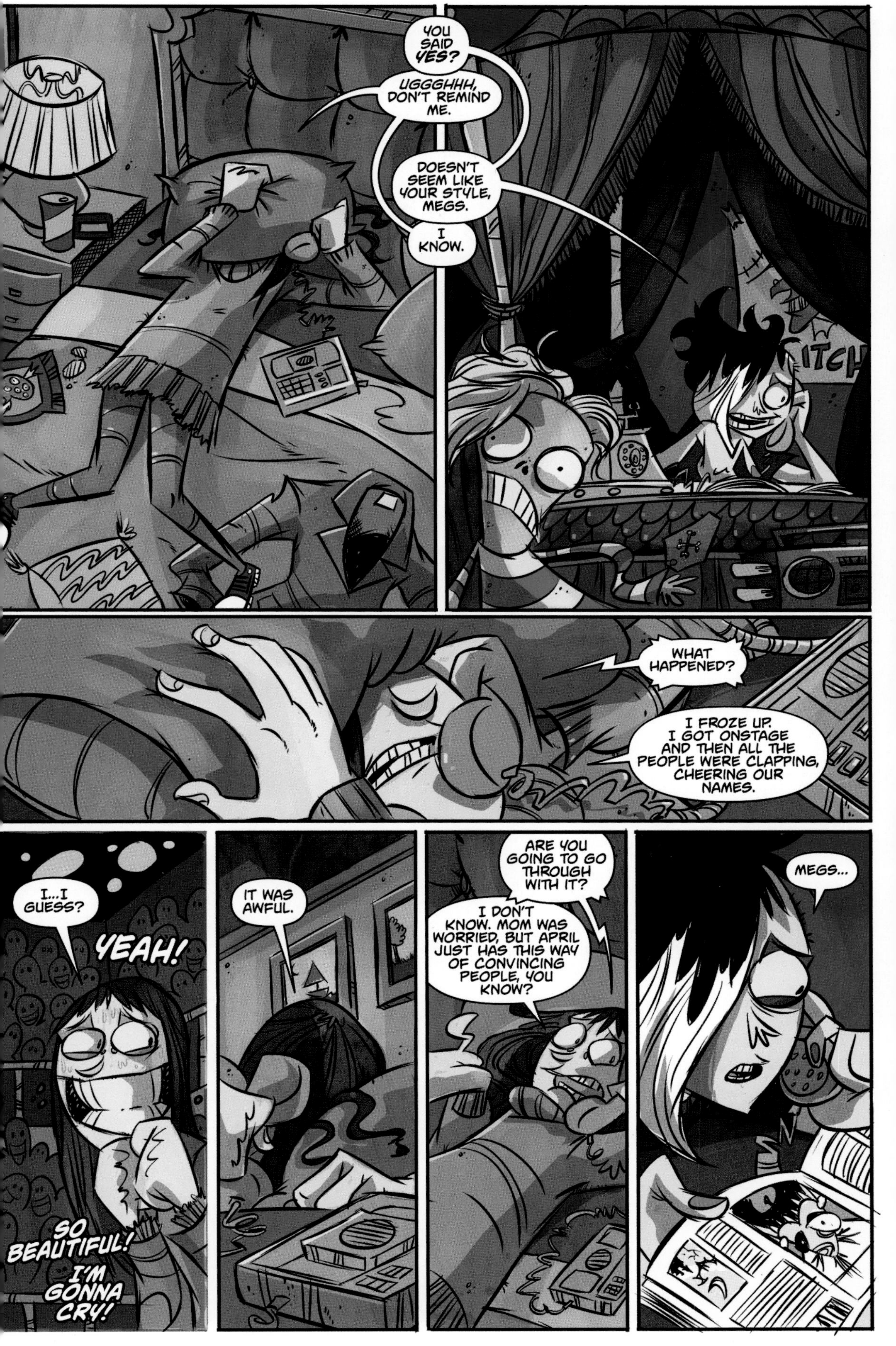
YOU SAID *YES?*
UGGGHHH, DON'T REMIND ME.
DOESN'T SEEM LIKE YOUR STYLE, MEGS.
I KNOW.
WHAT HAPPENED?
I FROZE UP. I GOT ONSTAGE AND THEN ALL THE PEOPLE WERE CLAPPING, CHEERING OUR NAMES.
I...I GUESS?
YEAH!
SO BEAUTIFUL!
I'M GONNA CRY!
IT WAS AWFUL.
ARE YOU GOING TO GO THROUGH WITH IT?
I DON'T KNOW. MOM WAS WORRIED, BUT APRIL JUST HAS THIS WAY OF CONVINCING PEOPLE, YOU KNOW?
MEGS...

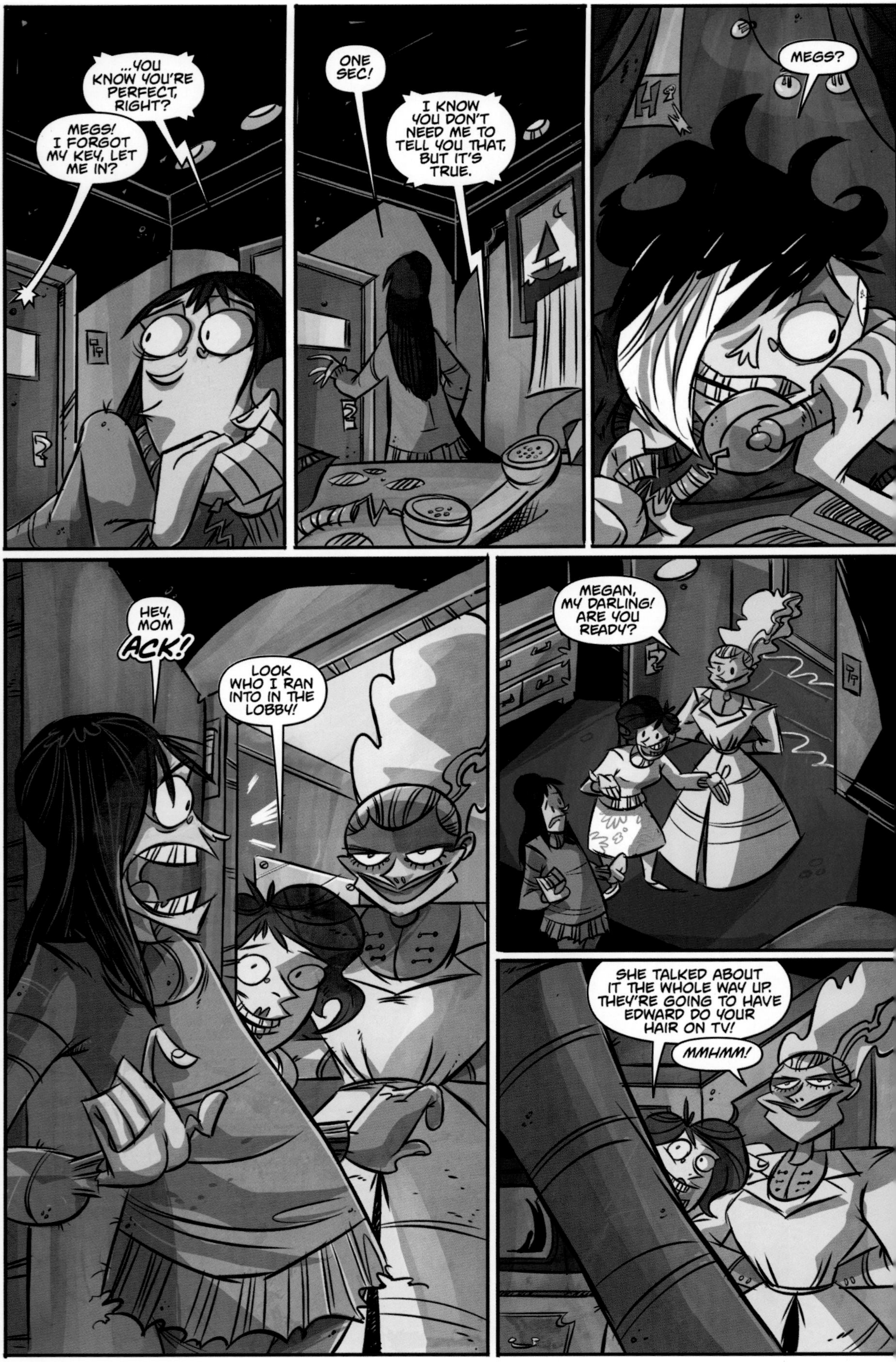

...YOU KNOW YOU'RE PERFECT, RIGHT?
MEGS! I FORGOT MY KEY, LET ME IN?
ONE SEC!
I KNOW YOU DON'T NEED ME TO TELL YOU THAT, BUT IT'S TRUE.
MEGS?
HEY, MOM ACK!
LOOK WHO I RAN INTO IN THE LOBBY!
MEGAN, MY DARLING! ARE YOU READY?
SHE TALKED ABOUT IT THE WHOLE WAY UP. THEY'RE GOING TO HAVE EDWARD DO YOUR HAIR ON TV!
MMHMM!

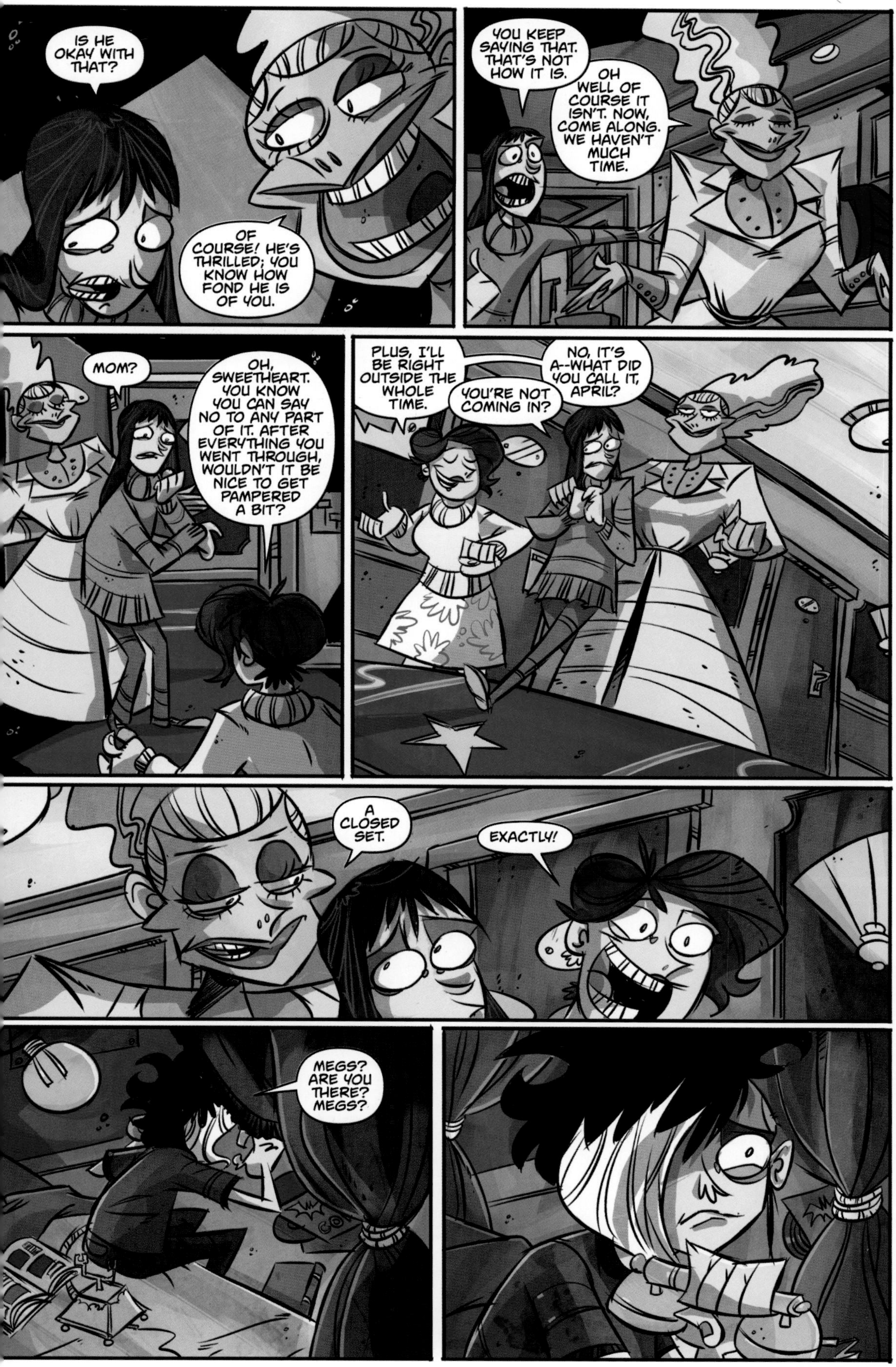
IS HE OKAY WITH THAT?
OF COURSE! HE'S THRILLED; YOU KNOW HOW FOND HE IS OF YOU.
YOU KEEP SAYING THAT. THAT'S NOT HOW IT IS.
OH WELL OF COURSE IT ISN'T. NOW, COME ALONG. WE HAVEN'T MUCH TIME.
MOM?
OH, SWEETHEART. YOU KNOW YOU CAN SAY NO TO ANY PART OF IT. AFTER EVERYTHING YOU WENT THROUGH, WOULDN'T IT BE NICE TO GET PAMPERED A BIT?
PLUS, I'LL BE RIGHT OUTSIDE THE WHOLE TIME.
YOU'RE NOT COMING IN?
NO, IT'S A--WHAT DID YOU CALL IT, APRIL?
A CLOSED SET.
EXACTLY!
MEGS? ARE YOU THERE? MEGS?

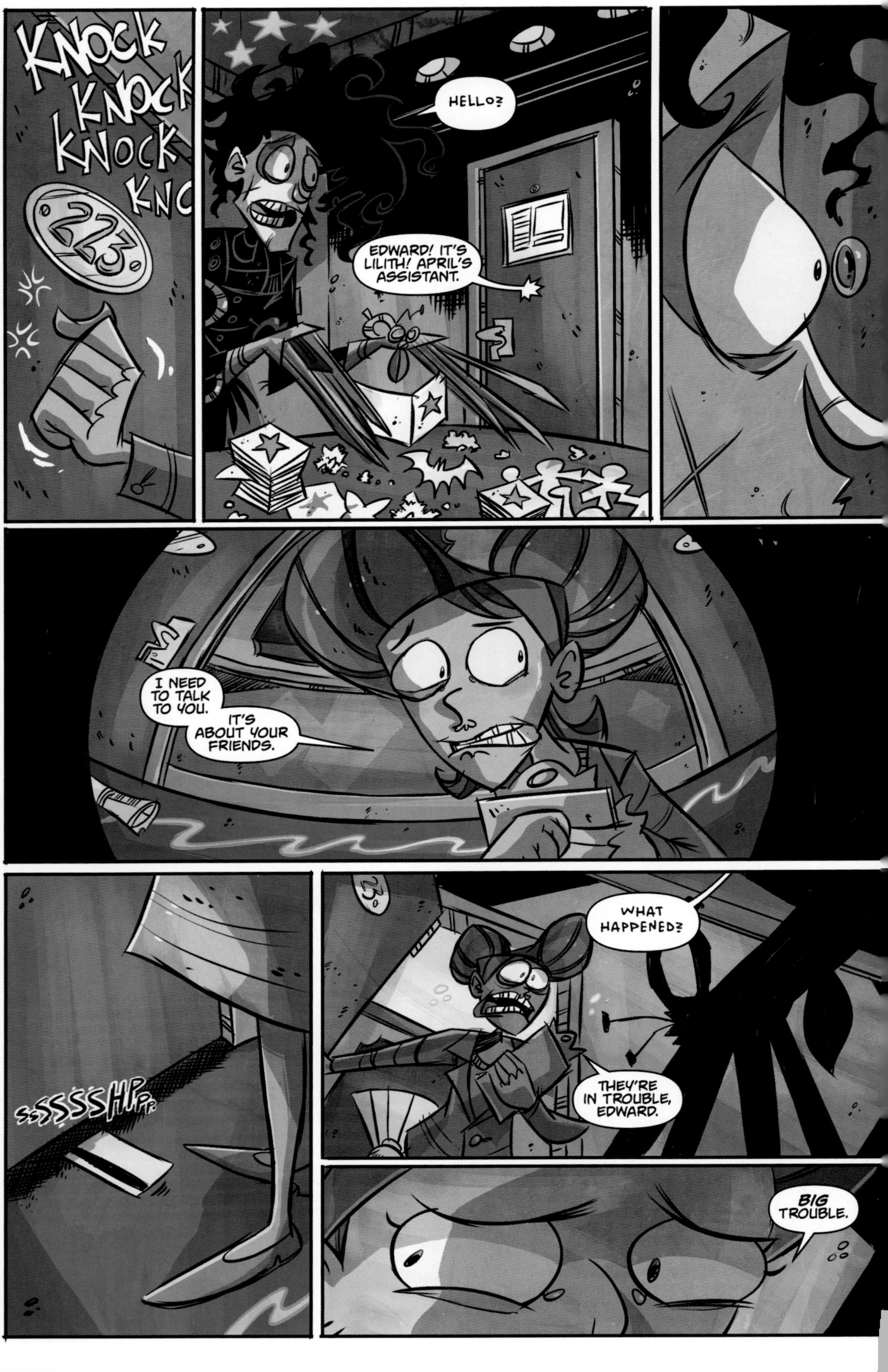
KNOCK KNOCK KNOCK KNC
223
HELLO?
EDWARD! IT'S LILITH! APRIL'S ASSISTANT.
I NEED TO TALK TO YOU.
IT'S ABOUT YOUR FRIENDS.
SSSSSSHPPP.
WHAT HAPPENED?
THEY'RE IN TROUBLE, EDWARD.
BIG TROUBLE.

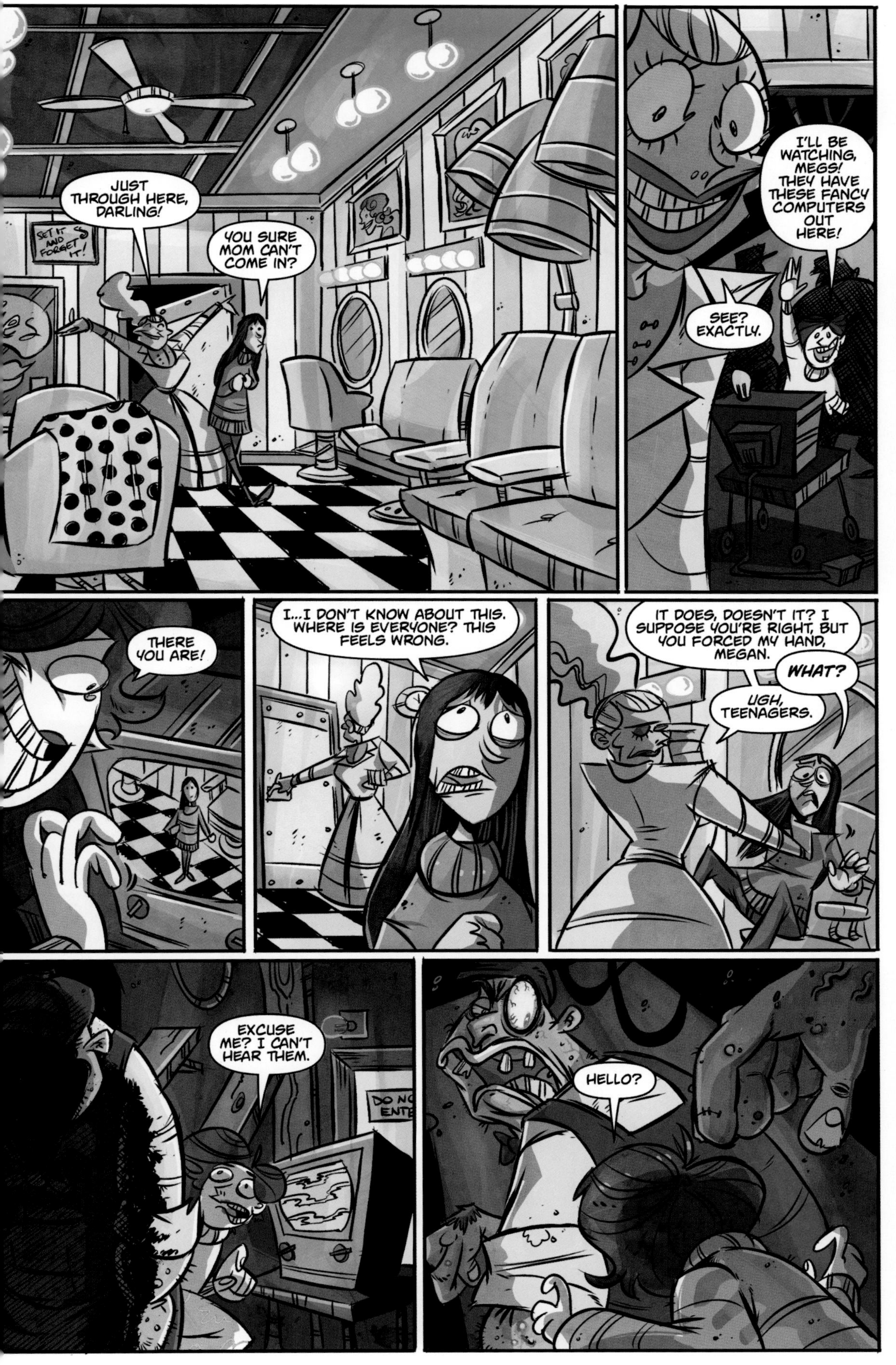
SET IT AND FORGET IT!
JUST THROUGH HERE, DARLING!
YOU SURE MOM CAN'T COME IN?
I'LL BE WATCHING, MEGS! THEY HAVE THESE FANCY COMPUTERS OUT HERE!
SEE? EXACTLY.
THERE YOU ARE!
I...I DON'T KNOW ABOUT THIS. WHERE IS EVERYONE? THIS FEELS WRONG.
IT DOES, DOESN'T IT? I SUPPOSE YOU'RE RIGHT, BUT YOU FORCED MY HAND, MEGAN.
WHAT?
UGH, TEENAGERS.
EXCUSE ME? I CAN'T HEAR THEM.
HELLO?

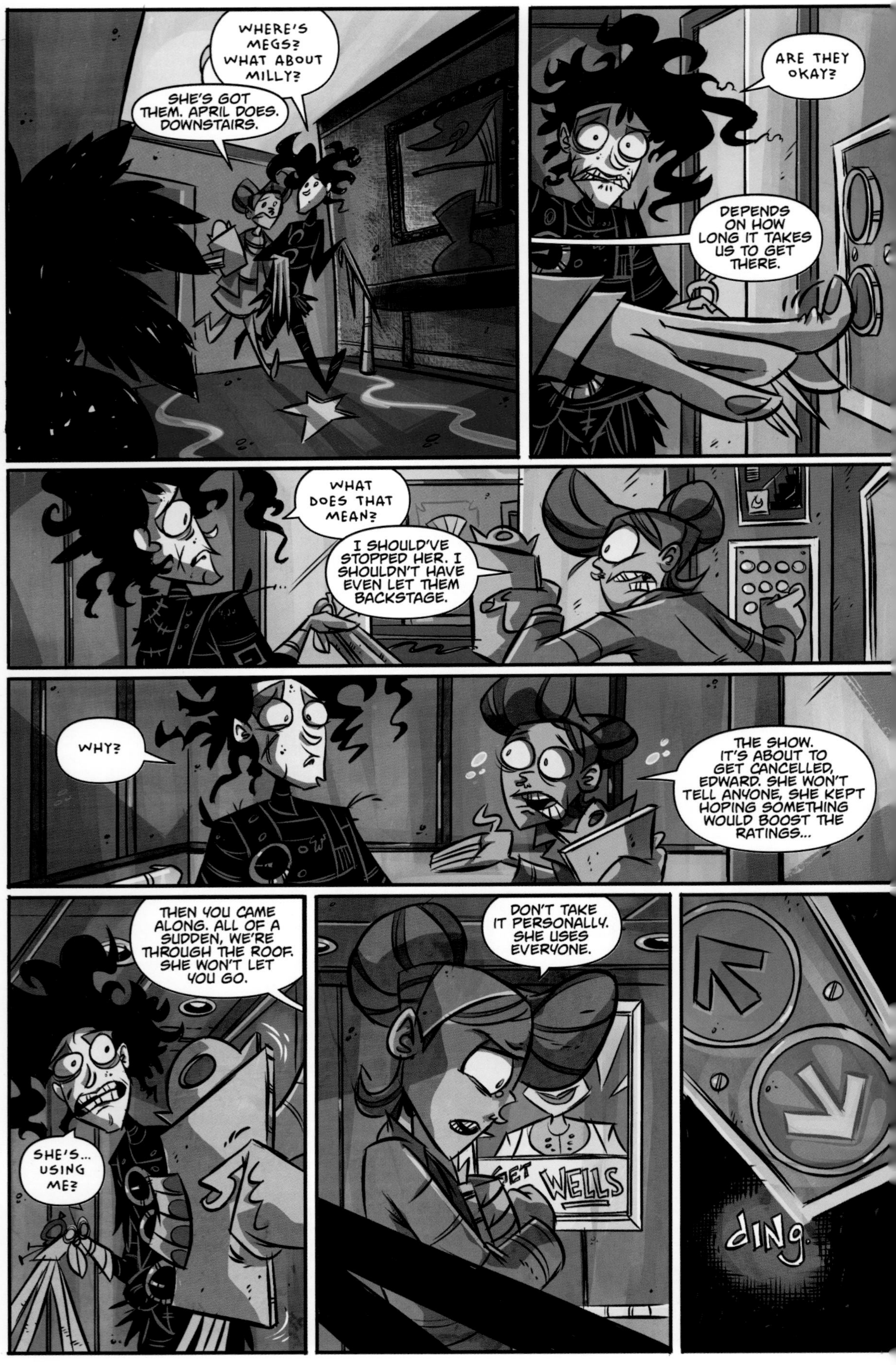
WHERE'S MEGS? WHAT ABOUT MILLY?
SHE'S GOT THEM. APRIL DOES. DOWNSTAIRS.
ARE THEY OKAY?
DEPENDS ON HOW LONG IT TAKES US TO GET THERE.
WHAT DOES THAT MEAN?
I SHOULD'VE STOPPED HER. I SHOULDN'T HAVE EVEN LET THEM BACKSTAGE.
WHY?
THE SHOW. IT'S ABOUT TO GET CANCELLED, EDWARD. SHE WON'T TELL ANYONE, SHE KEPT HOPING SOMETHING WOULD BOOST THE RATINGS...
THEN YOU CAME ALONG. ALL OF A SUDDEN, WE'RE THROUGH THE ROOF. SHE WON'T LET YOU GO.
SHE'S... USING ME?
DON'T TAKE IT PERSONALLY. SHE USES EVERYONE.
WELLS
ding.

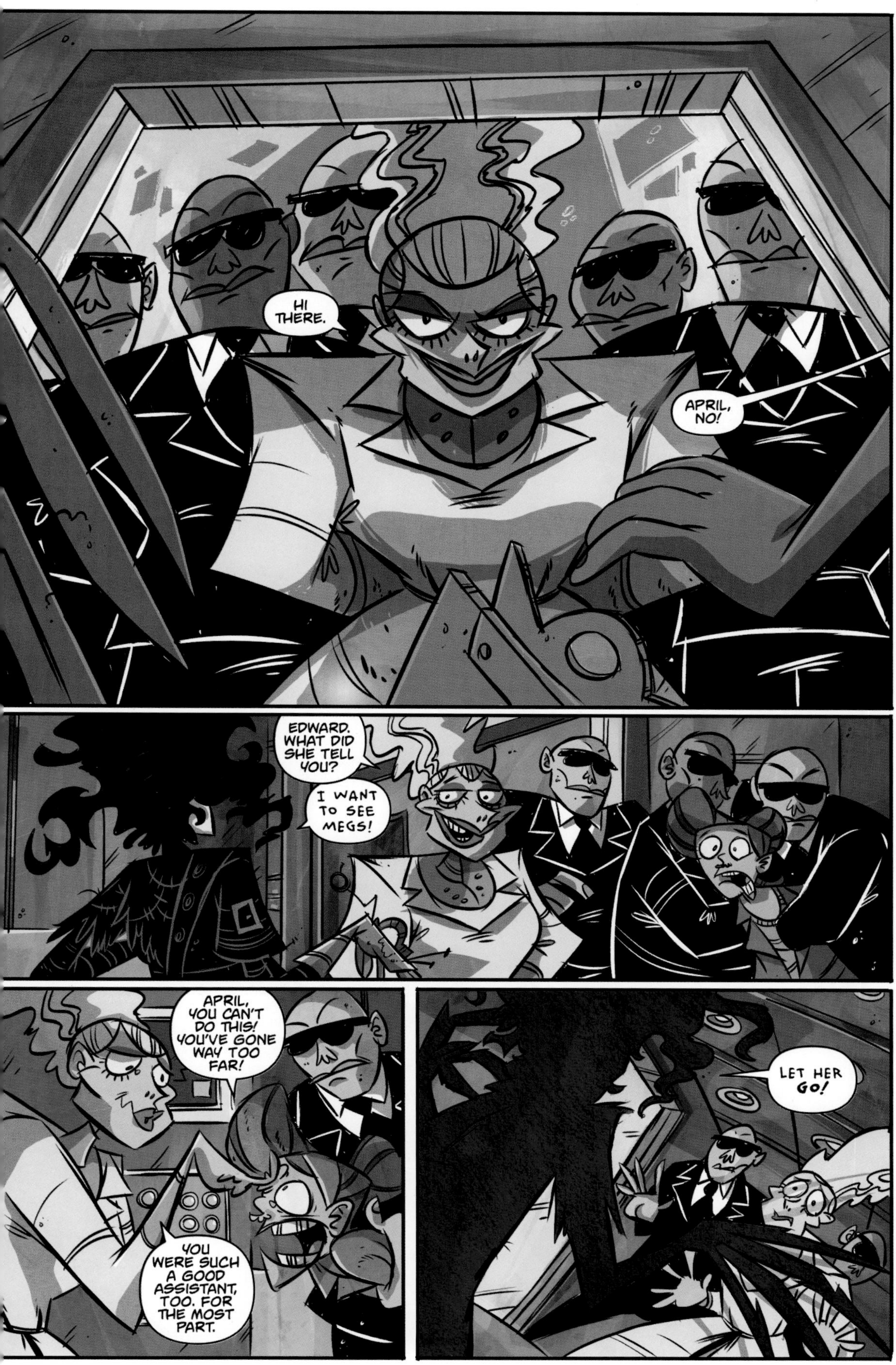
HI THERE.
APRIL, NO!
EDWARD. WHAT DID SHE TELL YOU?
I WANT TO SEE MEGS!
APRIL, YOU CAN'T DO THIS! YOU'VE GONE WAY TOO FAR!
YOU WERE SUCH A GOOD ASSISTANT, TOO. FOR THE MOST PART.
LET HER GO!

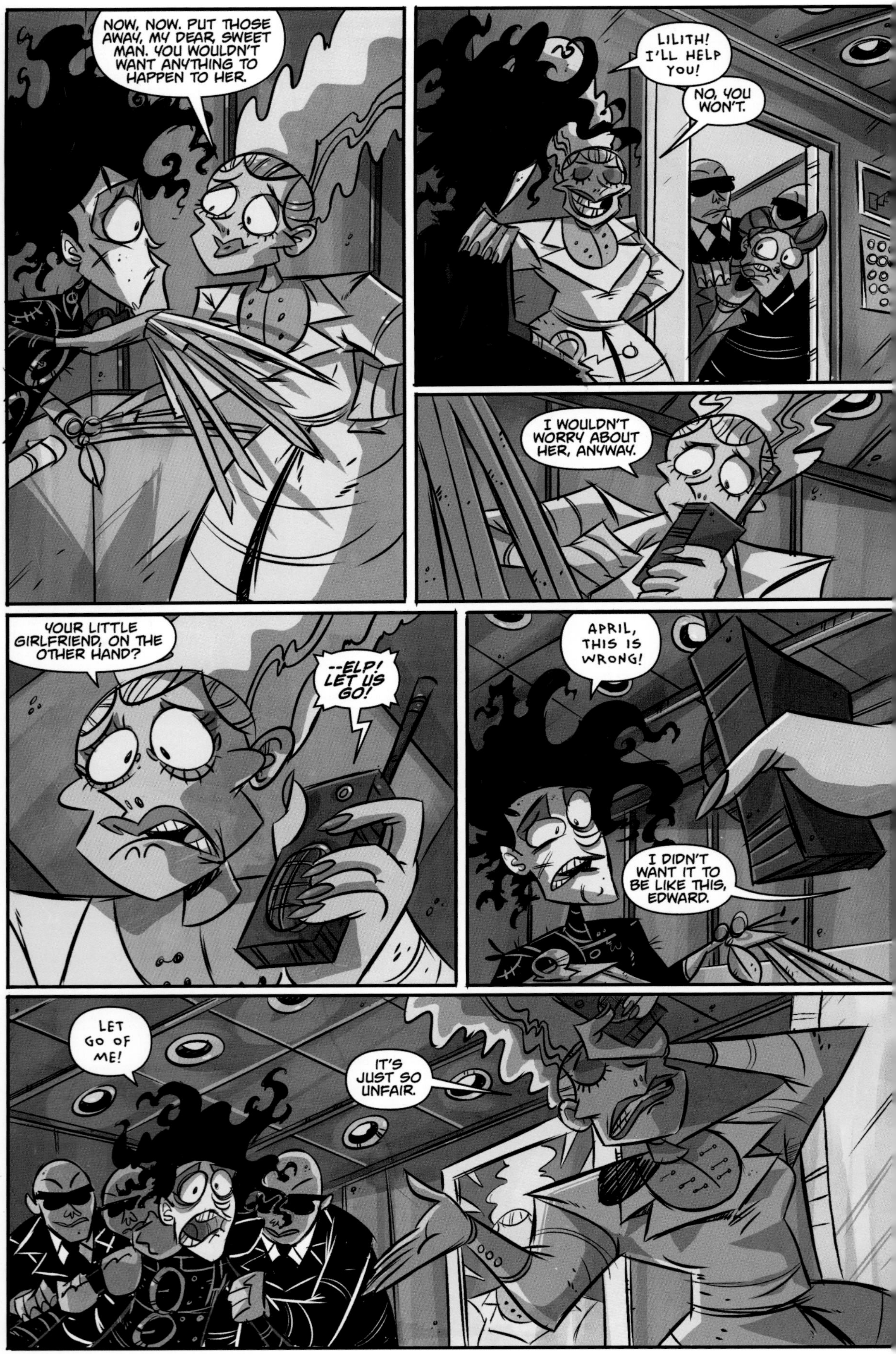
NOW, NOW. PUT THOSE AWAY, MY DEAR, SWEET MAN. YOU WOULDN'T WANT ANYTHING TO HAPPEN TO HER.
LILITH! I'LL HELP YOU!
NO, YOU WON'T.
I WOULDN'T WORRY ABOUT HER, ANYWAY.
YOUR LITTLE GIRLFRIEND, ON THE OTHER HAND?
--ELP! LET US GO!
APRIL, THIS IS WRONG!
I DIDN'T WANT IT TO BE LIKE THIS, EDWARD.
LET GO OF ME!
IT'S JUST SO UNFAIR.

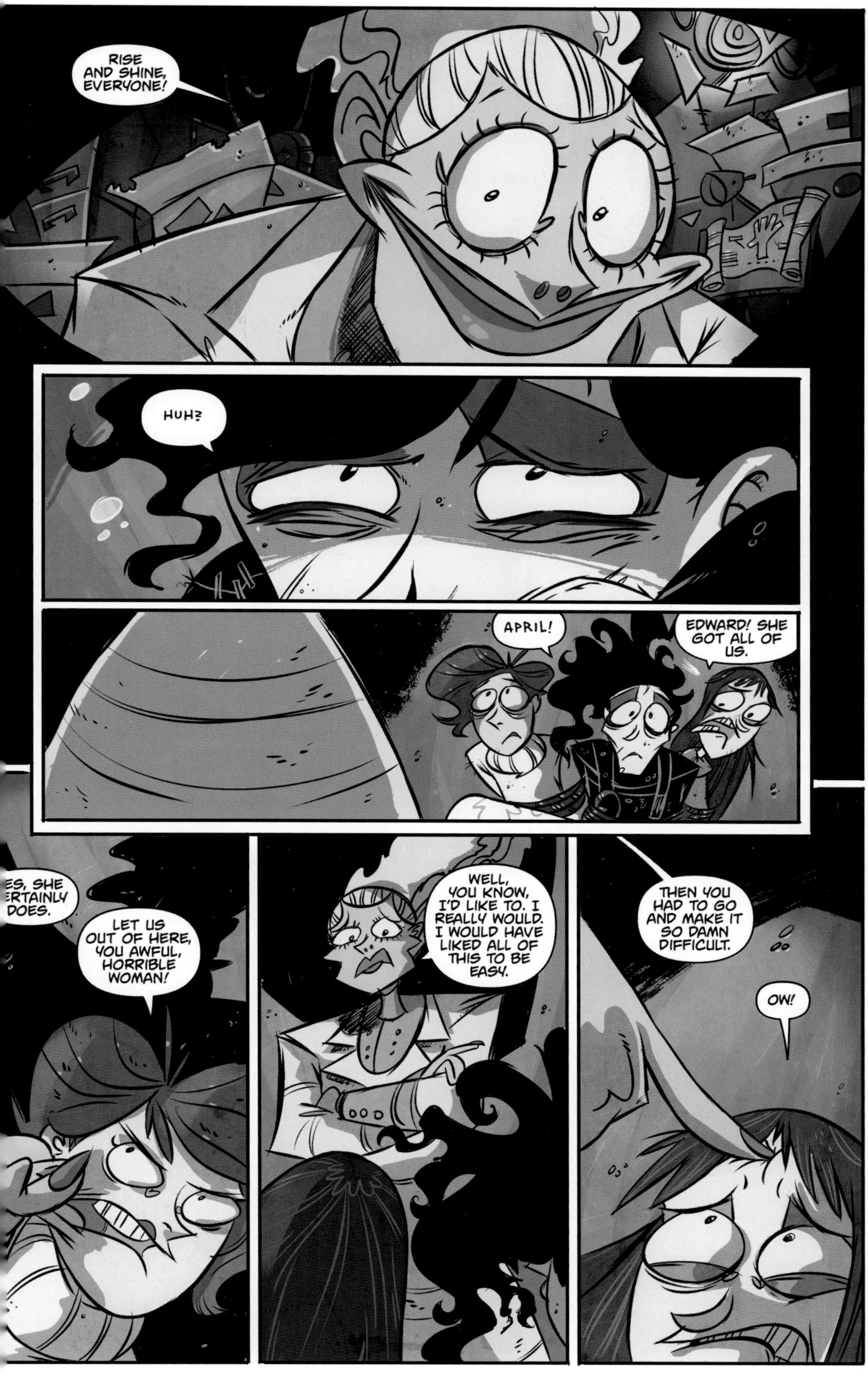
RISE AND SHINE, EVERYONE!
HUH?
APRIL!
EDWARD! SHE GOT ALL OF US.
ES, SHE ERTAINLY DOES.
LET US OUT OF HERE, YOU AWFUL, HORRIBLE WOMAN!
WELL, YOU KNOW, I'D LIKE TO. I REALLY WOULD. I WOULD HAVE LIKED ALL OF THIS TO BE EASY.
THEN YOU HAD TO GO AND MAKE IT SO DAMN DIFFICULT.
OW!

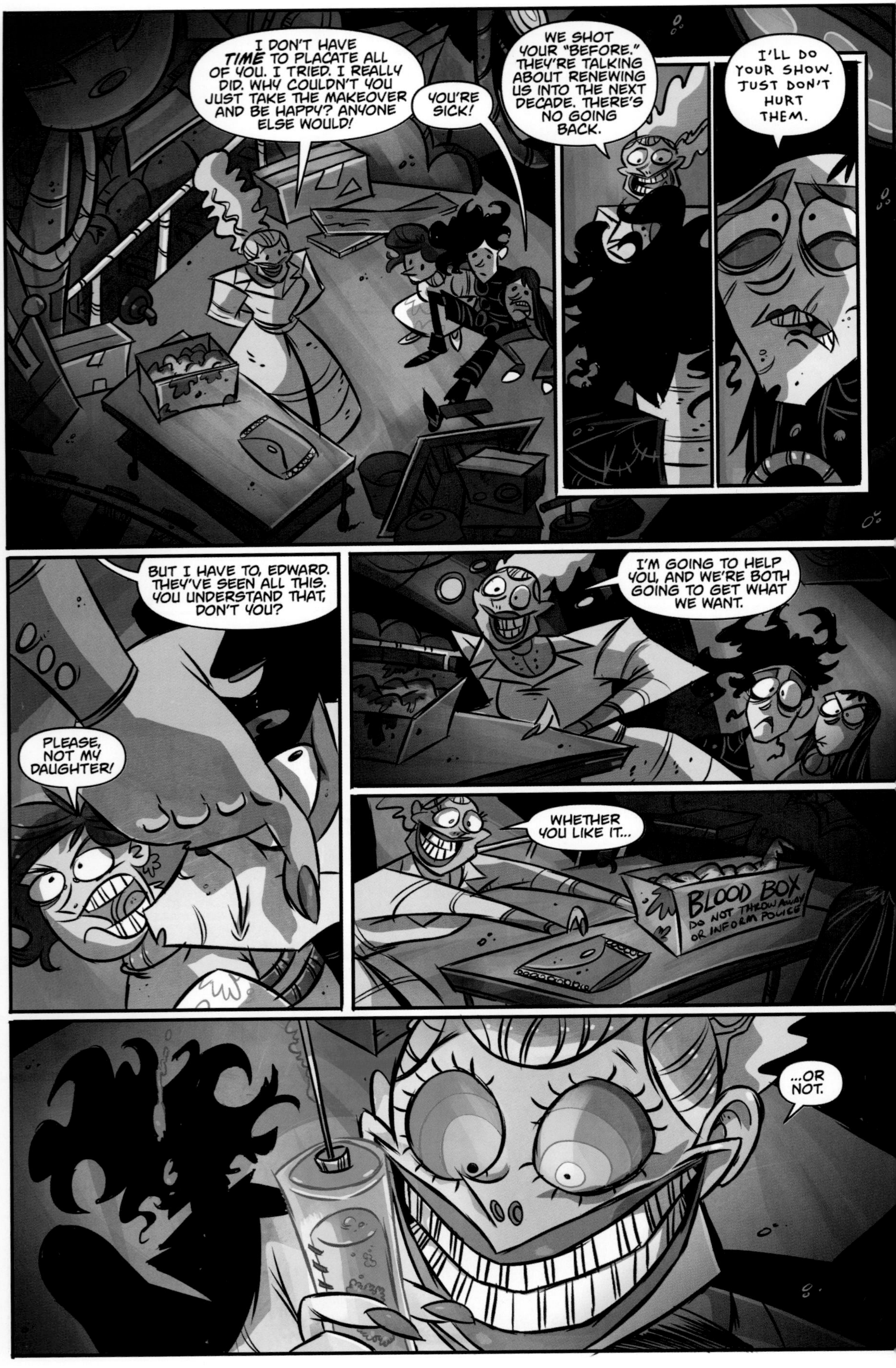

I DON'T HAVE TIME TO PLACATE ALL OF YOU. I TRIED. I REALLY DID. WHY COULDN'T YOU JUST TAKE THE MAKEOVER AND BE HAPPY? ANYONE ELSE WOULD!
YOU'RE SICK!
WE SHOT YOUR "BEFORE." THEY'RE TALKING ABOUT RENEWING US INTO THE NEXT DECADE. THERE'S NO GOING BACK.
I'LL DO YOUR SHOW. JUST DON'T HURT THEM.
BUT I HAVE TO, EDWARD. THEY'VE SEEN ALL THIS. YOU UNDERSTAND THAT, DON'T YOU?
PLEASE, NOT MY DAUGHTER!
I'M GOING TO HELP YOU, AND WE'RE BOTH GOING TO GET WHAT WE WANT.
WHETHER YOU LIKE IT...
BLOOD BOX
DO NOT THROW AWAY OR INFORM POLICE
...OR NOT.

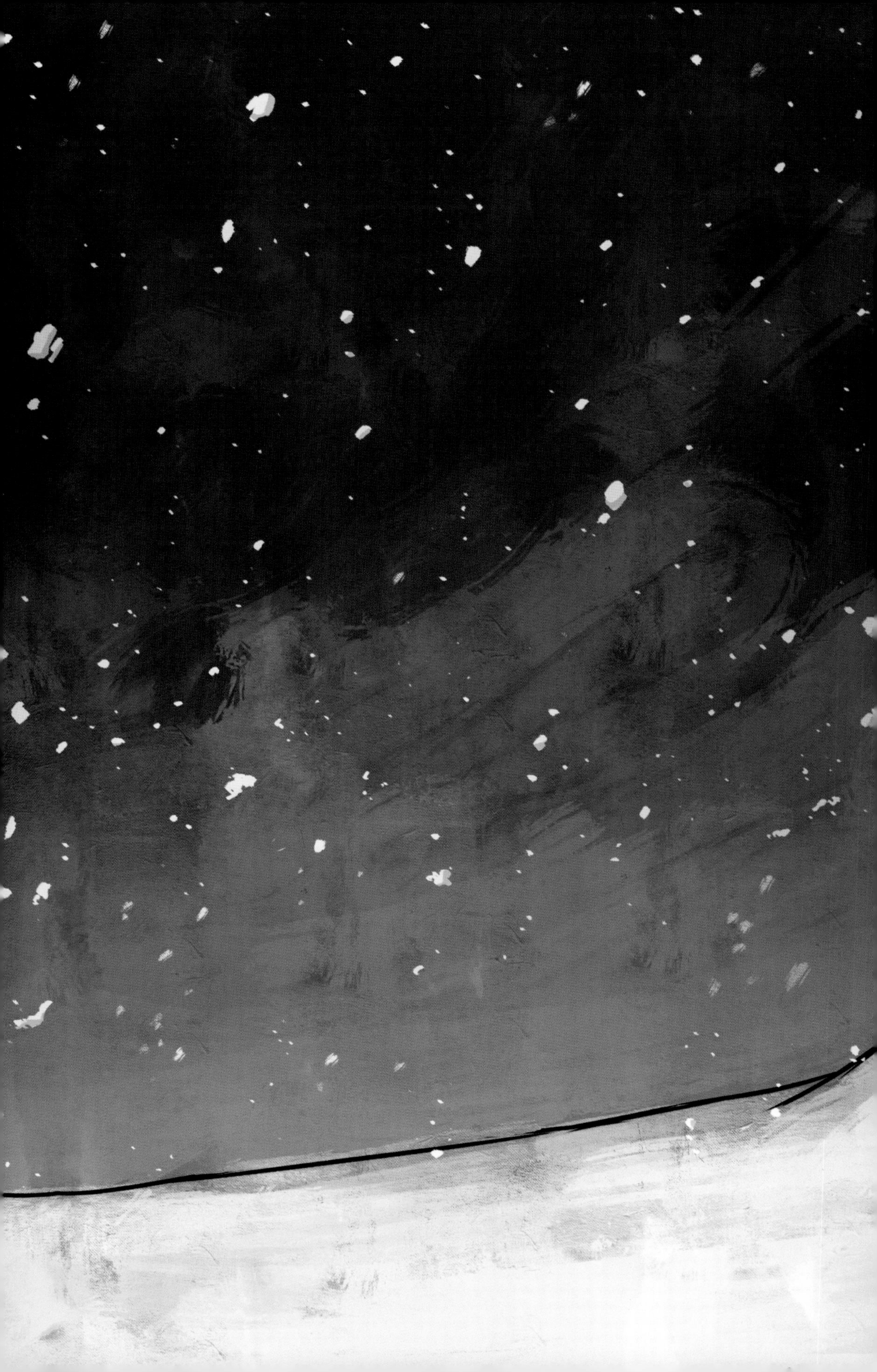

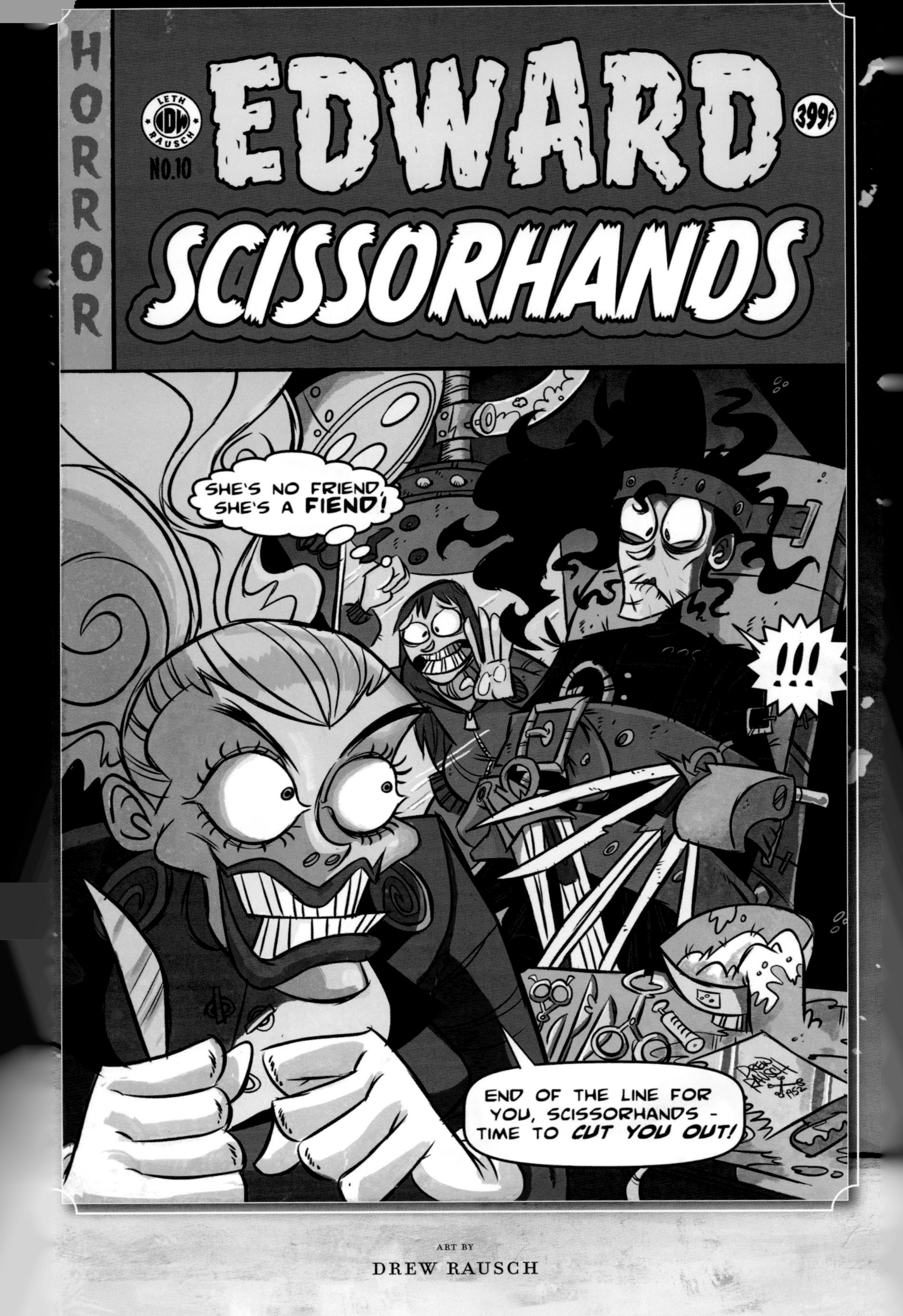
HORROR
NO.10
EDWARD
SCISSORHANDS
399¢
SHE'S NO FRIEND, SHE'S A FIEND!
!!!
END OF THE LINE FOR YOU, SCISSORHANDS - TIME TO CUT YOU OUT!

ART BY
DREW RAUSCH

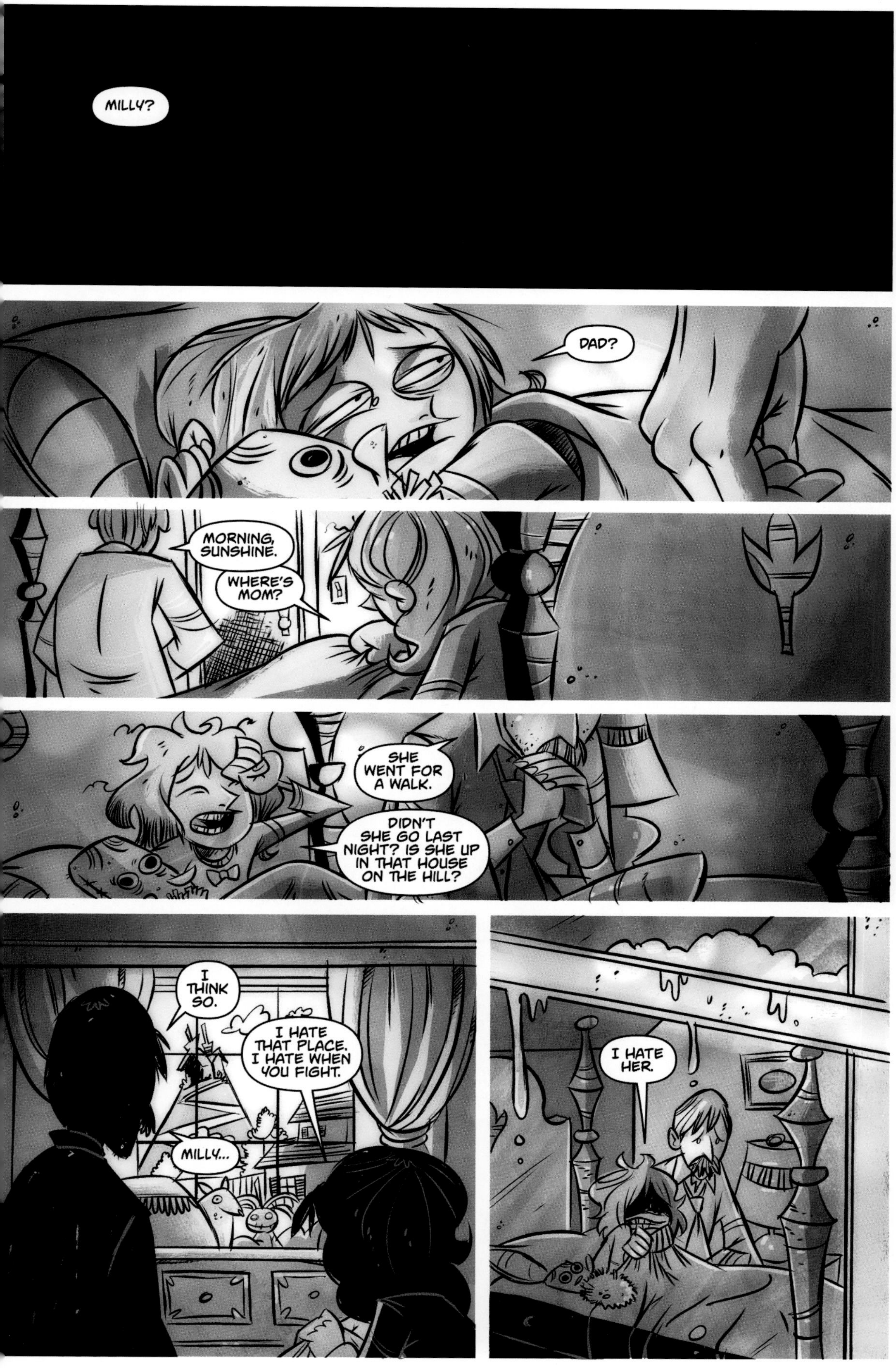
MILLY?
DAD?
MORNING, SUNSHINE.
WHERE'S MOM?
SHE WENT FOR A WALK.
DIDN'T SHE GO LAST NIGHT? IS SHE UP IN THAT HOUSE ON THE HILL?
I THINK SO.
I HATE THAT PLACE. I HATE WHEN YOU FIGHT.
MILLY...
I HATE HER.

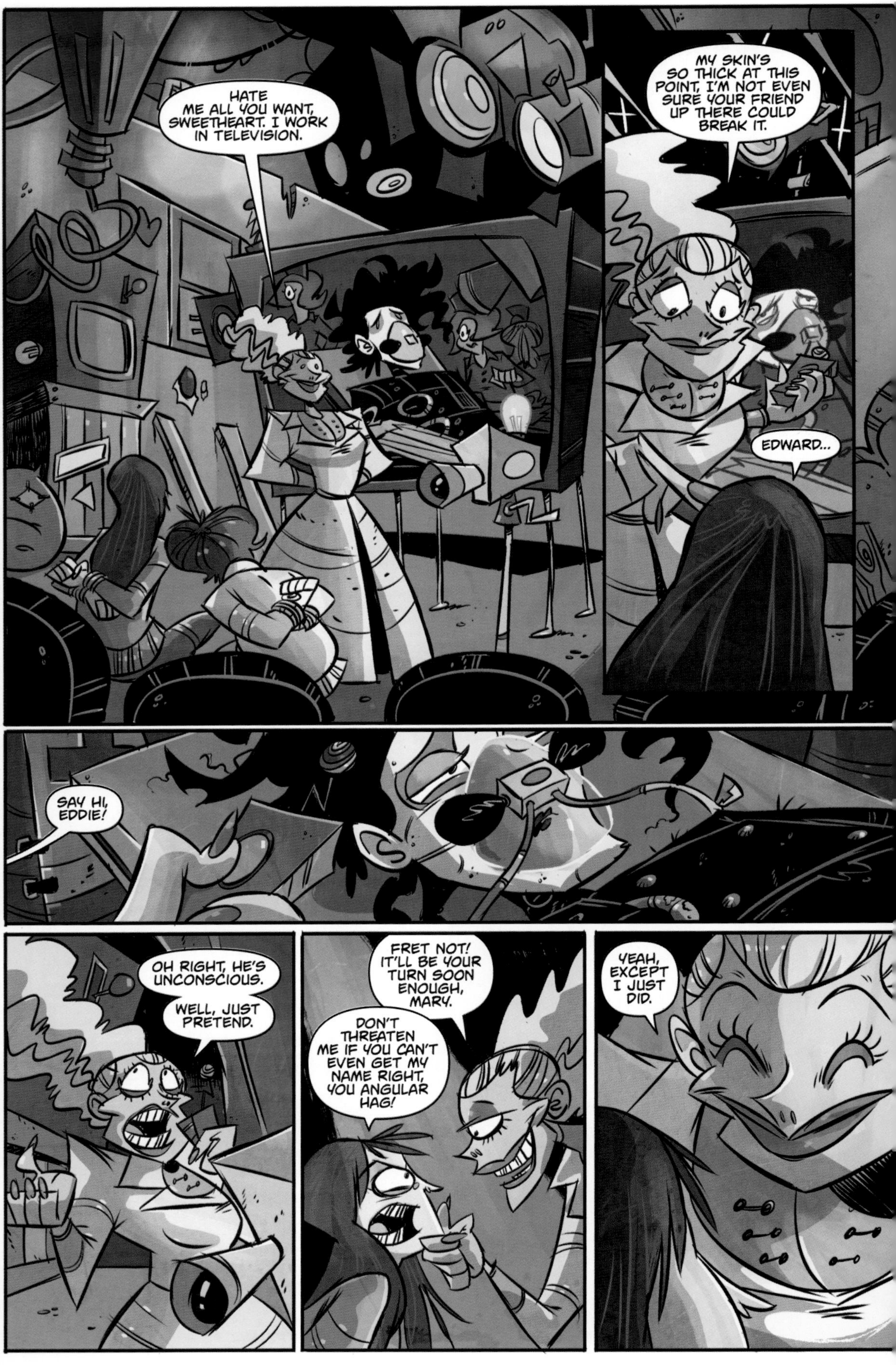
HATE ME ALL YOU WANT, SWEETHEART. I WORK IN TELEVISION.
MY SKIN'S SO THICK AT THIS POINT, I'M NOT EVEN SURE YOUR FRIEND UP THERE COULD BREAK IT.
EDWARD...
SAY HI, EDDIE!
OH RIGHT, HE'S UNCONSCIOUS.
WELL, JUST PRETEND.
FRET NOT! IT'LL BE YOUR TURN SOON ENOUGH, MARY.
DON'T THREATEN ME IF YOU CAN'T EVEN GET MY NAME RIGHT, YOU ANGULAR HAG!
YEAH, EXCEPT I JUST DID.

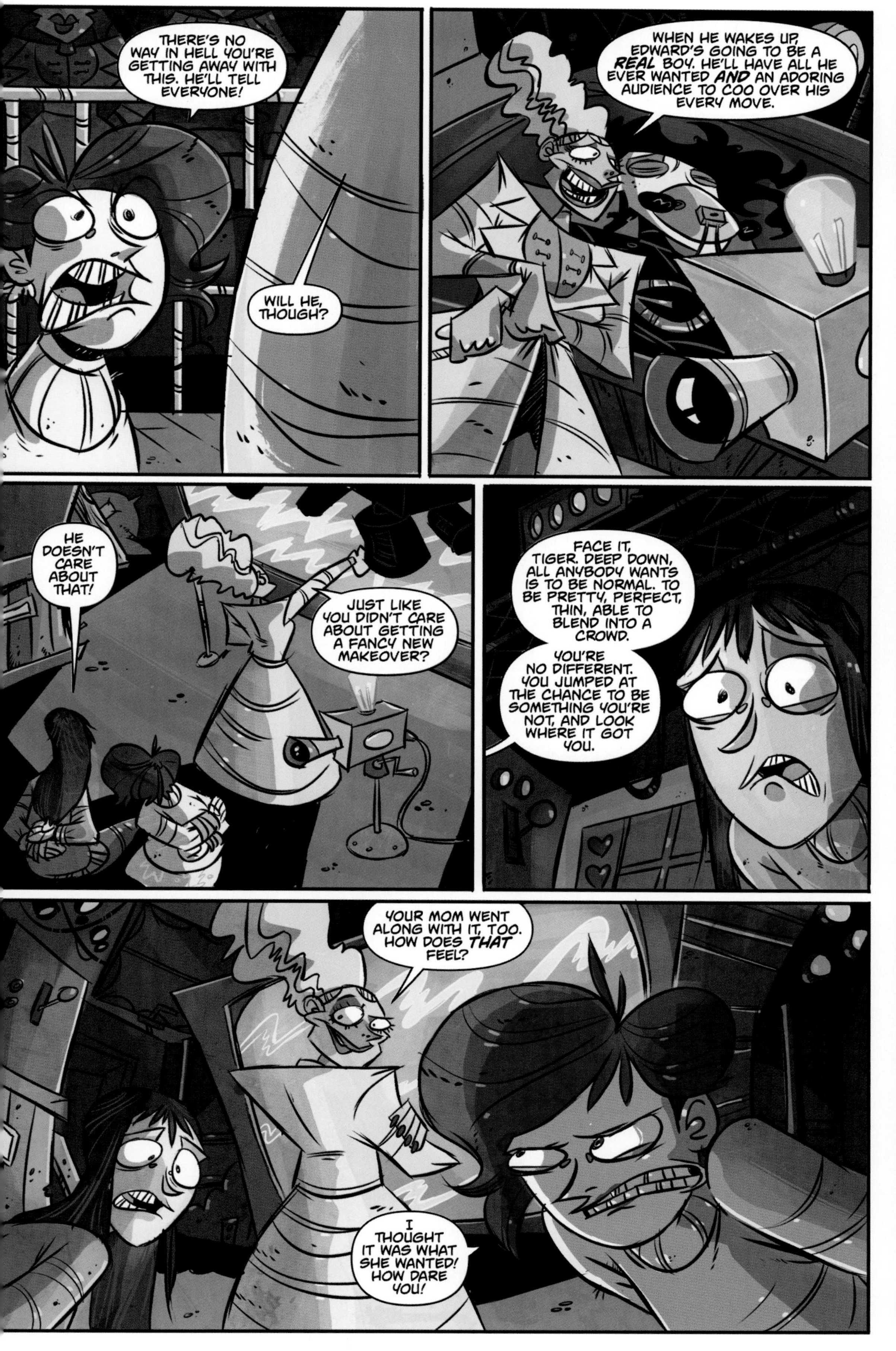
THERE'S NO WAY IN HELL YOU'RE GETTING AWAY WITH THIS. HE'LL TELL EVERYONE!
WILL HE, THOUGH?
WHEN HE WAKES UP, EDWARD'S GOING TO BE A *REAL* BOY. HE'LL HAVE ALL HE EVER WANTED *AND* AN ADORING AUDIENCE TO COO OVER HIS EVERY MOVE.
HE DOESN'T CARE ABOUT THAT!
JUST LIKE YOU DIDN'T CARE ABOUT GETTING A FANCY NEW MAKEOVER?
FACE IT, TIGER. DEEP DOWN, ALL ANYBODY WANTS IS TO BE NORMAL. TO BE PRETTY, PERFECT, THIN, ABLE TO BLEND INTO A CROWD.
YOU'RE NO DIFFERENT. YOU JUMPED AT THE CHANCE TO BE SOMETHING YOU'RE NOT, AND LOOK WHERE IT GOT YOU.
YOUR MOM WENT ALONG WITH IT, TOO. HOW DOES *THAT* FEEL?
I THOUGHT IT WAS WHAT SHE WANTED! HOW DARE YOU!

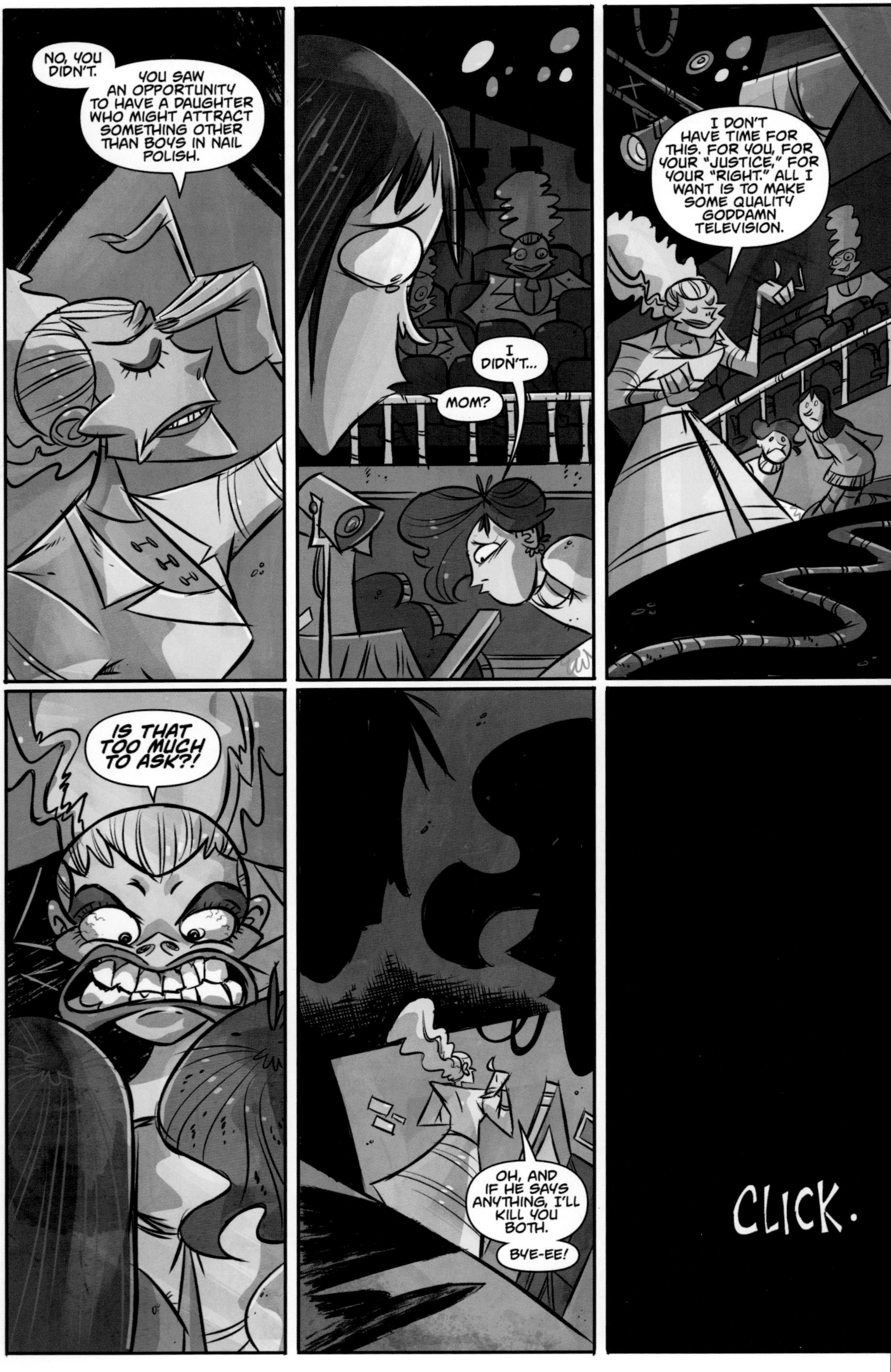
NO, YOU DIDN'T.
YOU SAW AN OPPORTUNITY TO HAVE A DAUGHTER WHO MIGHT ATTRACT SOMETHING OTHER THAN BOYS IN NAIL POLISH.
I DIDN'T...
MOM?
I DON'T HAVE TIME FOR THIS. FOR YOU, FOR YOUR "JUSTICE," FOR YOUR "RIGHT." ALL I WANT IS TO MAKE SOME QUALITY GODDAMN TELEVISION.
IS THAT TOO MUCH TO ASK?!
OH, AND IF HE SAYS ANYTHING, I'LL KILL YOU BOTH.
BYE-EE!
CLICK.

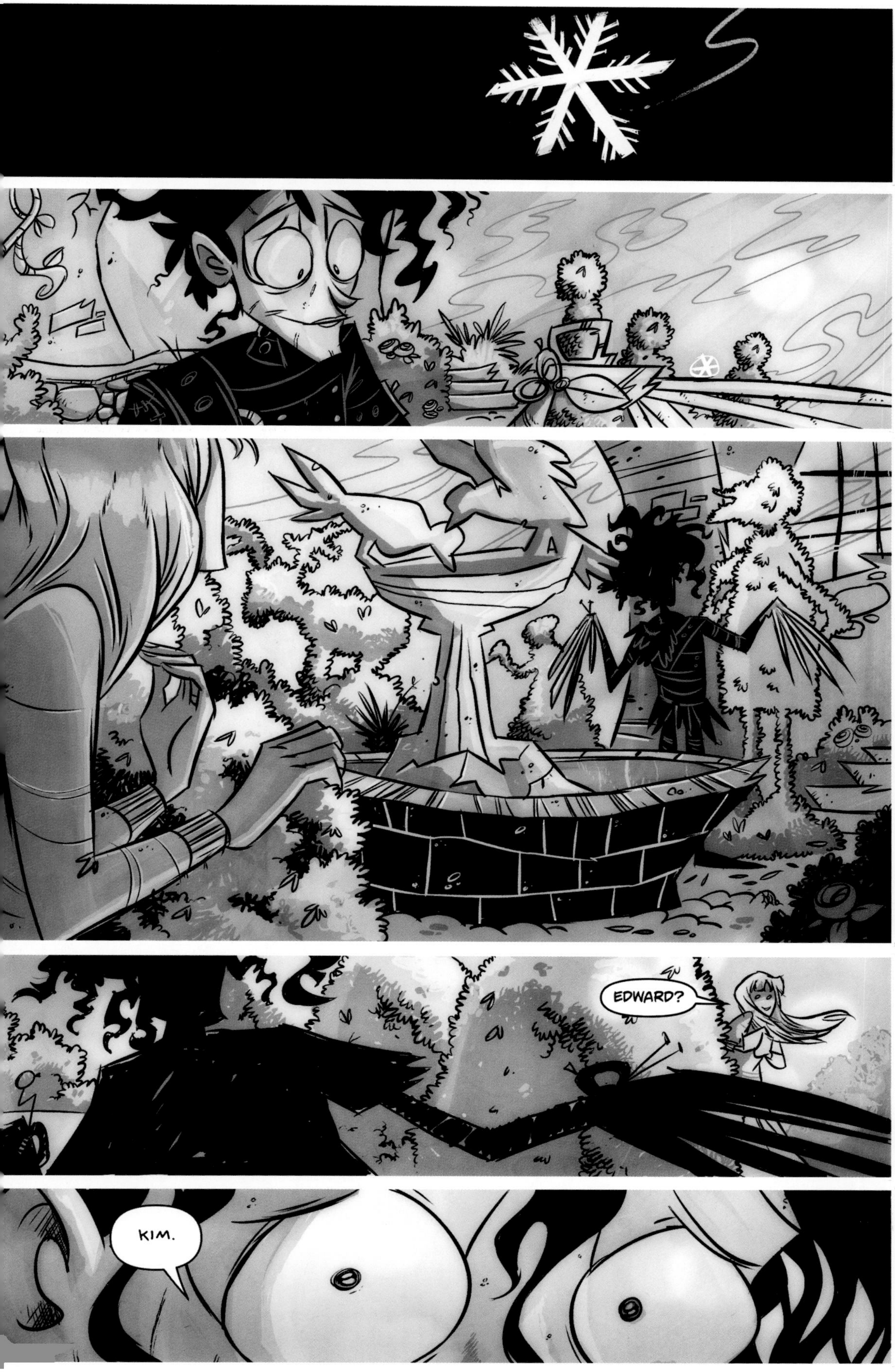
EDWARD?
KIM.

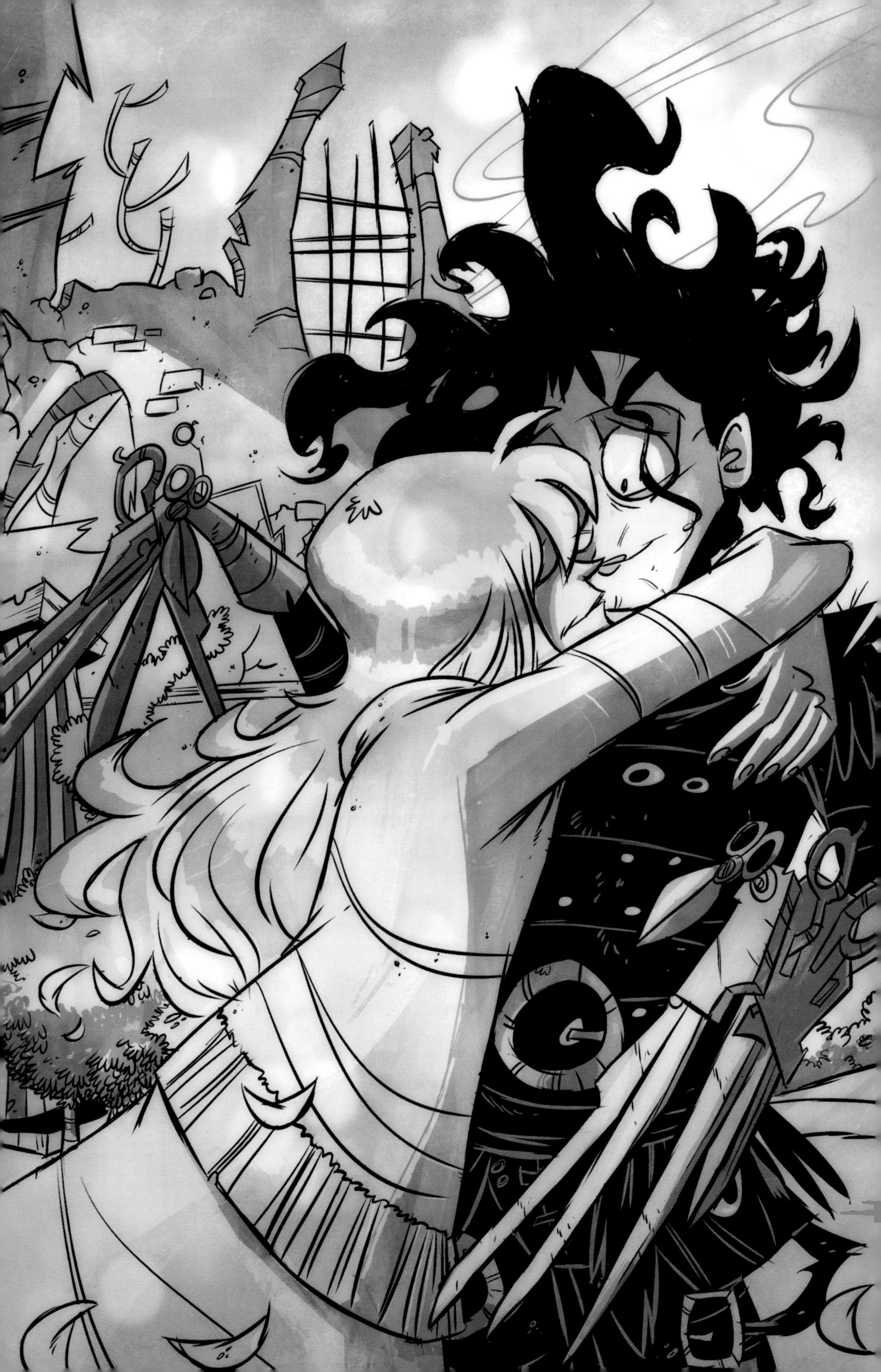

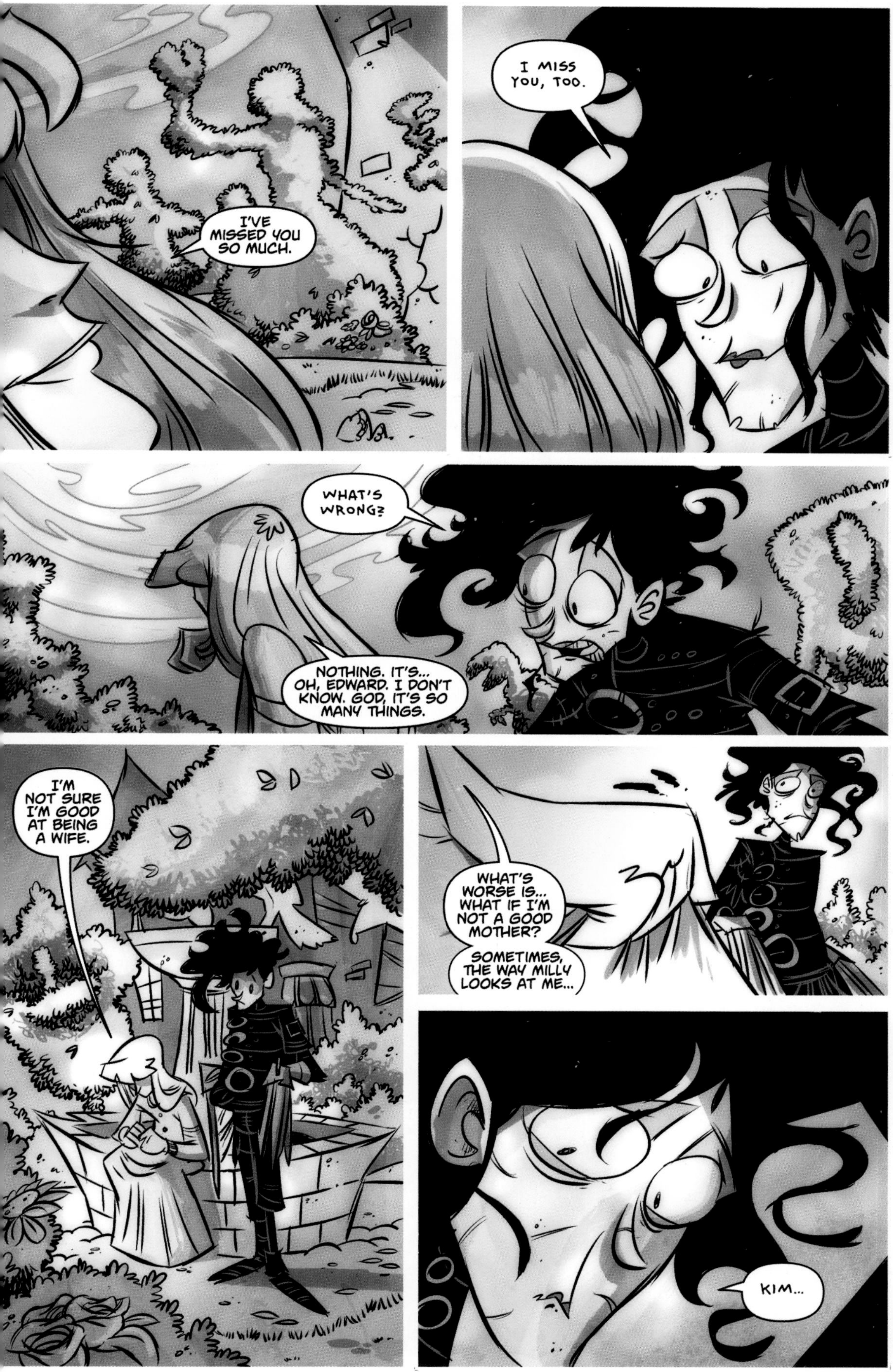
I'VE MISSED YOU SO MUCH.
I MISS YOU, TOO.
WHAT'S WRONG?
NOTHING. IT'S... OH, EDWARD. I DON'T KNOW. GOD, IT'S SO MANY THINGS.
I'M NOT SURE I'M GOOD AT BEING A WIFE.
WHAT'S WORSE IS... WHAT IF I'M NOT A GOOD MOTHER?
SOMETIMES, THE WAY MILLY LOOKS AT ME...
KIM...

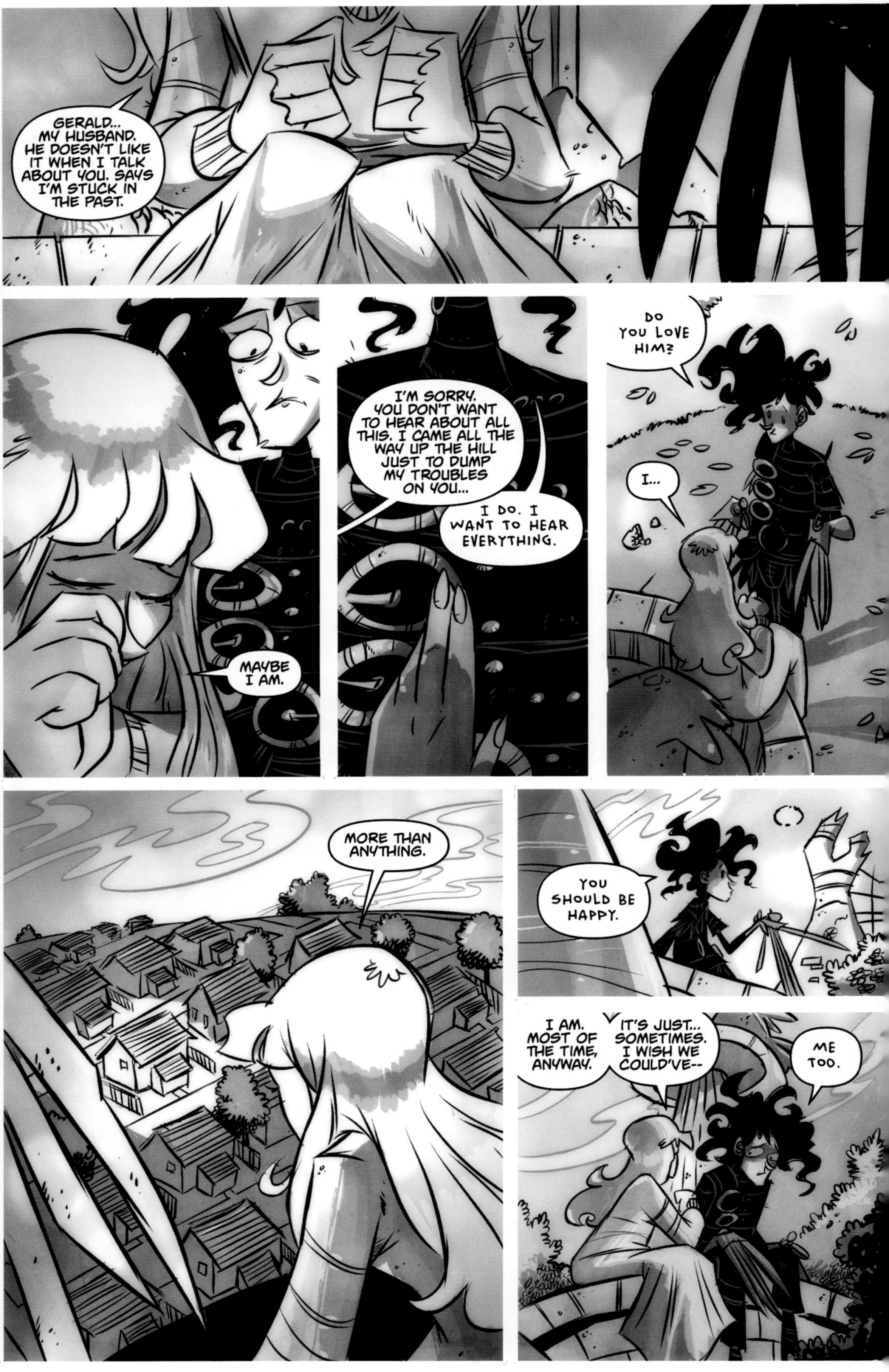
GERALD... MY HUSBAND. HE DOESN'T LIKE IT WHEN I TALK ABOUT YOU. SAYS I'M STUCK IN THE PAST.
MAYBE I AM.
I'M SORRY. YOU DON'T WANT TO HEAR ABOUT ALL THIS. I CAME ALL THE WAY UP THE HILL JUST TO DUMP MY TROUBLES ON YOU...
I DO. I WANT TO HEAR EVERYTHING.
DO YOU LOVE HIM?
I...
MORE THAN ANYTHING.
YOU SHOULD BE HAPPY.
I AM. MOST OF THE TIME, ANYWAY.
IT'S JUST... SOMETIMES. I WISH WE COULD'VE--
ME TOO.

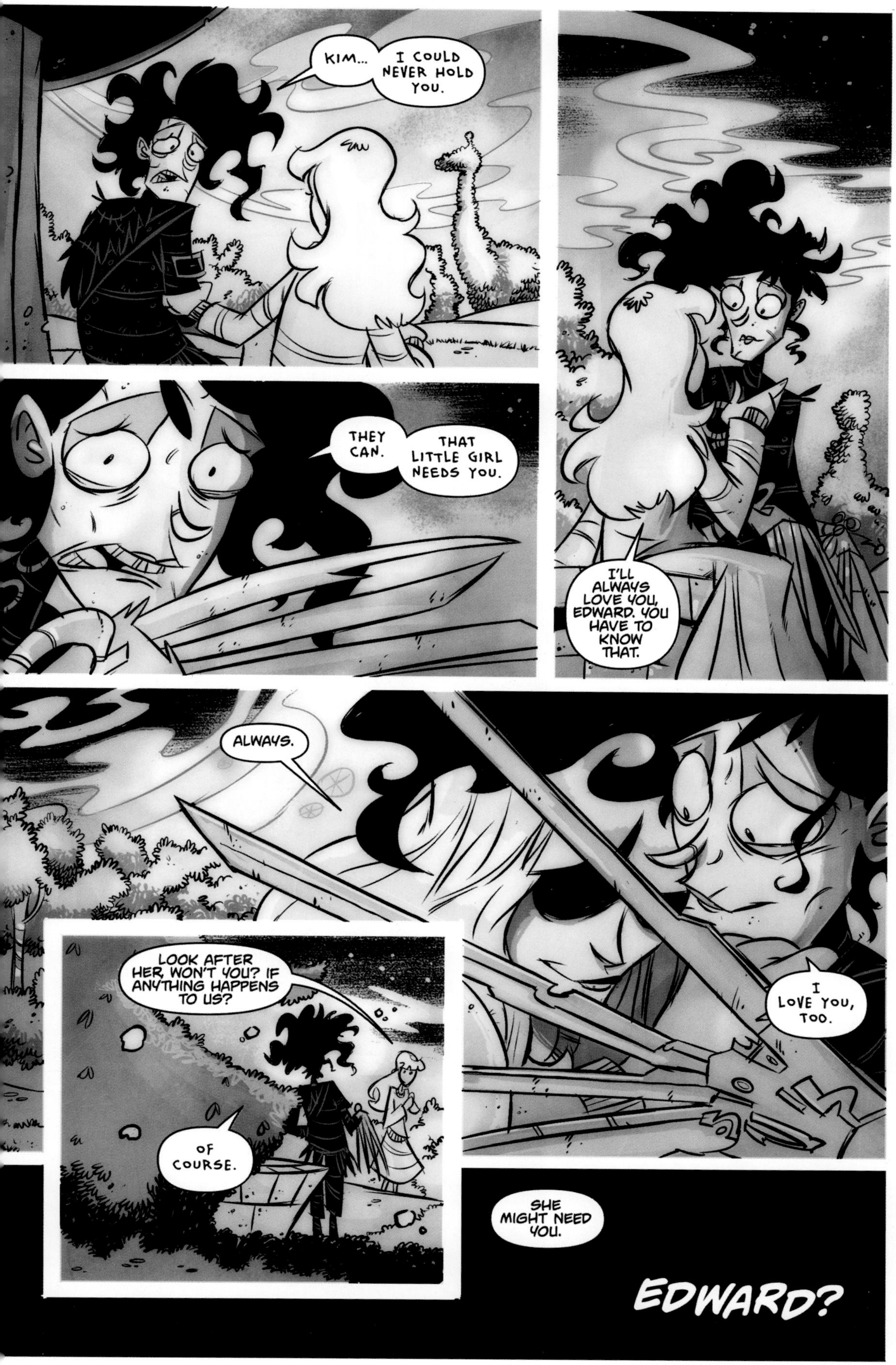
KIM...
I COULD NEVER HOLD YOU.
THEY CAN.
THAT LITTLE GIRL NEEDS YOU.
I'LL ALWAYS LOVE YOU, EDWARD. YOU HAVE TO KNOW THAT.
ALWAYS.
I LOVE YOU, TOO.
LOOK AFTER HER, WON'T YOU? IF ANYTHING HAPPENS TO US?
OF COURSE.
SHE MIGHT NEED YOU.
EDWARD?

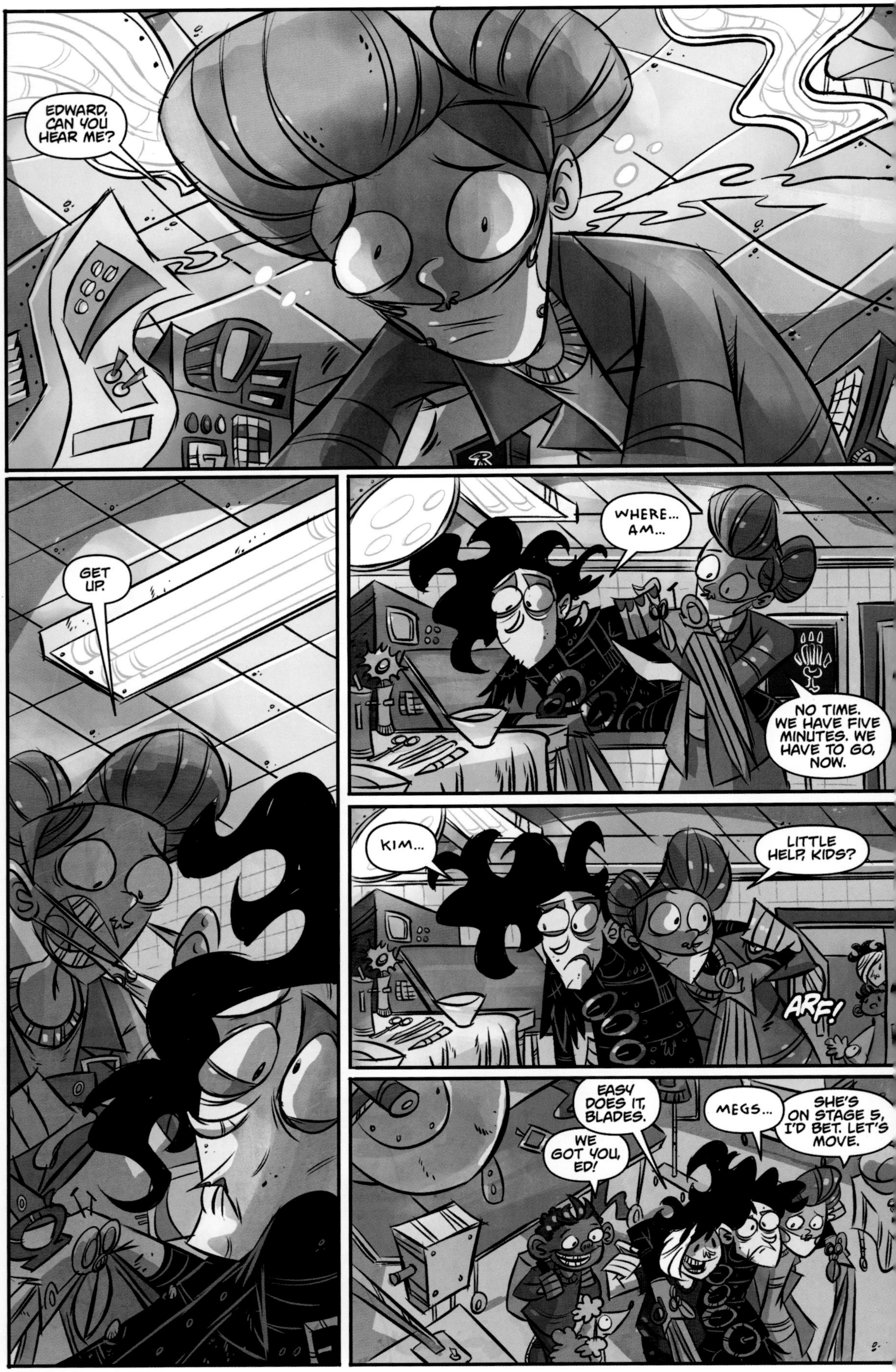
EDWARD, CAN YOU HEAR ME?
GET UP.
WHERE... AM...
NO TIME. WE HAVE FIVE MINUTES. WE HAVE TO GO, NOW.
KIM...
LITTLE HELP, KIDS?
ARF!
EASY DOES IT, BLADES.
WE GOT YOU, ED!
MEGS...
SHE'S ON STAGE 5, I'D BET. LET'S MOVE.

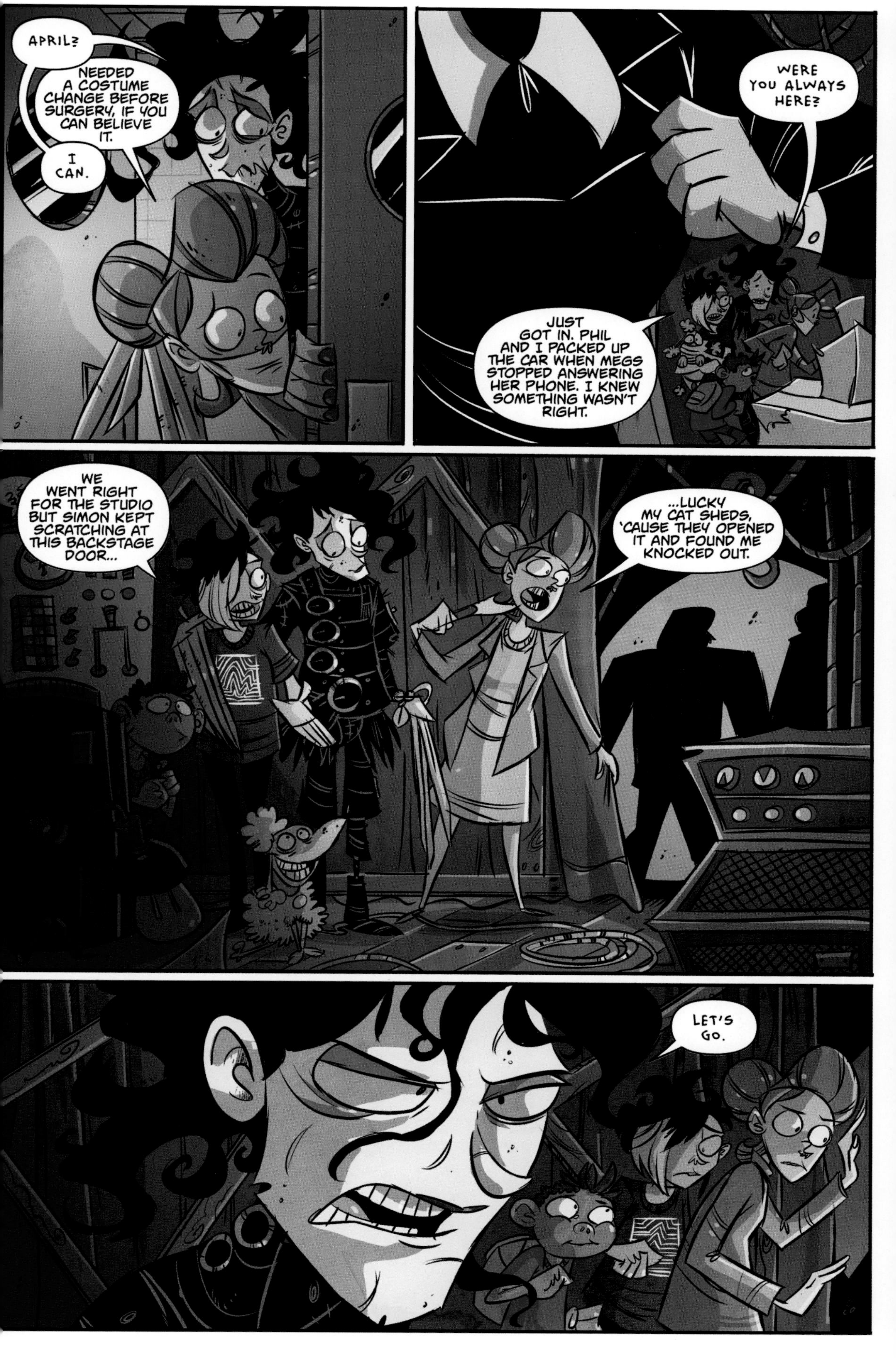

APRIL?
NEEDED A COSTUME CHANGE BEFORE SURGERY, IF YOU CAN BELIEVE IT.
I CAN.
WERE YOU ALWAYS HERE?
JUST GOT IN. PHIL AND I PACKED UP THE CAR WHEN MEGS STOPPED ANSWERING HER PHONE. I KNEW SOMETHING WASN'T RIGHT.
WE WENT RIGHT FOR THE STUDIO BUT SIMON KEPT SCRATCHING AT THIS BACKSTAGE DOOR...
...LUCKY MY CAT SHEDS, 'CAUSE THEY OPENED IT AND FOUND ME KNOCKED OUT.
LET'S GO.

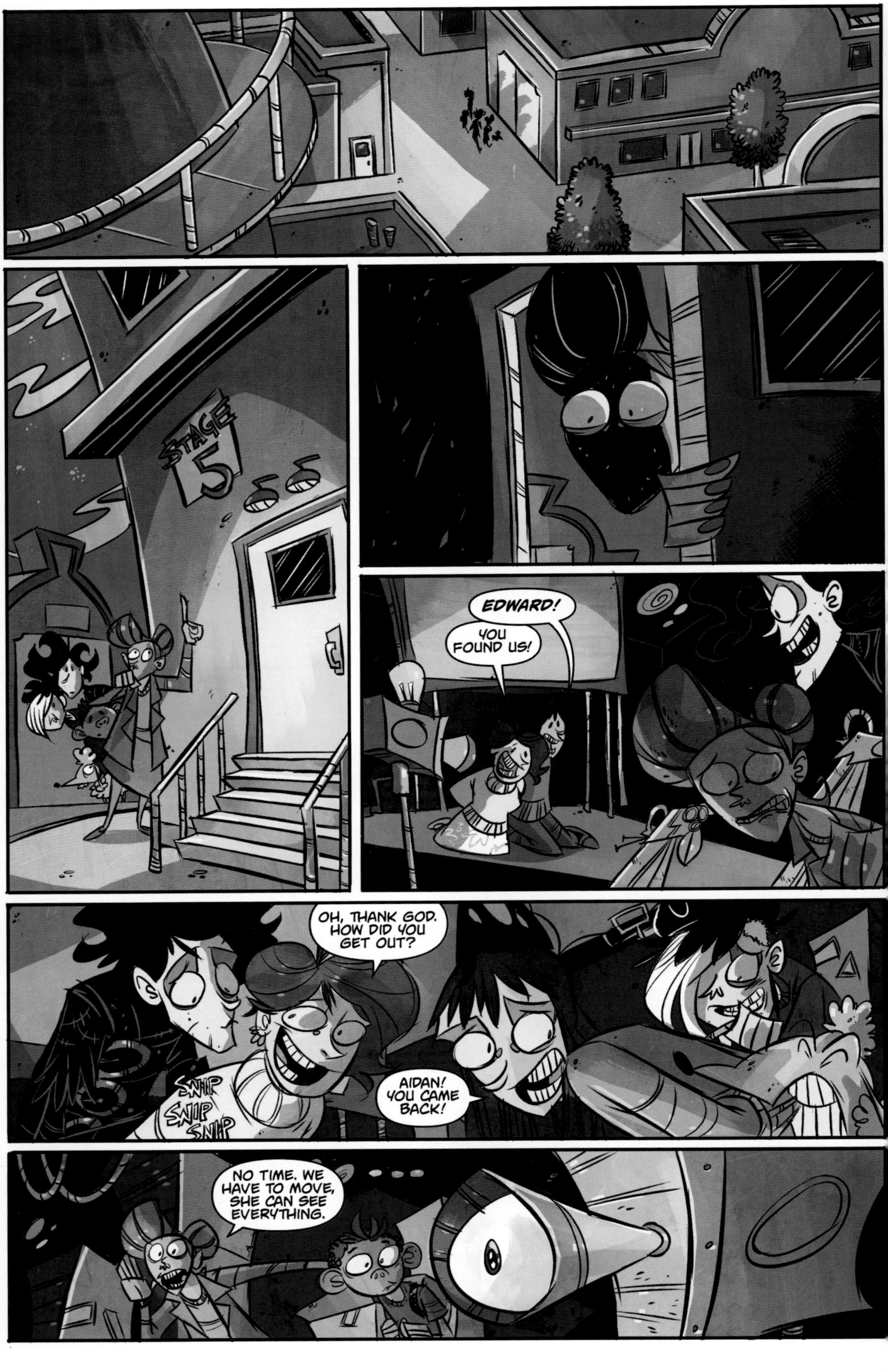
STAGE 5
EDWARD!
YOU FOUND US!
OH, THANK GOD. HOW DID YOU GET OUT?
SNIP SNIP SNIP
AIDAN! YOU CAME BACK!
NO TIME. WE HAVE TO MOVE, SHE CAN SEE EVERYTHING.

YEAH, SHE CAN.

APRIL!

HONESTLY, PEOPLE, WHAT AM I GOING TO DO WITH YOU?

SLAM!

SLAM

SLAM

SLAM!

SLAM

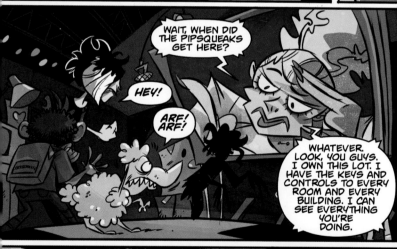

WAIT, WHEN DID THE PIPSQUEAKS GET HERE?

HEY!

ARF! ARF!

WHATEVER. LOOK, YOU GUYS. I OWN THIS LOT. I HAVE THE KEYS AND CONTROLS TO EVERY ROOM AND EVERY BUILDING. I CAN SEE EVERYTHING YOU'RE DOING.

CRUNCH!!

ZZZT

ZZZT

OH, WELL THAT'S ANNOYING.

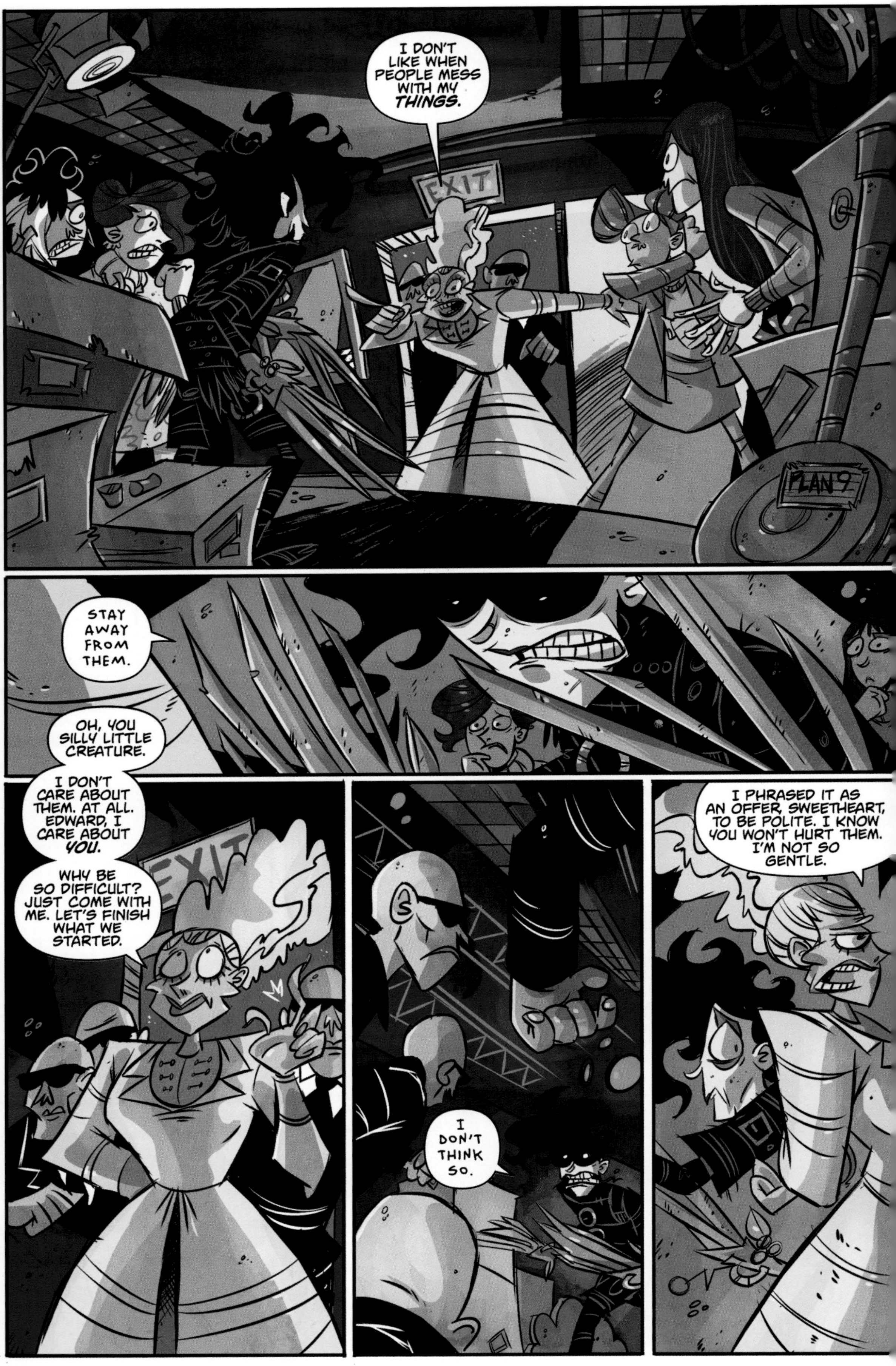

I DON'T LIKE WHEN PEOPLE MESS WITH MY *THINGS*.
EXIT
PLAN 9
STAY AWAY FROM THEM.
OH, YOU SILLY LITTLE CREATURE.
I DON'T CARE ABOUT THEM. AT ALL. EDWARD, I CARE ABOUT *YOU*.
WHY BE SO DIFFICULT? JUST COME WITH ME. LET'S FINISH WHAT WE STARTED.
EXIT
I DON'T THINK SO.
I PHRASED IT AS AN OFFER, SWEETHEART, TO BE POLITE. I KNOW YOU WON'T HURT THEM. I'M NOT SO GENTLE.

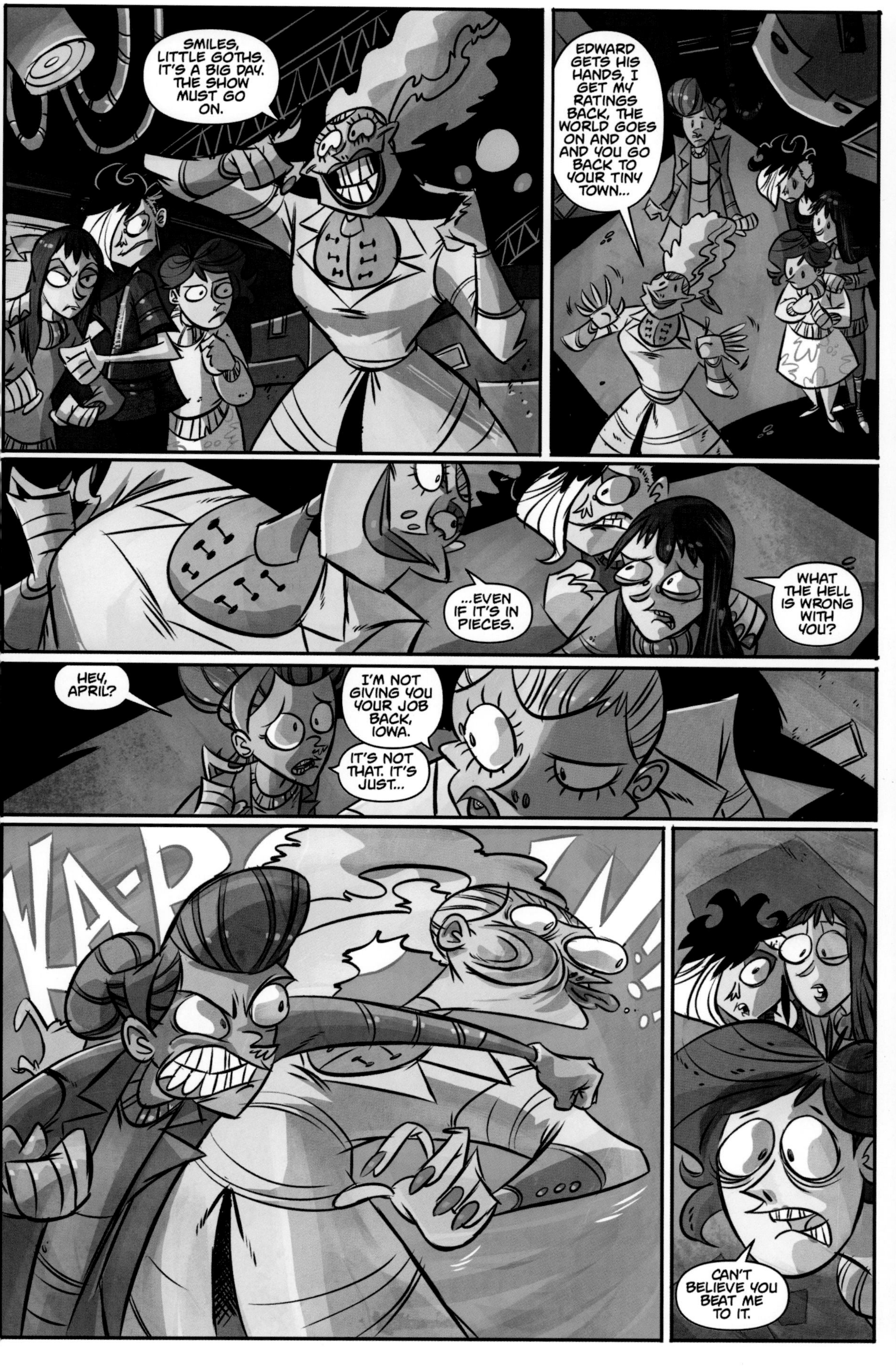
SMILES, LITTLE GOTHS. IT'S A BIG DAY. THE SHOW MUST GO ON.
EDWARD GETS HIS HANDS, I GET MY RATINGS BACK, THE WORLD GOES ON AND ON AND YOU GO BACK TO YOUR TINY TOWN...
...EVEN IF IT'S IN PIECES.
WHAT THE HELL IS WRONG WITH YOU?
HEY, APRIL?
I'M NOT GIVING YOU YOUR JOB BACK, IOWA.
IT'S NOT THAT. IT'S JUST...
CAN'T BELIEVE YOU BEAT ME TO IT.

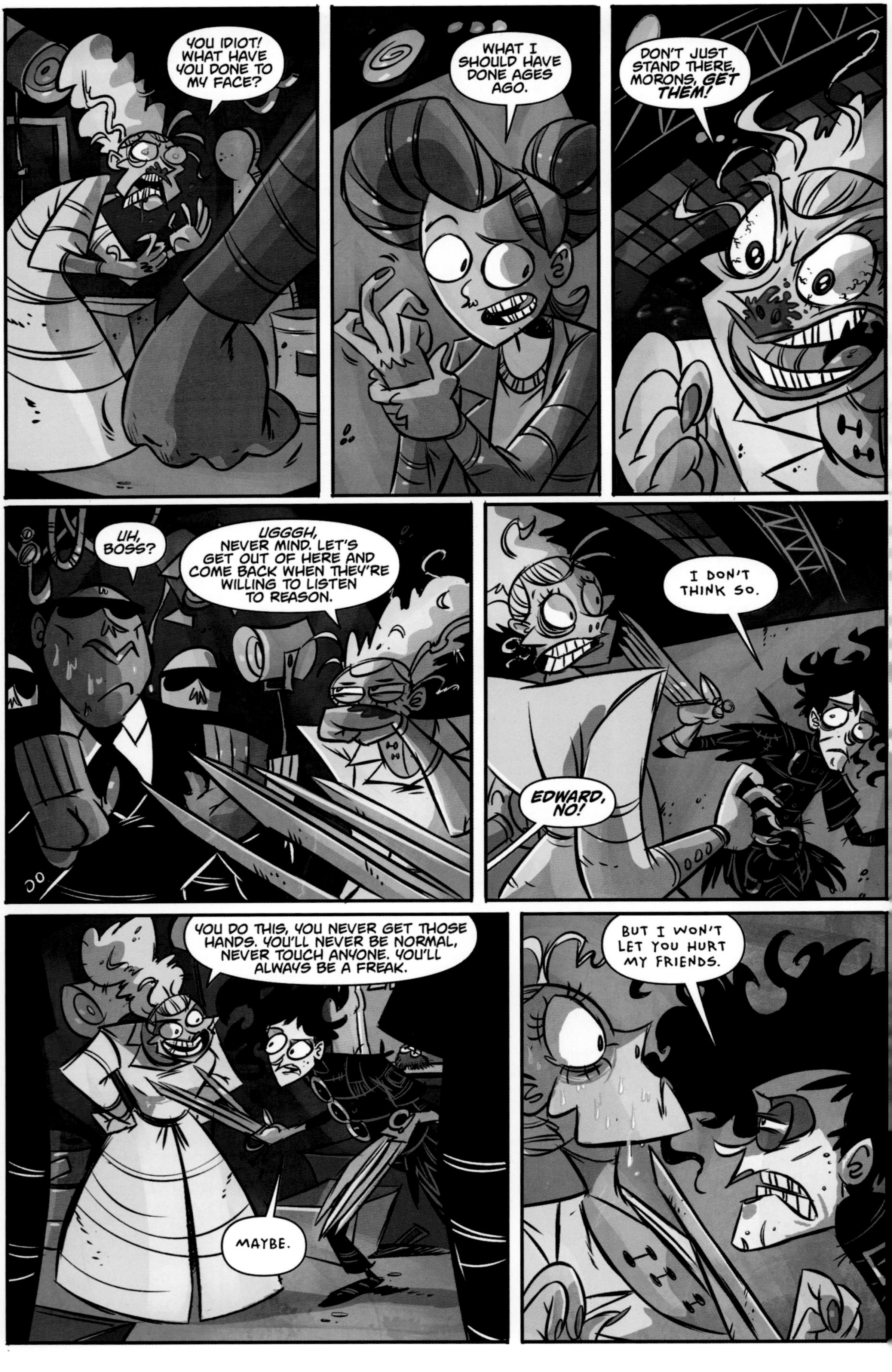

YOU IDIOT! WHAT HAVE YOU DONE TO MY FACE?
WHAT I SHOULD HAVE DONE AGES AGO.
DON'T JUST STAND THERE, MORONS, GET THEM!
UH, BOSS?
UGGGH, NEVER MIND. LET'S GET OUT OF HERE AND COME BACK WHEN THEY'RE WILLING TO LISTEN TO REASON.
I DON'T THINK SO.
EDWARD, NO!
YOU DO THIS, YOU NEVER GET THOSE HANDS. YOU'LL NEVER BE NORMAL, NEVER TOUCH ANYONE. YOU'LL ALWAYS BE A FREAK.
MAYBE.
BUT I WON'T LET YOU HURT MY FRIENDS.

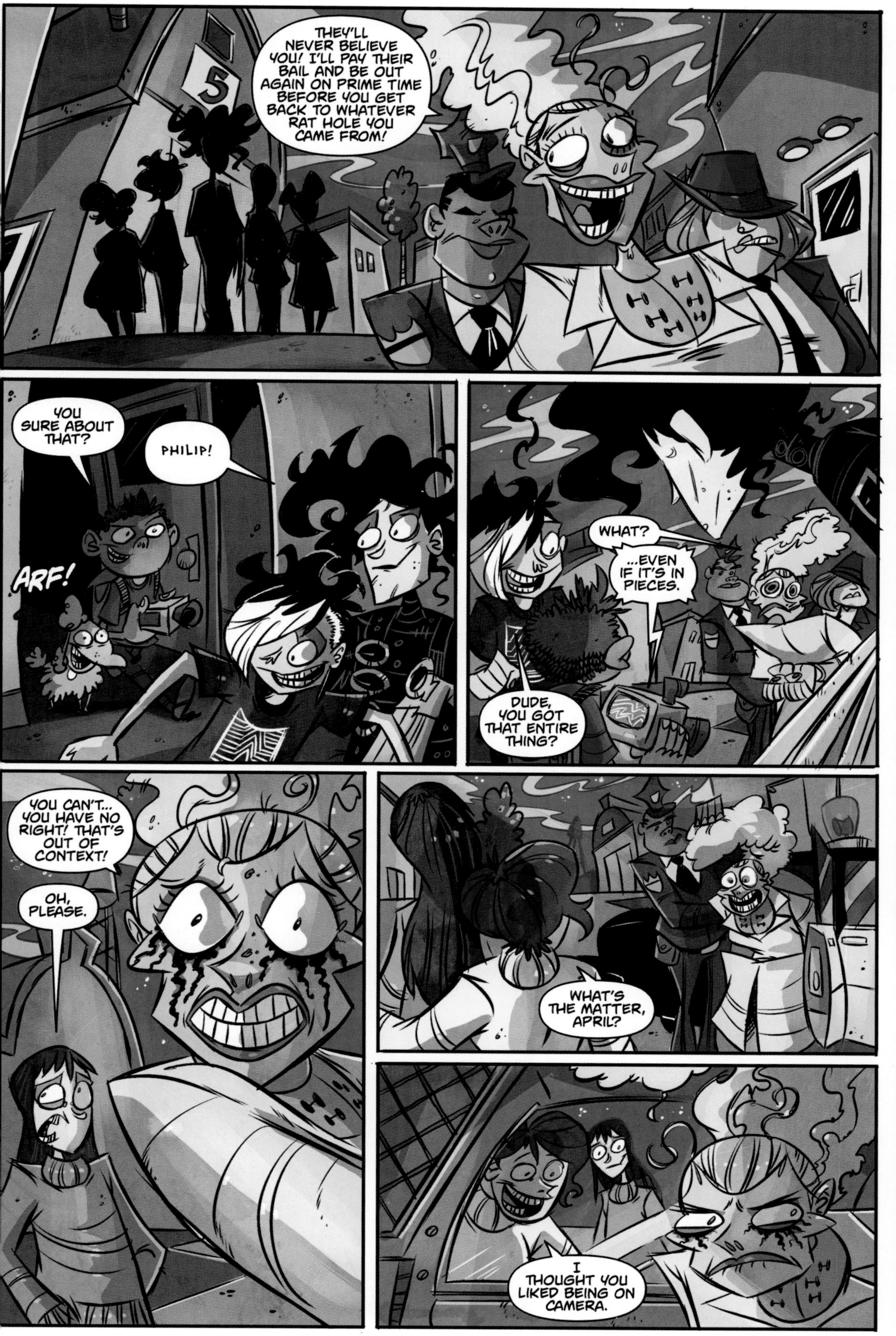
THEY'LL NEVER BELIEVE YOU! I'LL PAY THEIR BAIL AND BE OUT AGAIN ON PRIME TIME BEFORE YOU GET BACK TO WHATEVER RAT HOLE YOU CAME FROM!
YOU SURE ABOUT THAT?
PHILIP!
ARF!
WHAT?
...EVEN IF IT'S IN PIECES.
DUDE, YOU GOT THAT ENTIRE THING?
YOU CAN'T... YOU HAVE NO RIGHT! THAT'S OUT OF CONTEXT!
OH, PLEASE.
WHAT'S THE MATTER, APRIL?
I THOUGHT YOU LIKED BEING ON CAMERA.

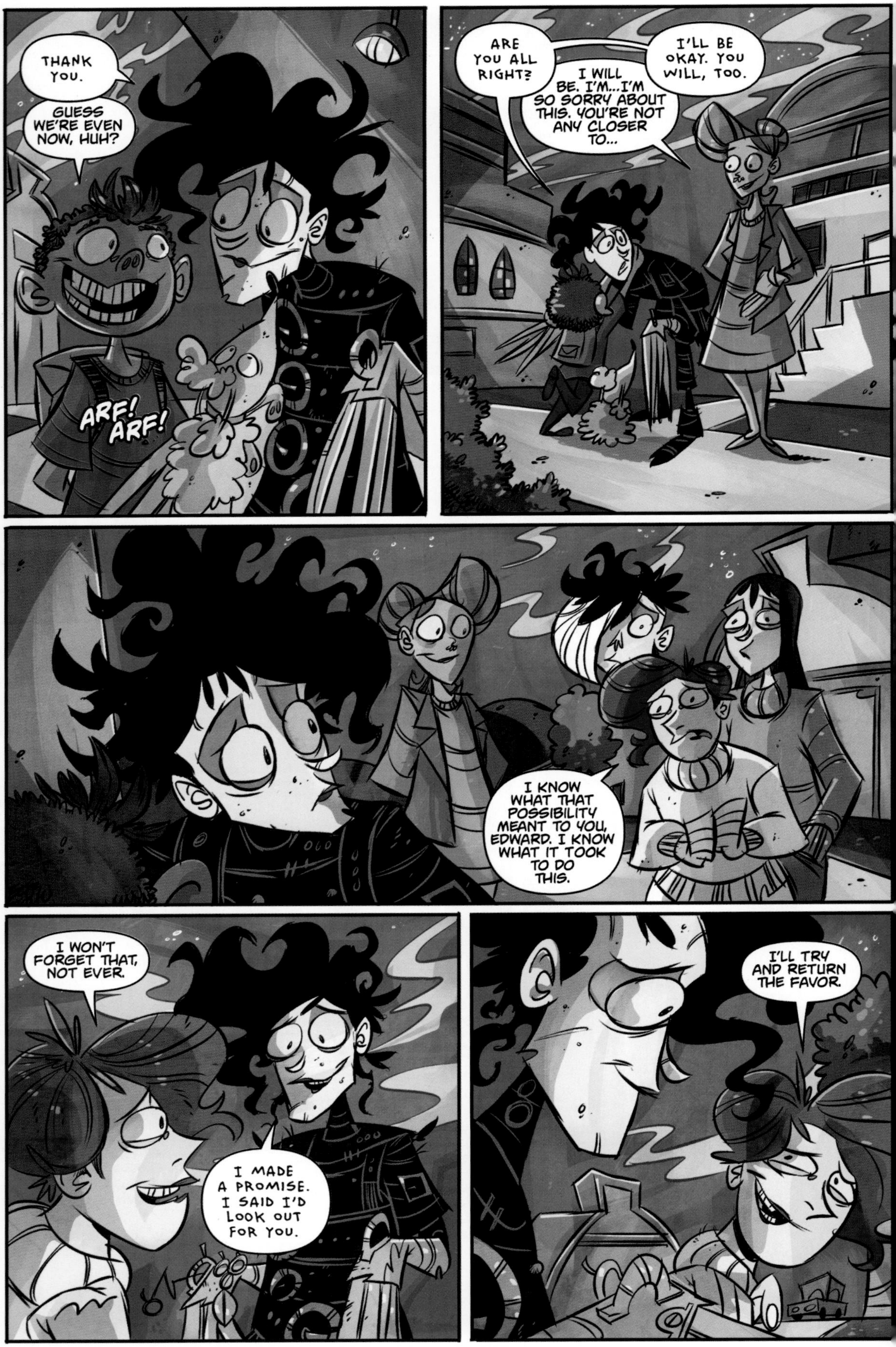
THANK YOU.
GUESS WE'RE EVEN NOW, HUH?
ARF! ARF!
ARE YOU ALL RIGHT?
I WILL BE. I'M...I'M SO SORRY ABOUT THIS. YOU'RE NOT ANY CLOSER TO...
I'LL BE OKAY. YOU WILL, TOO.
I KNOW WHAT THAT POSSIBILITY MEANT TO YOU, EDWARD. I KNOW WHAT IT TOOK TO DO THIS.
I WON'T FORGET THAT, NOT EVER.
I MADE A PROMISE. I SAID I'D LOOK OUT FOR YOU.
I'LL TRY AND RETURN THE FAVOR.

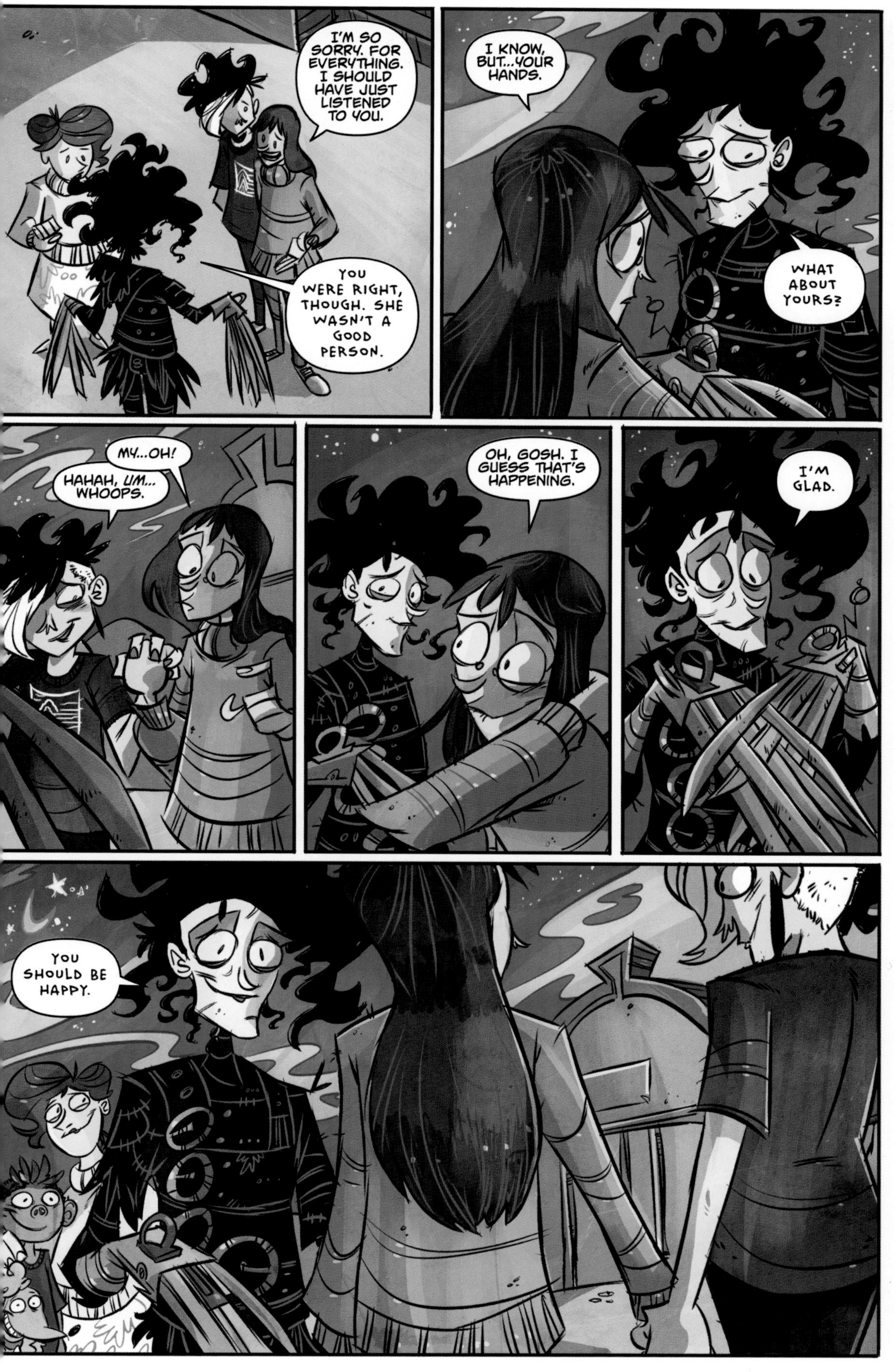
I'M SO SORRY. FOR EVERYTHING. I SHOULD HAVE JUST LISTENED TO YOU.
YOU WERE RIGHT, THOUGH. SHE WASN'T A GOOD PERSON.
I KNOW, BUT...YOUR HANDS.
WHAT ABOUT YOURS?
MY...OH!
HAHAH, UM... WHOOPS.
OH, GOSH. I GUESS THAT'S HAPPENING.
I'M GLAD.
YOU SHOULD BE HAPPY.

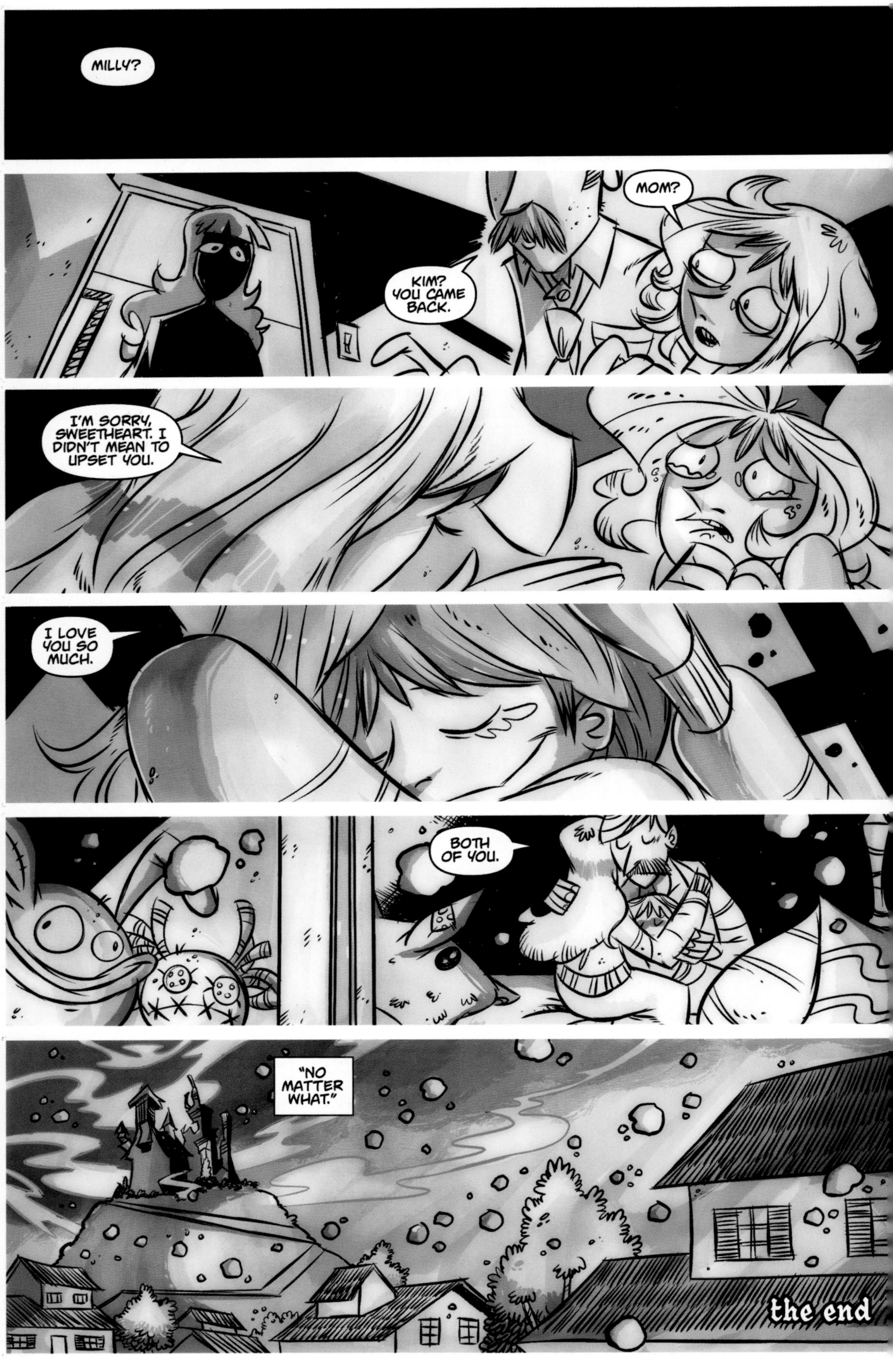
MILLY?
MOM?
KIM? YOU CAME BACK.
I'M SORRY, SWEETHEART. I DIDN'T MEAN TO UPSET YOU.
I LOVE YOU SO MUCH.
BOTH OF YOU.
"NO MATTER WHAT."
the end

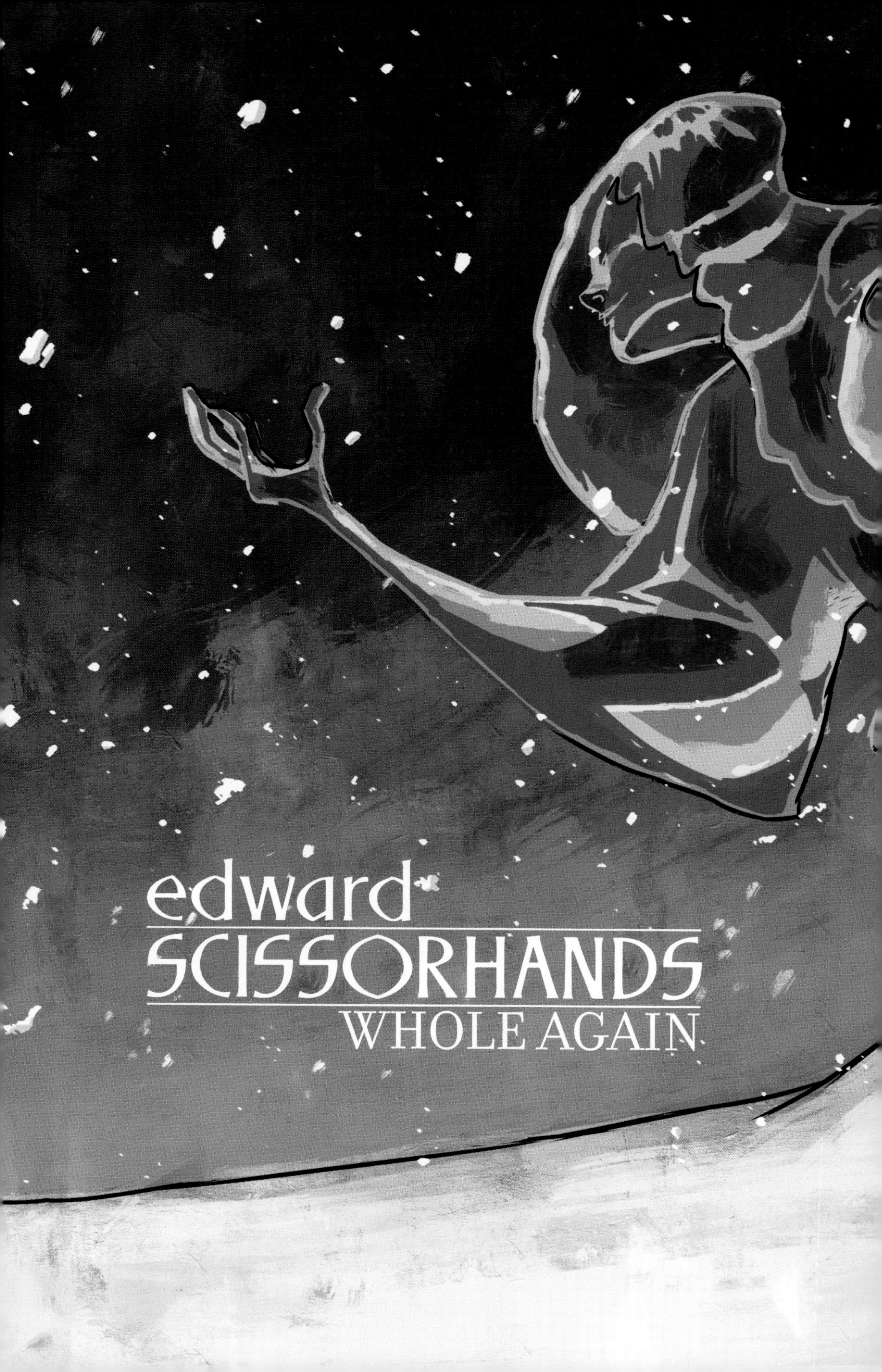
edward
SCISSORHANDS
WHOLE AGAIN

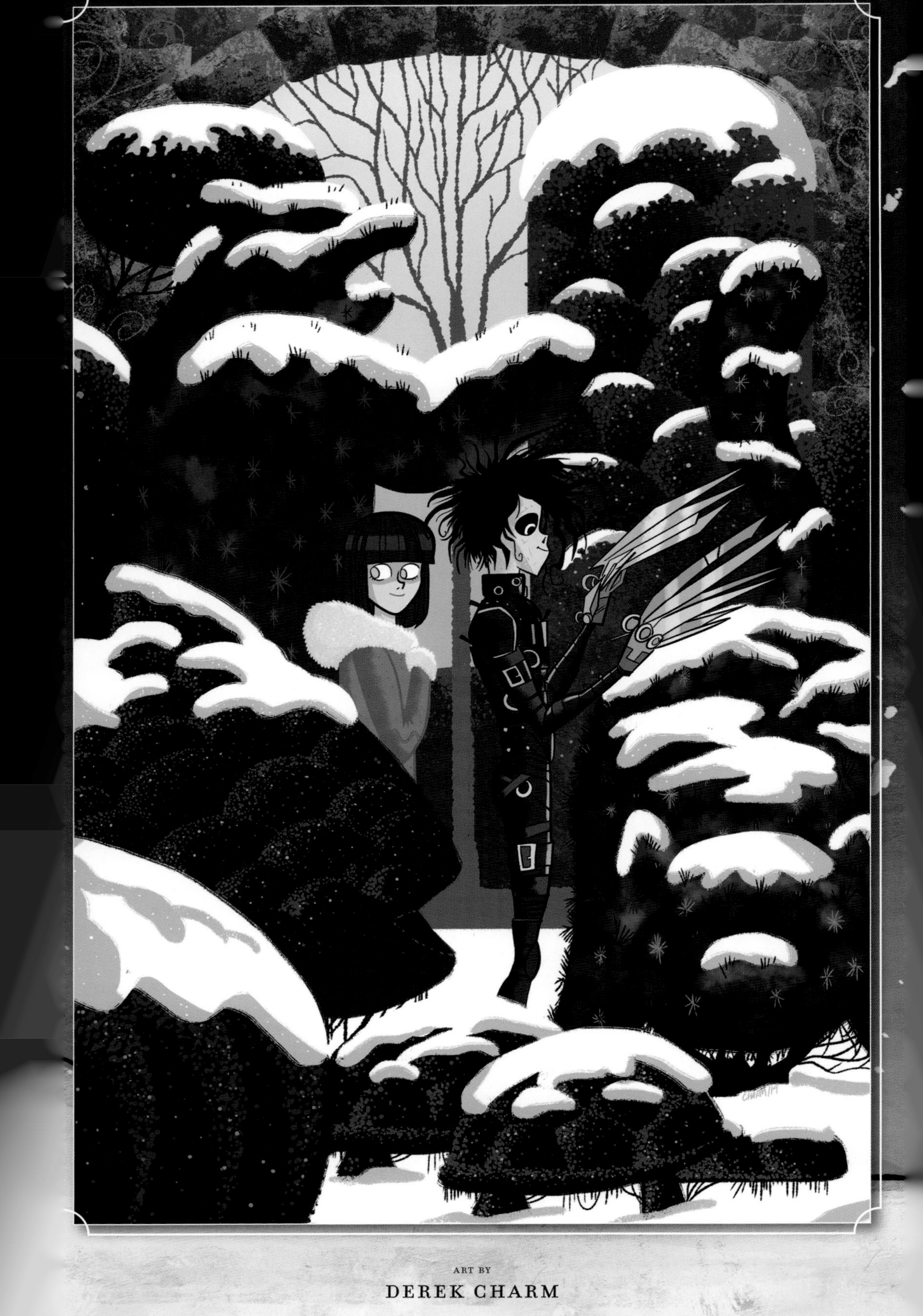

ART BY
DEREK CHARM

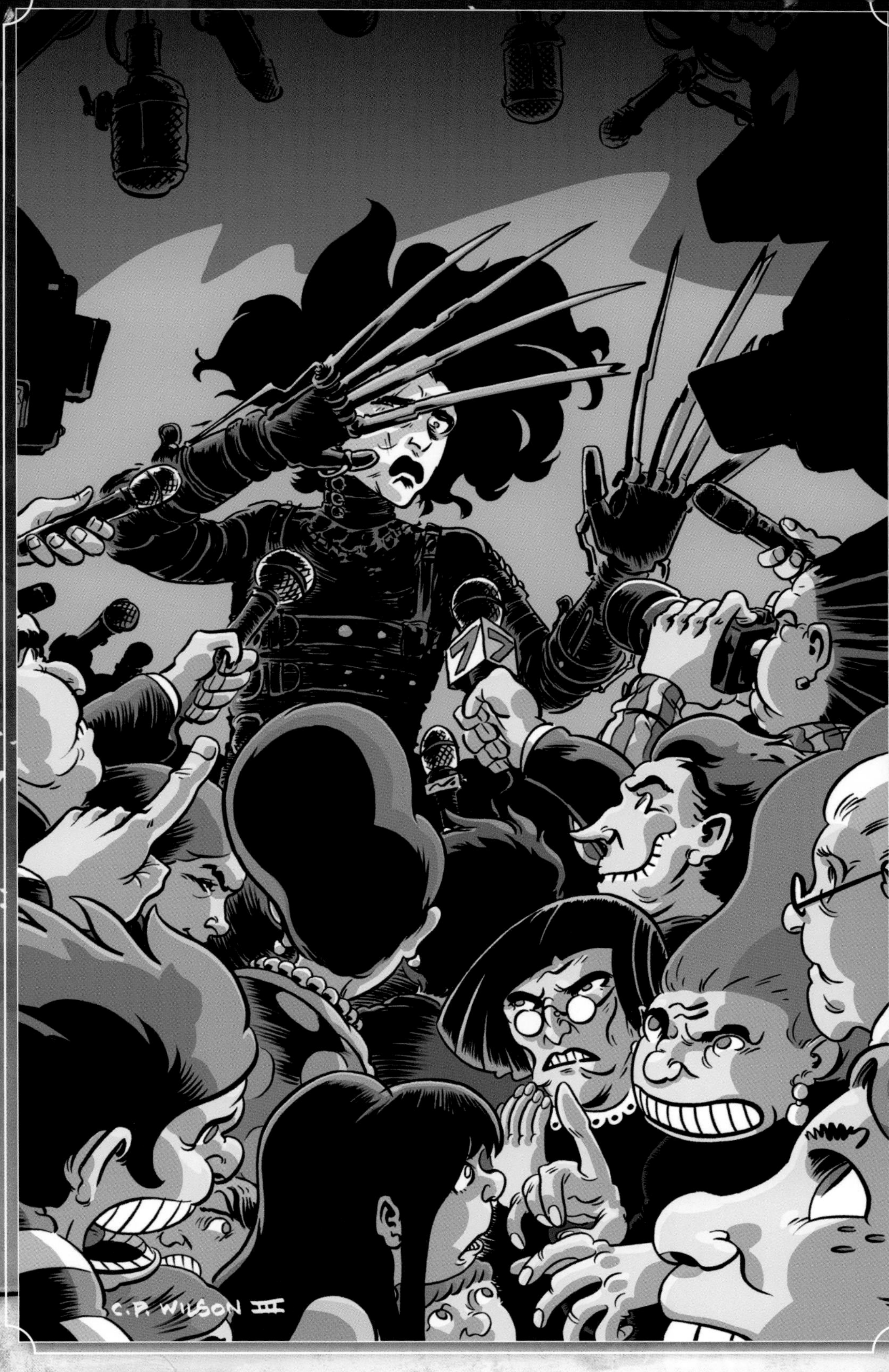
C.P. WILSON III

ART BY
C.P. WILSON III

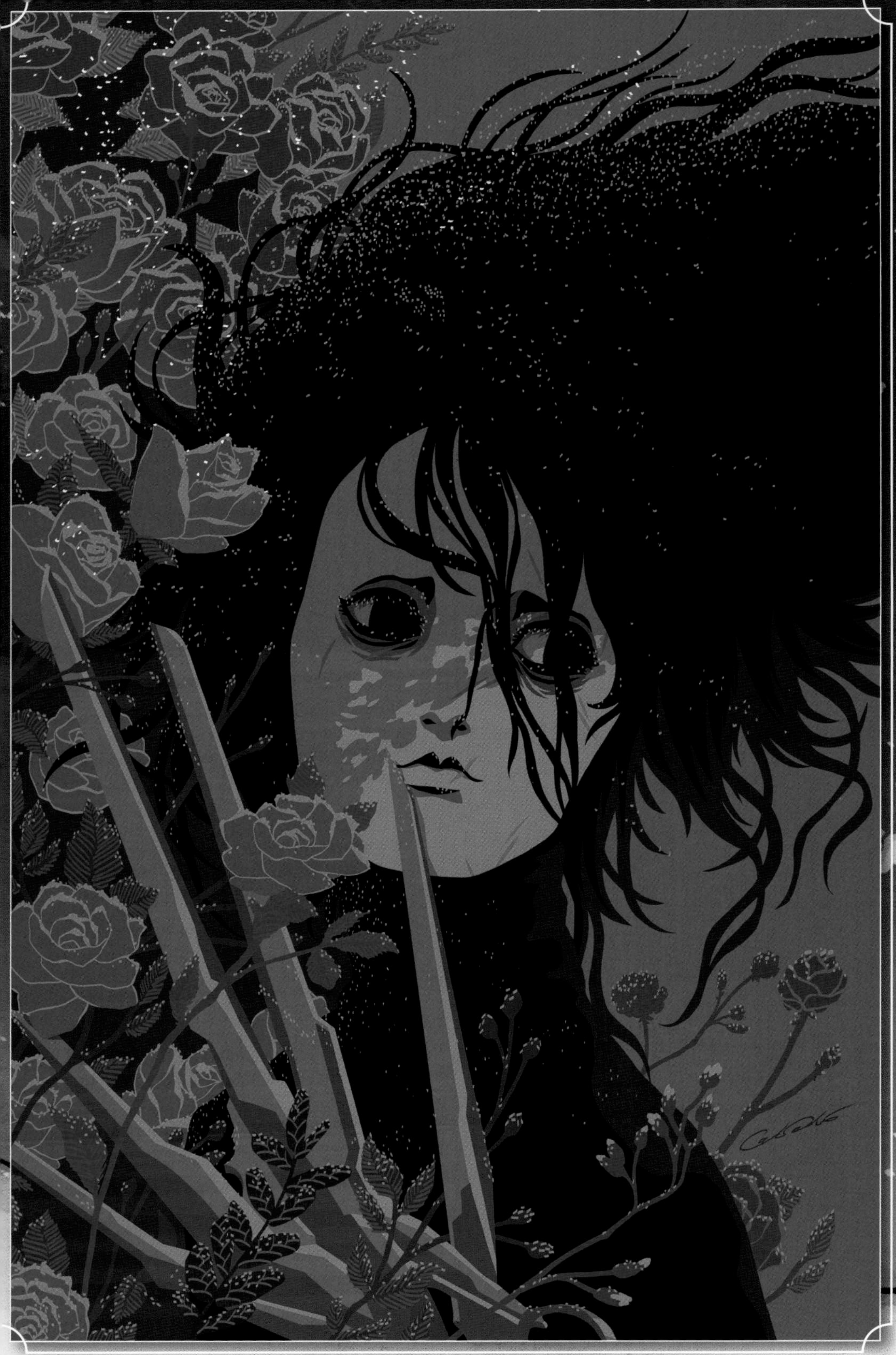

ART BY
GEORGE CALTSOUDAS

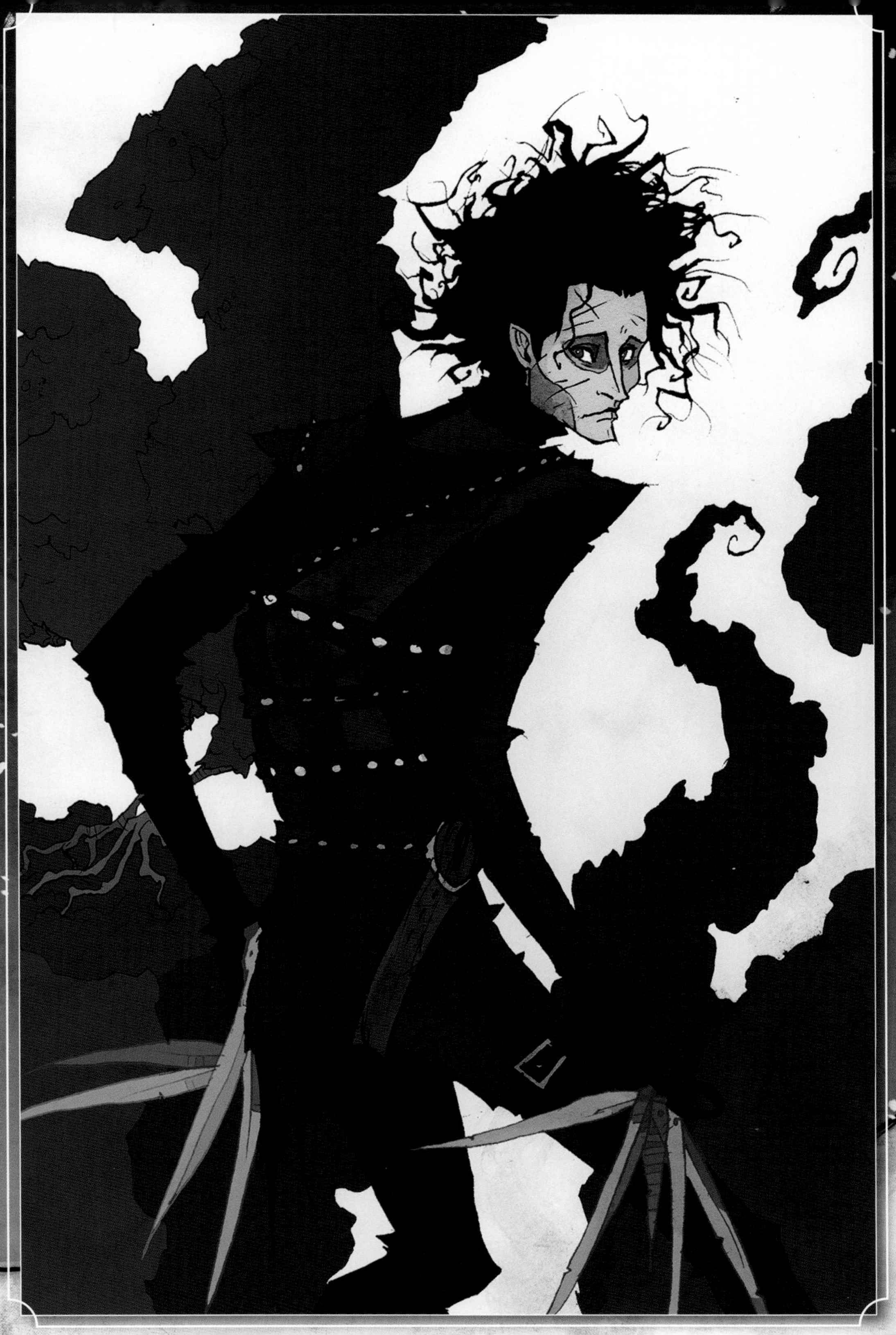

ART BY
ABIGAIL LARSON

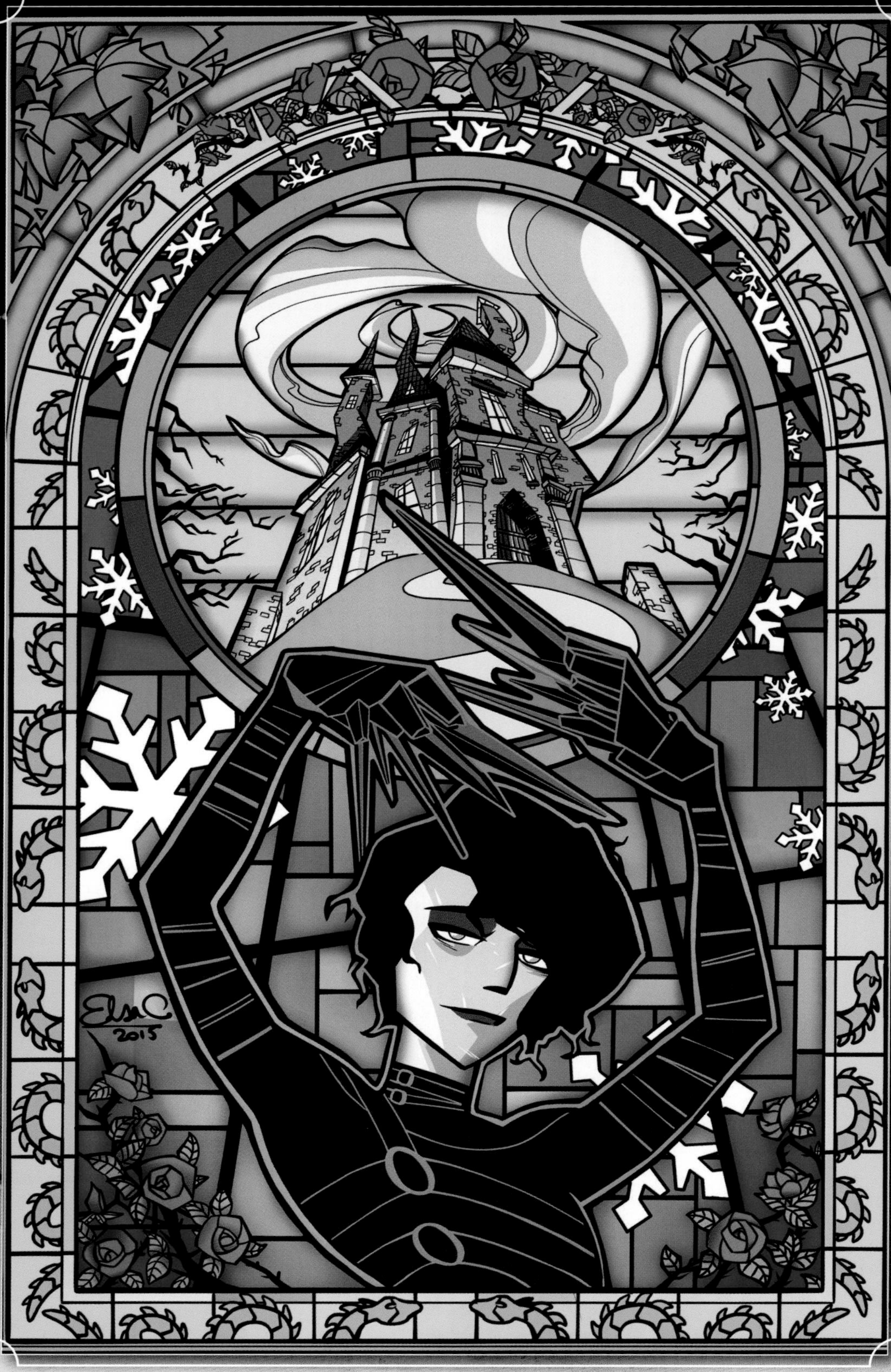
ElsaC.
2015

ART BY
ELSA CHARRETIER

CLIPPINGS

WELCOME BACK TO CLIPPINGS, WHERE THE TEAM BEHIND IDW'S EDWARD SCISSORHANDS COMICS CONNECTS WITH YOU, THE READER! I'M EDITOR SARAH GAYDOS (SG), WITH MEGA-WRITER KATE LETH (KL) AND UBER-ARTIST DREW RAUSCH (DR). THE CHARACTER OF EDWARD SPOKE TO SO MANY OF US IN OUR FORMATIVE YEARS FOR MANY REASONS: HIS OUTSIDER STATUS COMING INTO CONFLICT WITH HIS BIG HEART. HIS LONGING FOR SOMEONE TO UNDERSTAND HIM, AND SEE PAST HIS SCARS. HIS REALLY COOL HAIR. SEEING OURSELVES IN CHARACTERS LIKE EDWARD, AS WELL AS OTHER SPECIAL MOVIES, COMICS, POETRY, BOOKS AND PEOPLE, HELPED US ALL GET THROUGH PAINFUL PERIODS AND FIND COMMUNITIES OF LIKE-MINDED FOLKS. JOIN US FOR A FEW SELECTED LETTERS FROM READERS, PLUS INTERVIEWS WITH THE CREATIVE TEAM!

(SG) SARAH GAYDOS

(KL) KATE LETH

(DR) DREW RAUSCH

FIRST OFF, I'D LIKE TO SAY THANKS FOR TOSSING NOLA AND LOGANN'S PHOTOGRAPH INTO ISSUE THREE [**EDITOR'S NOTE:** ABSOLUTELY!]. THE GIRLS GOT A KICK OUT OF SEEING THEMSELVES IN A COMIC BOOK, AND I KNOW AS THE YEARS GO BY THAT THEY'LL JUST GROW TO APPRECIATE IT MORE.

AS FOR THE LATEST CHAPTER OF THE STORY, I ENJOYED ELI'S CREEPY SCENE WITH PHILIP. THE WHOLE "TRYING TO FIGURE OUT HOW IT WORKS ON THE INSIDE" FINISHED UP ON A POSSIBLY HORRIBLE NOTE? CURIOUS TO SEE HOW FAR THAT ENDED UP GOING.

SINCE THE RELEASE OF THE COMIC BOOK SERIES, I'VE THOUGHT A BIT MORE FROM AN ADULT PERSPECTIVE ABOUT WHAT INITIALLY APPEALED TO ME ABOUT EDWARD SCISSORHANDS AS A YOUNG FELLOW. AND OF COURSE, AS WITH MOST PEOPLE, IT WAS THE OVERALL LOOK OF THE CHARACTER THAT PULLED ME IN AS A START.

THE REASONING MIGHT BE A BIT DIFFERENT THAN OTHERS THOUGH. MY MOTHER RITA USED TO BOOK PUNK ROCK, METAL, HIP HOP, GOTH, THRASH, ART SHOWS, ETC. BACK IN THE 1980S AROUND THE DAYTON AREA. AS A CHILD, I WAS CONSISTENTLY AROUND A LOT OF REALLY CREATIVE PEOPLE WITH VERY DARK AND EXTREME STYLES.

EDWARD ACTUALLY REMINDS ME OF SOME OF THE MEN, AND WOMEN, THAT WERE FRIENDS OF MY MOM. THE PEOPLE AT VENUES THAT WOULD BE PLAYING WITH MY ACTION FIGURES, READING COMICS WITH ME WHILE THEIR BANDS WERE BETWEEN SETS. YOU KNOW, MINUS THE SCISSORS FOR HANDS THING.

I REMEMBER WATCHING THE MOVIE WITH MY MOTHER QUITE A BIT, ALONG WITH CRY-BABY. THOSE TWO JOHNNY DEPP TAPES WERE BURNING THE VCR OUT AROUND THAT TIME. I LOST MY MOM TO CANCER IN 2010, BUT THERE ARE A TON OF LITTLE THINGS THAT REMIND ME OF HER ALL THE TIME. EDWARD SCISSORHANDS JUST HAPPENS TO BE ONE OF THEM.

I'M INCLUDING A PHOTO OF MY MOTHER RITA PATRICK AND ME DURING MY FIRST MARDI GRAS, BACK IN 1992. THIS WAS AROUND THAT TIME WHEN WE WERE WEARING OUT THOSE VHS TAPES.

DARRICK PATRICK

(SG) DARRICK, THANKS FOR WRITING IN AGAIN, AND SHARING THIS BEAUTIFUL REMEMBRANCE OF YOUR MOTHER. SHE SOUNDS LIKE A FASCINATING WOMAN, AND EVEN FROM THIS ONE PHOTO YOU'VE PROVIDED, YOU CAN FEEL A BIT OF HER CHARACTER, IT SEEMS. I'M SO SORRY YOU'VE LOST HER. I KNOW YOUR GIRLS WILL BE ALL THE BETTER FOR HEARING STORIES ABOUT HER AND THE FOLKS YOU MET THROUGH HER. THANK GOODNESS FOR THE RITAS (AND EDWARDS) OF THE WORLD, RIGHT EVERYONE? THIS LETTERS PAGE IS DEDICATED TO HER!

(DR) I RAISE A GLASS OF SOMETHING DARK, PROBABLY RED, TO YOU AND YOUR MOTHER, DARRICK! AS I TYPE THIS RESPONSE, I HAVE JUST LEARNED, WITH A HEAVY HEART, THAT STEVE STRANGE OF VISAGE PASSED TODAY. HE, ALONG WITH KLAUS NOMI (WHO IS A PERSONAL STYLE HERO OF MINE), HELPED USHER IN THE NEW ROMANTIC MUSIC SCENE WHICH TURNED INTO WHAT I KNOW AS THE "GOTH." I HAVE NO DOUBT THAT YOUR MOTHER IS NOW SOMEWHERE WONDERFUL, BOOKING BANDS TO PLAY THE BEST SETS OF SONGS THAT INFLUENCED SO MANY, WITH CRY-BABY AND EDWARD SCISSORHANDS PLAYING ON A BIG SCREEN BEHIND THEM FOR SOME FORM OF ETERNITY. THANK YOU FOR SHARING YOUR STORY AND HER PICTURE. YOU GUYS ARE JUST TOO PERFECT FOR WORDS.

(KL) ABSOLUTELY, SARAH! THANK YOU, DARRICK. WHEN I FIRST SAW THE THUMBNAIL OF THIS PHOTO I THOUGHT IT MIGHT BE FAIRUZA BALK – AND BELIEVE ME, THAT IS THE HIGHEST OF COMPLIMENTS. I'M GLAD YOU'RE ENJOYING THE SERIES AND WE REALLY APPRECIATE YOUR SUPPORT!

DEAR CLIPPINGS,

MY NAME IS JOSHUA AND THIS COMIC BOOK IS A DREAM COME TRUE. I SAW EDWARD SCISSORHANDS *RIGHT AROUND THE TIME IT CAME OUT IN THEATERS IN 1990. I WAS 14 YEARS OLD AND MY FAMILY WAS SPENDING CHRISTMAS IN TEXAS VISITING FAMILY. I RECALL THAT MY MOTHER AND FOUR-YEAR-OLD SISTER WERE SPENDING THE DAY WITH MY GRANDPARENTS AND I WAS LEFT TO MY OWN DEVICES. I HAD SEEN ALL OF THE "EDWARD WAS HERE" POSTERS IN MY HOME TOWN AND OF COURSE SEEN THE TRAILERS FOR* EDWARD SCISSORHANDS *BY THIS TIME. I THOUGHT JOHNNY DEPP WAS AMAZING AND I HAD A HUGE CRUSH ON WINONA RYDER. I KNEW TIM BURTON FROM* PEE-WEE'S BIG ADVENTURE *AND, OF COURSE,* BATMAN *A YEAR BEFORE.*

I REMEMBER GOING TO THE MOVIES BY MYSELF THAT DAY TO SEE EDWARD. *I WALKED IN TO THE MOVIE THEATER FEELING A LITTLE BIT ALONE, AND AFTER THE CREDITS ROLLED, I WALKED OUT FEELING... STILL ALONE, BUT...UNDERSTOOD. ONLY YEARS AND YEARS LATER DID I UNDERSTAND WHAT BURTON AND DEPP AND RYDER HAD CREATED WITH THEIR STAGGERINGLY BEAUTIFUL FAIRYTALE — A STORY ABOUT WANTING TO BE LOVED AND ACCEPTED. A STORY ABOUT AN ARTIST WHO WANTS NOTHING MORE IN LIFE THAN TO CREATE AND HAVE THE WORLD THAT SURROUNDS HIM NOT JUDGE, OR FEAR OR QUESTION AND RIDICULE WHAT THEY DON'T UNDERSTAND.*

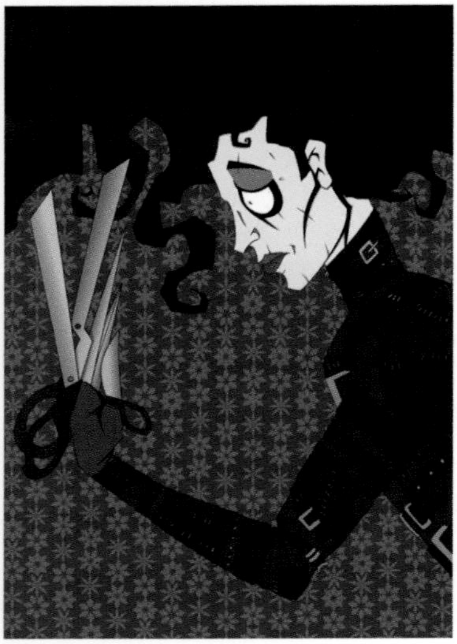

TO MY FOURTEEN-YEAR-OLD SELF IT WAS TRANSCENDENT, AND IT FELT LIKE THE MOVIE WAS SPEAKING DIRECTLY TO ME. EDWARD WAS ME! AWKWARD, ASHAMED AND CONFUSED BY MY AGE. FRIGHTENED OF GIRLS (AND OF BEING MYSELF) BUT DESPERATELY WANTING TO MAKE A MOVE AND FIT IN. IT WAS PAINFUL AND BEAUTIFUL TO WATCH AT THE SAME TIME. FOR THE REST OF THAT VACATION, ALL I COULD THINK ABOUT WAS THAT MOVIE...

THERE ARE ALWAYS A HANDFUL OF MOVIES, TV SHOWS AND BOOKS THAT REALLY SET PEOPLE OFF ON THE PATHS THEY END UP WALKING IN LIFE. EDWARD SCISSORHANDS *WAS ONE OF MINE. THE STORYTELLING AND STYLE SHAPED MY OWN ART AND MY OWN STYLES. THIS MOVIE LED ME DOWN THE ART AND MUSIC AND CULTURE RABBIT HOLE FROM EDWARD GOREY, AUBREY BEARDSLEY AND ROBERT BLAKE TO DEAD CAN DANCE, ROBERT SMITH AND MORRISSEY. IT WAS ONE OF THE KEY INFLUENCES THAT LED ME TO ART SCHOOL AND THEN INTO MY CAREER OF EDITING AND ART DIRECTING AND PRODUCING AND LICENSING.*

I'M SO PLEASED TO SEE THE RECEPTION TO THE EDWARD SCISSORHANDS *COMIC AND HOW IT HAS REACHED SO MANY PEOPLE. I CAN'T EVEN BEGIN TO EXPRESS MY GRATITUDE TO DREW AND KATE AND SARAH AND CHRIS AND GREG [EDITOR'S NOTE: CHRIS IS IDW'S EDITOR IN CHIEF, GREG IS OUR PRESIDENT!] FOR TAKING A RISK AND CREATING THIS BEAUTIFUL AND HAUNTING AND SINCERE SERIES. FOR MY WHOLE LIFE I HAVE HARBORED A SECRET BUCKET LIST OF LICENSES AND WORLDS AND STORIES AND PROJECTS THAT I HAVE WANTED TO WORK ON. THANKS TO THE AMAZING TEAM ON THIS BOOK, I CAN CROSS OFF A PROJECT THAT I HAVE BEEN DREAMING ABOUT FOR 25 YEARS...*

JOSHUA IZZO

- - - - - - - - - - - - - - - - - -

SG JOSHUA! THANK YOU SO MUCH FOR MAKING THIS PIECE OF ART FOR US. I HAD A FEELING ABOUT HOW MUCH THIS MOVIE (AND NOW COMIC) MEANS TO YOU, BUT READING THIS LETTER AND SEEING THE ART JUST DEEPENS THAT SO MUCH MORE. AND THANK YOU FOR EVERYTHING YOU DO BEHIND THE SCENES TO MAKE THIS BOOK HAPPEN, DAY AFTER DAY, WEEK AFTER WEEK! GO TEAM EDWARD!

KL JOSHUA! OUR GRATITUDE IS WITH YOU. I THINK WE'RE ALL PRETTY EQUALLY THRILLED TO BE WORKING ON SUCH A WONDERFUL AND WEIRD STORY. THANKS FOR YOUR LOVELY ART AND ALL YOU DO - I THINK WE'RE ALL PRETTY GLAD TO BE WORKING TOGETHER ON THIS BEAST.

- - - - - - - - - - - - - - - - - -

SG HERE'S SOME FREE-FLOWING INTERVIEWS WITH OUR CREATIVE TEAM, STARTING WITH WRITER-EXTRAORDINAIRE KATE LETH!

- - - - - - - - - - - - - - - - - -

SARAH: GOOD MORNING, KATE! THANKS FOR JOINING ME ON THE INTERNETS DOT COM FOR A LITTLE CHAT ABOUT THE EDWARD SCISSORHANDS SERIES, NOW THAT IT IS COMING TO A (HOPEFULLY TEMPORARY) CLOSE AFTER ISSUE #10.

KATE: *YOU'RE WELCOME, SARAH!*

SARAH: SO, THE READERS JUST FINISHED UP ISSUE #9, THE PENULTIMATE ISSUE OF THE SERIES... I THOUGHT IT WOULD BE A GOOD TIME TO LOOK BACK AT WHERE WE'VE BEEN SO FAR.

KATE: *THAT SOUNDS GREAT! LET'S REMINISCE.*

SARAH: OK, SO YOU TITLED THE FIRST ARC OF THE SERIES "PARTS UNKNOWN." I THINK THAT'S A GREAT PLACE TO START, BECAUSE NOT ONLY DO WE THINK OF EDWARD ("PARTS"- SORRY, EDWARD), BUT MORE SPECIFICALLY, "UNKNOWN." HE DOESN'T KNOW MEGS, AND MEGS DOESN'T REALLY KNOW HIM. THE TOWNSFOLK THINK THEY KNOW ABOUT EDWARD, BUT THEY REALLY DON'T... ALL THEY KNOW IS THIS SHADOWY URBAN

LEGEND FIGURE ON A HILL.

BUT, WE ALL KNOW EDWARD. HE'S A POP CULTURE ICON. THAT'S WHY I LOVE MEGS, BECAUSE WE GET TO SEE EDWARD THROUGH NEW EYES. HOW DID MEGS COME TO BE?

KATE: *EDWARD IS SUCH AN INCREDIBLE CHARACTER BECAUSE OF HOW HE INTERACTS WITH THE PEOPLE AND THE WORLD AROUND HIM. HE'S SO OUT OF PLACE, THIS SPECTACULARLY WEIRD CREATURE IN A SUBURBAN WORLD, AND THAT'S WHAT SO MANY PEOPLE IDENTIFY WITH. I THOUGHT IT WOULD BE GREAT, IN A SORT OF "MODERN" VERSION, TO PAIR HIM WITH THE SORT OF PERSON WHO WOULD'VE WATCHED THE MOVIE AND THOUGHT "THAT'S ME, I GET THAT."*

PLUS, WITH HER BEING KIM'S GRANDDAUGHTER, THERE'S A SENSE OF CONNECTION TO THE FILM AND A KIND OF WEIGHT TO THEIR RELATIONSHIP.

SARAH: ABSOLUTELY. I AM MEGS, TOO — WE CAN ALL RELATE TO MEGS — I THINK WE ALL "GET IT" AS WELL. SO ALTHOUGH SHE'S AWFULLY CLOSE TO THE STORY AT HAND, SHE'S OUR ENTRE INTO EDWARD'S WORLD.

I'M REALLY GLAD YOU CREATED HER AND HER MOM, BECAUSE WE NEEDED A WAY TO APPROACH EDWARD IN A NEW WAY, TO REALLY MAKE THIS RESONATE.

MILLY, HER MOM, IS A GREAT CHARACTER, BECAUSE SHE'S GOT ONE FOOT IN EACH WORLD. THE MODERN WORLD, WHERE UNTIL NOW, EDWARD WAS JUST A LEGEND. BUT SHE ALSO REMEMBERS THINGS ABOUT HER MOM, KIM, AND HER HISTORY... AND IT ISN'T ALL GREAT.

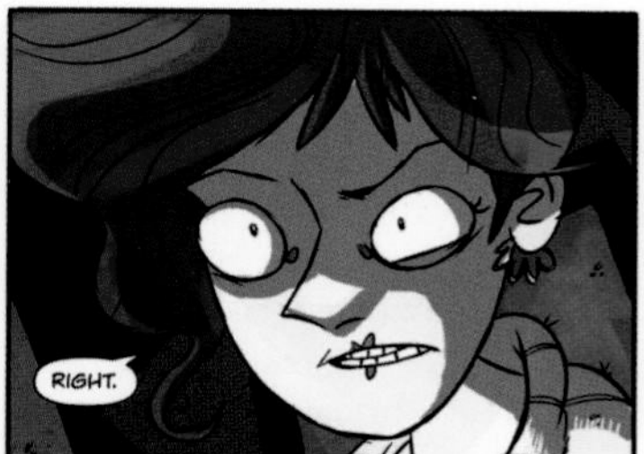
RIGHT.

SHE'S OBVIOUSLY DEFENSIVE OF HER FAMILY UNIT. HOW DID YOU DECIDE TO APPROACH THAT?

KATE: *I CAME TO LOVE MILLY SO MUCH AS I WAS WRITING THIS SERIES. IT'S NOT REALLY A SECRET THAT, IN MANY WAYS, SHE'S BASED ON MY MOM. I WANTED HER TO BE A VERY REALISTIC CHARACTER, AND I FIND MOMS ARE QUITE OFTEN TYPECAST. SHE HAS A COMPLICATED RELATIONSHIP WITH HER OWN MOTHER, AND WITH HER DAUGHTER, TOO. SHE WANTS TO DO WHAT'S RIGHT, BUT SHE HAS A CHIP ON HER SHOULDER ABOUT QUITE A FEW THINGS AND CAN'T ALWAYS SEE IT.*

I THINK, ESPECIALLY AS WE COME TOWARDS THE END OF THIS SECOND ARC, WE GET TO SEE WHERE THAT COMES FROM AND WHY SHE IS THE WAY SHE IS. THE FAMILIES IN THE ORIGINAL FILM ARE ALMOST CARTOONISHLY NUCLEAR - I WANTED TO SHOW THE CRACKS UNDERNEATH THAT.

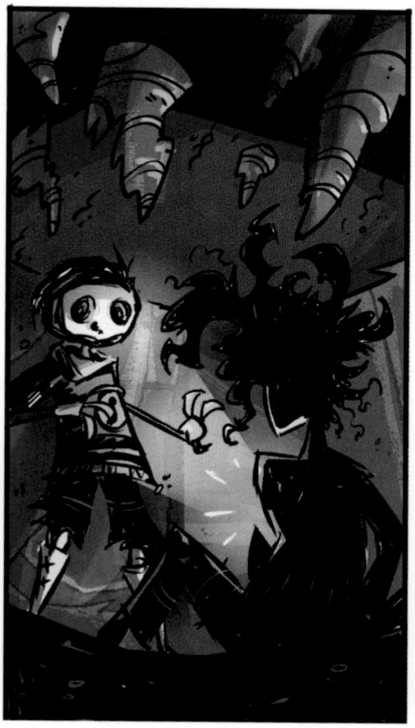

SARAH: I THINK YOU HAVE THE IDEA THAT A LOT OF MILLY'S REMEMBRANCES OF EDWARD, AT LEAST THE ONES WE SEE IN FLASHBACK — ARE SHOWN THROUGH THE LENS OF CHILDHOOD MEMORY, WHICH IS SO FAULTY.

IT APPEARS (AT LEAST UP TO THIS POINT) THAT MILLY WAS AN ONLY CHILD, AND WHEN YOU'RE AN ONLY CHILD (HI, WORLD!), YOU ONLY HAVE THESE WEIRD SHARDS OF MEMORY TO THINK BACK UPON — THERE WAS NO ONE ELSE AROUND TO CHECK IN WITH AND SAY, "DO YOU REMEMBER THIS? DO YOU REMEMBER THEM FIGHTING ABOUT THAT?"

KATE: *YEAH, EXACTLY! CHILDHOOD MEMORIES CAN BE SO INTENSE. I THINK, WHEN YOU'RE A KID, IT NEVER OCCURS TO YOU TO LOOK OUTSIDE YOURSELF AND THINK ABOUT HOW OTHER PEOPLE FELT, OR WHY THEY ACTED THE WAY THEY DID.*

SARAH: TOTALLY... YOU HAVE NO CONCEPT OF ADULT RELATIONSHIPS OTHER THAN WHAT YOU SEE, AND WHAT YOU READ ABOUT/WATCH.

KATE: *I'M ALSO AN ONLY CHILD, TOO! THE WAY YOUR PARENTS INTERACT CAN BE SO VITAL (OR DESTRUCTIVE) WHEN THEY'RE ALL YOU'VE GOT. YEAH, THAT'S IT.*

SARAH: SO REALLY, MEGS GREW UP IN THIS WORLD WHERE A) EDWARD WAS THIS URBAN LEGEND, NOT EVEN REALLY ON THE RADAR ANYMORE... BUT ALSO B) ANY TIME SHE WANTED TO TALK

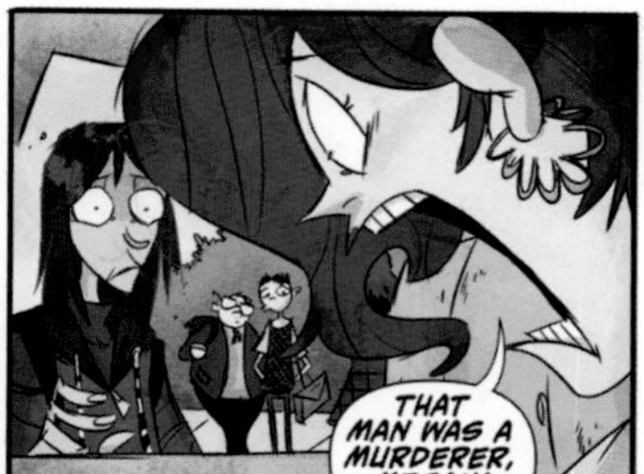
THAT MAN WAS A MURDERER, MEGAN!

ABOUT HER GRANDMOTHER AND HER LIFE, SHE'D RUN INTO IMMEDIATE TENSION WITH HER OWN MOTHER, SORT OF CONTINUING THE CHAIN OF MISINFORMATION AND BAD FEELINGS.

BUT MEGS IS SPECIAL, AND KNEW HER GRANDMOTHER WAS A GREAT WOMAN, AND WANTED TO KNOW MORE

KATE: *YEAH. I THINK SHE COULD TELL, FROM A PRETTY YOUNG AGE, THAT HER MOM WASN'T EVEN WILLING TO THINK ABOUT THE WAY SHE SAW HER OWN MOM, OR HER OWN CHILDHOOD EXPERIENCES. AS MEGS GOT OLDER, SHE GOT MORE CURIOUS, AS WELL AS MORE FRUSTRATED BY CONTINUALLY HITTING A WALL WHEN SHE ASKED QUESTIONS.*

I HAD THIS WHOLE IDEA I WANTED TO PLAY WITH, SHOWING MEGS AS A KID, DEALING WITH BULLIES TEASING HER ABOUT HER GRANDMOTHER, ABOUT EDWARD, AND HER BEING SO CONFUSED BECAUSE HER MOM WOULDN'T TELL HER WHY.

SARAH: AH, BUT THERE'S NEVER ENOUGH TIME, IS THERE?

KATE: *NEVER! STILL, IT STUCK WITH ME, HOW THAT WOULD CREATE EVEN MORE TENSION BETWEEN HER AND HER MOTHER. BEING BULLIED IS HARD ENOUGH, BUT YOUR MOM NOT TAKING YOUR SIDE... THAT CAN BUILD A LOT OF RESENTMENT.*

SARAH: SO, DEAR READERS, THANKS FOR STICKING THROUGH THE TALK OF MILLY AND MEGS RATHER THAN OUR STAR, EDWARD, BECAUSE I THINK IT IS IMPORTANT THAT WE UNDERSTAND THAT THEY ARE THE FRAME IN WHICH WE COME TO RE-MEET EDWARD.

I THINK IT WAS IMPORTANT WE FOUND A NEW WAY TO APPROACH HIM, BECAUSE HE'S SUCH A GIANT, SOLID, ALBEIT QUIET, FIGURE IN OUR POP CULTURE SPHERE.

SO, KATE, WHEN MY BOSS CHRIS RYALL ASKED FOR A PITCH, HOW DID YOU COME TO THIS PLACE?

KATE: *YES! I WAS ORIGINALLY GOING TO SAY, THOUGH I GET VERY EXCITED TO TALK ABOUT MILLY AND MEGS, THAT I WANTED TO CREATE THESE CHARACTERS BECAUSE EDWARD COMES ALIVE IN HIS REACTIONS AND INTERACTIONS WITH THE PEOPLE AROUND HIM. HE'S SO QUIET, SO SUBTLE, THAT YOU KIND OF HAVE TO HAVE SOME BOISTEROUS FRIENDS FOR HIM TO PLAY OFF OF.*

SARAH: THAT'S TOTALLY TRUE. I THINK HE'S ALSO A CHARACTER SORT OF "OUT OF TIME..." SO IF WE JUST APPROACHED HIM BACK IN HIS CASTLE, IT WOULD HAVE BEEN A LOT HARDER TO GROUND HIM IN ANY SORT OF STORYLINE.

KATE: *I KIND OF... THE ATTEMPT, ANYWAY, WAS TO CREATE A WORLD IN WHICH EVERYONE IS AN OUTSIDER, WHERE EDWARD IS THE ONLY ONE IN THE FILM. THAT'S OUR WORLD, YOU KNOW? NOBODY "FITS IN," NOBODY'S DOING EVERYTHING RIGHT, AND I THINK EDWARD KIND OF FINDS HIS PEOPLE IN THAT. THEY'RE MUCH MORE ACCEPTING OF HIM THAN THE TOWN IN THE MOVIE WAS, JUST LIKE HOW FOLKS WITH PIERCINGS AND TATTOOS WORK BANK JOBS NOW. THAT'S THE BIGGEST DIFFERENCE, MUCH MORE SO THAN THE OUTFITS AND TECHNOLOGY.*

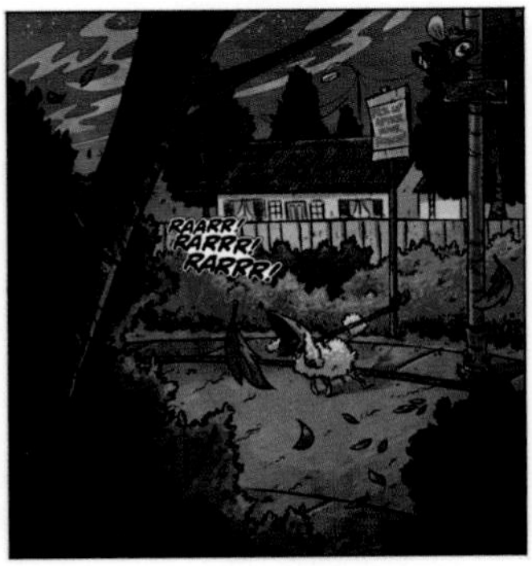
RAARR!
RARRR!
RARRR!

I JUST WANT HIM TO BE HAPPY, DANGIT!

SARAH: SPEAKING OF OUT OF TIME, I KNOW YOU MADE A DELIBERATE CHOICE TO NOT SET THE STORY TOO DEEPLY IN ANY YEAR OR SITUATION.

KATE: *I DID!*

SARAH: YES WE SEE THINGS LIKE CCTV AND NEIGHBORHOODS BEING RECORDED, BUT WE DON'T SEE THINGS LIKE CELL PHONES EVERYWHERE. WHAT WAS YOUR THINKING ON THAT?

KATE: *THAT WAS VERY DELIBERATE, ABSOLUTELY, AND I WAS HAPPY IT WAS SOMETHING THE WHOLE TEAM AGREED ON AT THE START, HAHA.*

ONE OF THE BIGGEST POINTS ABOUT THE MOVIE IS THAT IT'S ANACHRONISTIC. IT COULD BE THE FIFTIES, BUT WE SEE VCRS. IT'S NOT SET IN ANY POINT IN TIME. THE TOWN ISN'T NAMED. THAT WHOLE ELEMENT MAKES IT SEEM MUCH MORE LIKE A FAIRYTALE.

I WANTED TO CARRY THAT OVER, IT WAS THE ONLY WAY THAT A "MODERN" VERSION WAS GOING TO FEEL TRUE TO THAT WORLD. SO YES, WE SEE CAMERAS AND RECORDING EQUIPMENT EVERYWHERE, BECAUSE I THINK THAT'S HOW A SUBURB WOULD EVOLVE OVER TIME. EVERYONE STAYING PICTURE-PERFECT ON THE OUTSIDE, BUT BEING INCREASINGLY PARANOID.

AS FOR CELL PHONES, THE MAKES AND MODELS CHANGE SO MUCH THAT WHEN YOU DRAW THEM, IT IMMEDIATELY TIES THE COMIC TO A PARTICULAR YEAR. I WANTED TO AVOID THAT. ALSO, CELL PHONES MAKE EVERYTHING TOO EASY! TAKE 'EM OUT!

SARAH: HAH! I TOTALLY AGREE.

KATE: *SO WHERE THE MOVIE COULD BE ANYWHERE FROM THE '50s–'80s, THE COMIC COULD BE ANYWHERE FROM THE '90s–2010s.*

SARAH: EDWARD JUST SEEMS TO FIT IN ANYWHERE, TOO, WHICH IS SORT OF NEAT, CONSIDERING HOW SENSITIVE HE IS.

KATE: *YES, HE'S SO WONDERFUL THAT WAY. AND IN ALL WAYS.*

SARAH: WHAT WAS THE HARDEST THING TO DO, WHEN IT CAME TO WRITING HIM?

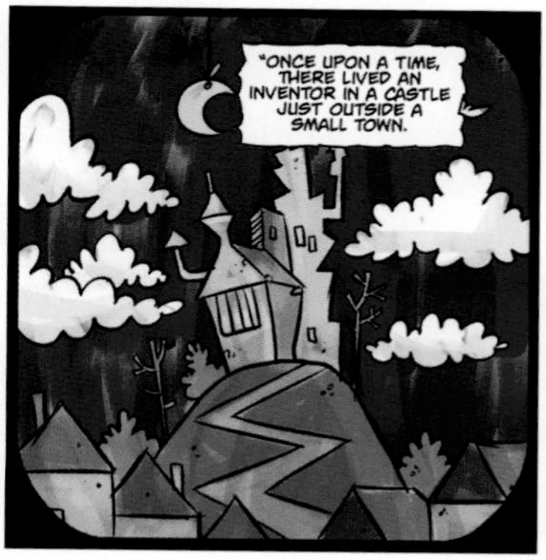
"ONCE UPON A TIME, THERE LIVED AN INVENTOR IN A CASTLE JUST OUTSIDE A SMALL TOWN.

KATE: *HIS DIALOGUE!!*

EDWARD SPEAKS SO INFREQUENTLY, AND IN SHORT SENTENCES. HE'S NOT FLOWERY, NEVER AGGRESSIVE, AND ALWAYS A BIT SELF-CONSCIOUS. ANY LINE HE SPOKE HAD TO BE NECESSARY.

SARAH: FORTUNATELY, DREW IS ABLE TO GET A LOT ACROSS WITH A LOOK AND A GESTURE... WHICH BRINGS ME TO OUR ART TEAM!

KATE: *OH, ABSOLUTELY. DREW TRANSLATES MY CONFUSING DESCRIPTIONS OF EXPRESSIONS AND REACTIONS SO WELL.*

SARAH: WHEN I STARTED LOOKING AT DIFFERENT ARTISTS FOR THIS PROJECT, DREW JUST FIT FOR ME. YES, HE KNEW THE CHARACTER SO WELL, AND WAS ABLE TO CAPTURE HIM TO MAKE THE LICENSORS HAPPY, BUT HE ALSO BROUGHT SOMETHING OF HIMSELF TO THE TABLE — WHICH, IF YOU ARE ALLOWED TO DO IT IN LICENSED BOOKS, I PREFER.

KATE: *MHM, ABSOLUTELY.*

SARAH: I KNOW ONE OF THE FIRST THINGS WE DID WAS HAVE HIM DO SOME CHARACTER DESIGNS. WHAT WAS IT LIKE TO SEE MEGS AND MILLY COME TO LIFE?

KATE: *IT WAS AMAZING! HE CAPTURED THE IDEAS I HAD SO WELL, CONTINUES TO. THE FIRST SKETCHES I SAW OF MEGS WERE SO REAL. MY FAVORITE IS AIDAN, THOUGH. AIDAN IS PERFECT.*

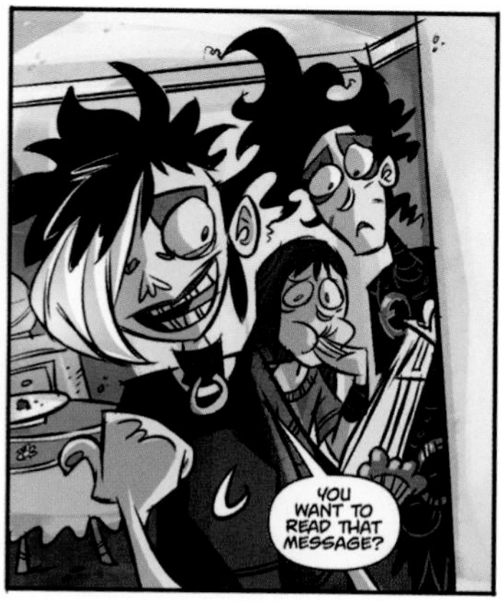
YOU WANT TO READ THAT MESSAGE?

SARAH: YES, LET'S TALK ABOUT AIDAN. WHERE DID HE COME FROM?

KATE: *LET'S.*

ORIGINALLY, HE WAS A CHARACTER OF NECESSITY. I NEEDED SOMEONE TO DRIVE PHIL HOME FROM SCHOOL, HAHA!

I KIND OF FELL FOR HIM, THOUGH, AS YOU DO. AIDAN, MUCH MORE SO THAN MEGS, IS A MODERN EMO GOTH KID. YOU KNOW HE SHOPS AT HOT TOPIC. HE WEARS NAIL POLISH AND BLEACHES HIS HAIR, LISTENS TO OPERATIC METAL AND BOY BANDS. HIS SEXUALITY IS AMBIGUOUS. HE'S KIND OF MY IDEA OF A TEEN DREAMBOAT.

SARAH: AND, HE'S A TOTAL SWEETIE

KATE: *YES, HE IS. THAT WAS REALLY IMPORTANT. HE CARES ABOUT PHIL, ABOUT HIS BROTHER, ABOUT EDWARD AND MEGS, TOO. I FIND THAT THE EMPHASIS ON "LOVE INTERESTS" IS RARELY ON THEM BEING GOOD PEOPLE... IF THAT MAKES SENSE!*

SARAH: IT DOES! AND AS WE SEE IN THIS ARC, I LOVE THAT YOU MESS WITH THE IDEA OF MEGS AND EDWARD AS A COUPLE BEING THE DEFAULT. IF THIS WAS A CHEESY HOLLYWOOD MOVIE, THAT MIGHT BE THE CASE — DESPITE THE INSANE AGE GAP!

KATE: *YES! EVERYONE WANTS TO ACCUSE THEM OF IT – HAHA, SECRETLY, THIS WAS MY RESPONSE TO EVERYONE WHO REVIEWED THE EARLY ISSUES AND HOPED FOR ROMANCE BETWEEN MEGS AND EDWARD. GROSS, GUYS! SHE'S 16!*

...ALTHOUGH I GUESS KIM WAS, TOO?

SARAH: AGHHH, HMM... BUT I FEEL LIKE EDWARD WAS YOUNG THEN, TOO.

KATE: *YEAH. MUCH MORE BOYISH. IT MAKES SENSE IN THE MOVIE, BUT NOT FOR MODERN TIMES. EDWARD'S IMMORTAL, IN MY HEAD, BUT HE'S STILL AT LEAST 50 NOW.*

SARAH: THAT MAKES SENSE. LET'S TALK ABOUT ELI, OUR "VILLAIN" FROM ARC ONE. ELI IS SCARY, BUT YOU ALSO FOUND A WAY FOR US TO FEEL SOME EMPATHY FOR HIM. THAT'S NOT EASY.

KATE: *ELI! AH, THERE'S AN EVEN STRONGER CASE FOR HOW AMAZING DREW'S ART IS – WE CAME UP WITH A VILLAIN WHO DOESN'T EVEN TALK.*

SARAH: YUP. AND THE COLORISTS THAT HAVE WORKED

ON THIS BOOK, AS WELL — DREW, JEREMY COLWELL, RIKI SIMONS, ALSO HAVE A HUGE ROLE IN THAT.

***KATE:** SO INCREDIBLE! ALL OF THEM!*

SARAH: WE ARE A VERY LUCKY TEAM TO HAVE THEIR TALENTS ON OUR SIDE.

***KATE:** DAMN SKIPPY WE ARE.*

SARAH: AND ONE CANNOT FORGET LETTERER TRAVIS LANHAM, WHO NAILED IT WITH THAT FONT FOR EDWARD.

***KATE:** IT'S SO FANTASTIC! I START THINKING ABOUT IT AND I GET VERY OVERWHELMED.*

YOU HEAR HIS VOICE WHEN YOU SEE THOSE LETTERS, YOU KNOW? THAT'S NO SMALL FEAT.

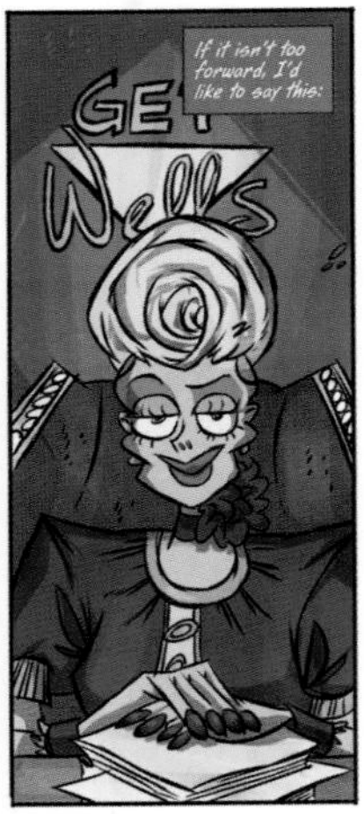
If it isn't too forward, I'd like to say this:

SARAH: YUP. WE ARE IN HIS DEBT. SO, LET'S TALK ABOUT DR. WELLS, OUR BIG-BAD FOR THIS SECOND ARC.

WE MET HER IN ISSUE #6, AND I THINK WE KNEW IMMEDIATELY THAT NOT ALL WAS WELL...

***KATE:** NOT ALL WAS... WELLS.*

(THIS IS ME TURNING TO CAMERA THREE AND GRINNING.)

SARAH: BWAHHHH!

***KATE:** BUT, YES! DR. WELLS IS A VILLAIN IN COMPLETE CONTRAST TO ELI. ELI WAS UNDERSTATED, SILENT, CREEPING IN THE SHADOWS. DR. WELLS IS BRIGHT, LOUD, CONFIDENT, AND ABOUT AS SUBTLE AS A CAR WRECK.*

SARAH: AND YET, PEOPLE WOULD FOLLOW HER ANYWHERE.

***KATE:** WHEN DREW AND I WERE TALKING CHARACTER DESIGNS, WE BOTH AGREED SHE WAS SOMEWHERE BETWEEN HARLEY QUINN AND EFFIE TRINKET (FROM THE* HUNGER GAMES*). I THINK HE NAILED THAT.*

SO YES. HER PERSONALITY IS UTTERLY CAPTIVATING. SHE'S PERFECT FOR TELEVISION!

SARAH: AND YET AGAIN, IT IS MEGS WHO WE TURN TO, TO CUT THROUGH THE NOISE AND GET TO THE HEART OF THE MATTER. SHE'S THE ONE WHO SEES THROUGH IT.

***KATE:** SHE DOES, BUT SHE'S NOT FULLY CONFIDENT IN HER SUSPICIONS. SHE STARTS OUT THE ARC DETERMINEDLY AGAINST HER, AND AGAINST EDWARD'S WISHES TO GO ON HER SHOW, BUT SHE SLOWLY STARTS TO UNDERSTAND HOW IMPORTANT IT IS TO EDWARD TO LIVE A "NORMAL" LIFE. SHE WANTS TO TAKE THE STANCE THAT HE'S FINE THE WAY HE IS, BUT SHE REALIZES THAT IT'S NOT HER CHOICE TO MAKE.*

SARAH: I THINK THAT'S ONE OF THE HARDEST THINGS TO SEE IN THIS ARC — EDWARD DEALING WITH HOW TO MAKE HIS LIFE "BETTER."

***KATE:** IT'S TRICKY TO WRITE, TOO.*

SARAH: HE'S GOT FRIENDS NOW, BUT IT ISN'T ENOUGH?

***KATE:** EXACTLY. HIS TRAGEDY, WHICH WE KIND OF DON'T DEAL WITH IN THE FIRST ARC, IS THAT AT THE END OF THE DAY HE CAN'T LIVE A NORMAL LIFE. HE CAN'T TOUCH.*

IT'S WHAT MAKES HIM SPECIAL, AND THAT'S WHAT MEGS SEES - SHE SEES THE GOOD IN EVERYONE, DEEP DOWN - BUT INSIDE, PART OF HIM JUST WANTS TO BE LIKE EVERYONE ELSE.

SARAH: THERE'S LOTS OF LITTLE WAYS YOU SHOW THAT: HE CAN'T HAVE A NORMAL TV REMOTE. HE CAN'T OPEN DOORS. HE CAN'T PAINT. THOSE LITTLE THINGS JUST KILL ME.

***KATE:** I'M TRYING TO BREAK YOUR HEART!*

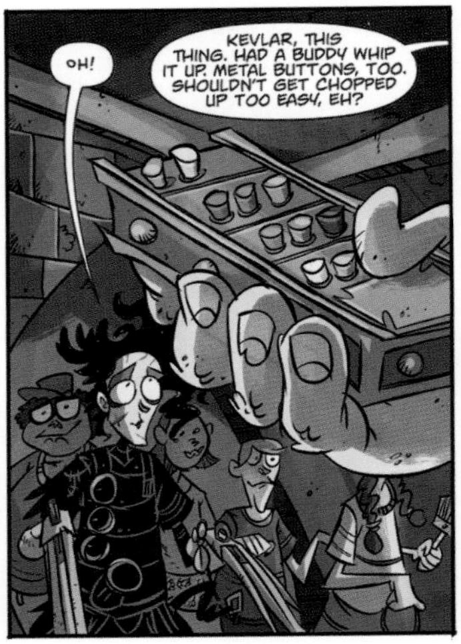
OH!
KEVLAR, THIS THING. HAD A BUDDY WHIP IT UP. METAL BUTTONS, TOO. SHOULDN'T GET CHOPPED UP TOO EASY, EH?

SARAH: IT IS WORKING.

***KATE:** GOOD.*

SARAH: MEAN.

I COULD TALK ABOUT EDWARD FOREVER, BUT I WANTED TO TOUCH ON THE LETTERS PAGE IN THE SERIES SO FAR. WHAT AN AWESOME THING IT GREW INTO.

***KATE:** OH MAN, WERE WE EVER LUCKY WITH THAT!*

SARAH: I FEEL LIKE PEOPLE SENT US GIFTS EVERY MONTH, BY TELLING THEIR STORIES.

***KATE:** ME, TOO. I GOT SO EMOTIONAL READING THEM, EVERY TIME!*

I ALSO LOVED READING YOUR RESPONSES, AND DREW'S. IT WAS SUCH A BONDING EXPERIENCE.

SARAH: A BIG THANK YOU TO EVERYONE WHO SENT IN LETTERS.

KATE: *YEAH. YOU'RE ALL THE BEST. NONE MORE GOTH, ETC.*

SARAH: SO, BEFORE WE GO, ANYTHING ELSE YOU'D LIKE TO SAY TO OUR FAIR READERS? NEXT MONTH, I'M GOING TO INTERVIEW DREW!

KATE: *OH, YAY! I CAN'T WAIT TO READ THAT! HMM. I WOULD SAY... THANK YOU, THANK YOU SO MUCH, FOR TRUSTING US WITH THIS WORLD AND THESE CHARACTERS. FOR YOUR LETTERS AND YOUR SUPPORT. I HOPE YOU'VE HAD AS MUCH FUN WITH IT AS WE HAVE. STAY SPOOKY!!!*

SARAH: YAY! THANKS KATE!

KATE: *NO PROBS, SARAH! YOU'RE THE BEST!*

SG AND NOW, A WEE CHAT WITH SERIES ARTIST DREW RAUSCH!

SARAH: HI, DREW! THANKS FOR JOINING ME THIS GLOOMY SUNDAY MORNING FOR A CHAT ABOUT EDWARD.

DREW: *HI, SARAH! THE GLOOM IS JUST DELIGHTFUL. FITTING, ISN'T IT?*

SARAH: SO, THIS IS OUR LAST ISSUE... FOR NOW, HOPEFULLY! I WANTED TO TAKE SOME TIME TO REFLECT A BIT ABOUT HOW WE GOT HERE, TO ISSUE #10. WE'VE BEEN THROUGH SOME NUTTY STUFF WITH EDWARD.

DREW: *OOOOOOO – GOING BACK IN TIME, BENDING THE FABRIC OF REALITY AND SUCH. THIS MIGHT REQUIRE SOME SPECIAL MAGIKS. AND MORE COFFEE (BLACK, OF COURSE).*

SARAH: BUT OF COURSE! WHEN I WAS FIRST HANDED THE (WONDERFUL) TASK OF EDITING *EDWARD*, YOUR NAME CAME UP JUST ABOUT INSTANTLY. YES, BECAUSE OF YOUR ART STYLE, BUT ALSO BECAUSE YOU ALSO KNEW AND LOVED THE CHARACTER. HOW DID YOU FIRST COME INTO CONTACT WITH IDW?

DREW: *AND MY HAIR, OBVIOUSLY.*

SARAH: WELL, THE HAIR IS AWESOME. I CANNOT LIE.

DREW: *IT HOLDS SECRETS. SO YEAH – I HAVE TO THANK DAVID HEDGECOCK FOR PUTTING ME WITHIN EYESIGHT OF THE POWERS THAT BE AT IDW, SINCE I ONLY APPEAR IN THE CORNER OF ONE'S EYE AND AS BLURRED IMAGES IN PHOTOGRAPHS FROM THE 1920S. I'VE KNOWN DAVID FOR CLOSE TO A DECADE – HE WAS THE ONE WHO BASICALLY GAVE ME MY PROFESSIONAL START IN COMICS AS PUBLISHER / EDITOR OF MY FIRST COMIC* SULLENGREY. *I SHOULD GIVE THAT GUY AN EXTRA TURN ON THE RACK FOR ALL HE'S DONE FOR ME!*

SARAH: DAVID HAD SUCH WONDERFUL THINGS TO SAY ABOUT YOU, AND AFTER LINKING ME TO YOUR WORK, AND THEN MEETING YOU AT A CONVENTION... I HAD A FEELING THAT YOU'D BE PERFECT. I HAD YOU DO A FEW SAMPLES. I REMEMBERED BEING REALLY CURIOUS ABOUT HOW YOU'D HANDLE THE SUBURBAN NEIGHBORHOOD, AND, OF COURSE, YOU NAILED IT.

DREW: *AW THANKS! I HAD THE OPPORTUNITY TO TEST OUT FOR TWO BOOKS –* FEAR AND LOATHING IN LAS VEGAS *AND* EDWARD SCISSORHANDS. *WORKING ON A TIM BURTON PROPERTY IS DEFINITELY A "BUCKET LIST" PROPERTY FOR ME, SO I WAS FREAKING OUT THAT I GOT THE CALLBACK FOR IT. I REMEMBER YOU WANTING TO SEE MY RENDITIONS OF A TOWN WITH A STARBUCKS ON*

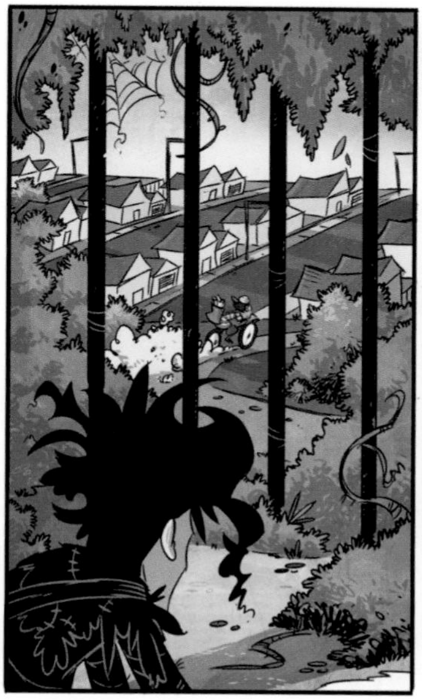

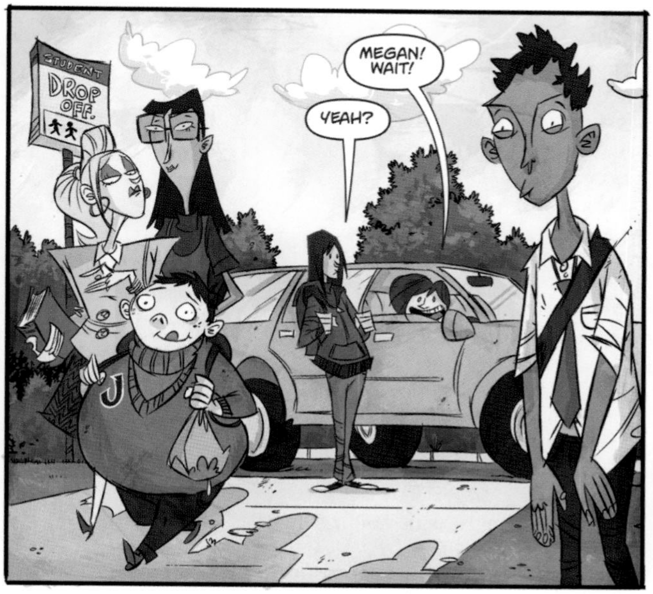
STUDENT DROP OFF.
MEGAN! WAIT!
YEAH?

EVERY CORNER AND PASTEL SUVS PARKED AS FAR AS THE EYE COULD SEE.

SARAH: HAH YES, WE SORTA PULLED BACK ON THAT, TO MAKE IT SORT OF MORE "TIMELESS," WHICH I THINK WAS A GOOD IDEA. SO, SPEAKING OF YOUR SAMPLES...

DREW: *WELL, THAT'S ONE OF THE GREAT THINGS ABOUT THE MOVIE AND OUR STORIES – THEY DON'T TAKE PLACE IN A SPECIFIC TIME PERIOD. ACTUALLY, IT'S REALLY KIND OF UNNERVING TO THINK THAT THE TOWN, AFTER ALL THESE YEARS, STILL LIVES IN THIS ISOLATED VACUUM. WHEN WE WERE KICKING AROUND IDEAS, I HAD THIS THOUGHT THAT IF THERE WAS GOING TO BE PHONES, THEY WERE ALL GOING TO BE OBNOXIOUSLY NOVELTY-SIZED AND RETRO-LOOKING. THE KIDS WOULD HAVE BEEN REAL EXCITED ABOUT USING DIALUP TO CONNECT TO THIS THING CALLED THE INTERNET. BUT YEAH, I LOVED YOUR IDEA OF THE PASTEL SUVS, WHICH ENDED UP BEING THE MOM-MOBILE MILLY DRIVES, BECAUSE IT SEEMED LIKE A NATURAL PROGRESSION FROM THE STATION WAGONS THAT EVERYONE DROVE IN THE MOVIE.*

SARAH: HAHA, YES. ANYWAY, YOUR SAMPLES FLEW THROUGH THE APPROVAL SYSTEM WITH FOX, WHO LOVES YOUR WORK! AND THEN WE GOT TO WORK ON WHAT I CONSIDER MAYBE THE MOST FUN PART OF ANY PROJECT... THE CHARACTER DESIGNS!

CAN YOU TALK A BIT ABOUT HOW YOU APPROACHED THOSE, ONCE YOU GOT DESCRIPTIONS FROM KATE?

DREW: *I'LL BE HONEST – I WAS SUPER NERVOUS ABOUT THE APPROVAL SYSTEM WITH FOX. MOVIE-BASED COMICS TEND TO LEAN HEAVILY ON ACTOR LIKENESSES, WHICH IS DEFINITELY NOT MY STRONG SUIT. SO WHEN IT CAME TO EDWARD, I BASED HIS DESIGN MORESO ON TIM BURTON'S EARLY CHARACTER SKETCHES. BASICALLY TRYING TO CAPTURE THE LOOK OF THE CHARACTER OF EDWARD AND NOT JOHNNY DEPP THE ACTOR. THANKFULLY FOX WANTED EXACTLY THAT. I REMEMBER BREATHING A HEAVY SIGH OF RELIEF, BECAUSE BURTON'S DRAWING OF EDWARD'S ACTUAL SCISSOR HANDS WERE JUST SOME SCRIBBLY LINES. THE REST OF THE CAST WAS A LITTLE TRICKIER SINCE WE WERE CREATING NEW LIFE ESSENTIALLY.*

FOREMOST, I REALLY WANTED TO GET MEGS RIGHT. SHE WAS GOING TO BE THE AUDIENCE'S INTRO INTO THE WORLD SO IT WAS REALLY IMPORTANT TO MAKE HER THE MOST RELATABLE. I ENDED UP BASING HER ON A CROSS BETWEEN WYNONA RYDER, (WHICH MADE SENSE TO ME BECAUSE SHE WOULD BE A DESCENDANT OF KIM) AND A FRIEND OF MINE WHO HAS THAT QUIET WALLFLOWER QUALITY THAT I THINK KATE WAS LOOKING FOR.

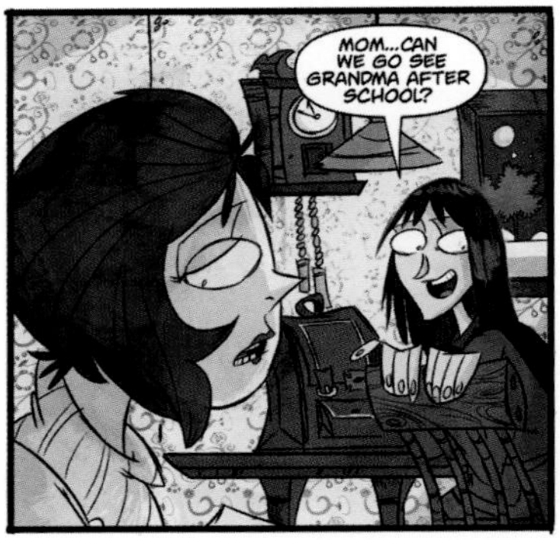
MOM...CAN WE GO SEE GRANDMA AFTER SCHOOL?

SARAH: ABSOLUTELY. EDWARD IS THE HEART OF THE STORY, AS WITH THE MOVIE, BUT MEGS... MEGS IS ALL OF US.

DREW: *THE ONE I STRUGGLED MOST WITH WAS ELI. I THINK AT THE POINT I WAS BROUGHT ON, WE WEREN'T REALLY SURE WHERE THE STORY WAS HEADED. KATE'S DESCRIPTION*

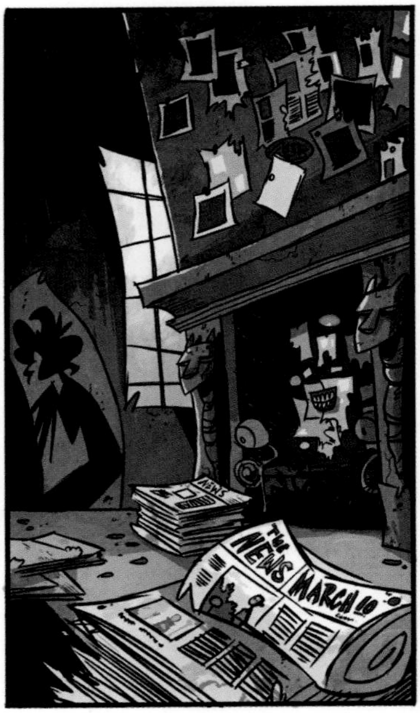
NEWS
THE NEWS
MARCH 10

WAS KIND OF VAGUE, HE DIDN'T EVEN HAVE A NAME – IT WAS JUST "THE CREATURE," BUT THERE WAS ONE BIT THAT STUCK AND THAT WAS IT WOULD BE COOL IF WE CREATED SOMETHING SOMEONE WOULD WANT TO COSPLAY AS AT A CONVENTION. MY ORIGINAL CONCEPT WAS IF THIS WAS GOING TO BE AN ACTUAL FILM I WANTED ELI TO BE DONE IN STOP MOTION WITH JUST A WEIRD COLLECTION OF ANTIQUE WIND-UP TINKERTOY PARTS, SORT OF "BROTHERS QUAY" STYLE. SO IN MY EARLIER SKETCHES HE WAS REALLY BENDY, KIND OF HAD THIS QUIRKY JERKY MOVEMENT THAT I COULD PLAY WITH. SINCE HE DIDN'T TALK, HE NEEDED TO BE ABLE TO EMOTE THROUGH BODY LANGUAGE. I PROBABLY WOULD HAVE WANTED SOMEONE REALLY WELL KNOWN TO DO SOME CREEPY HEAVY BREATHING

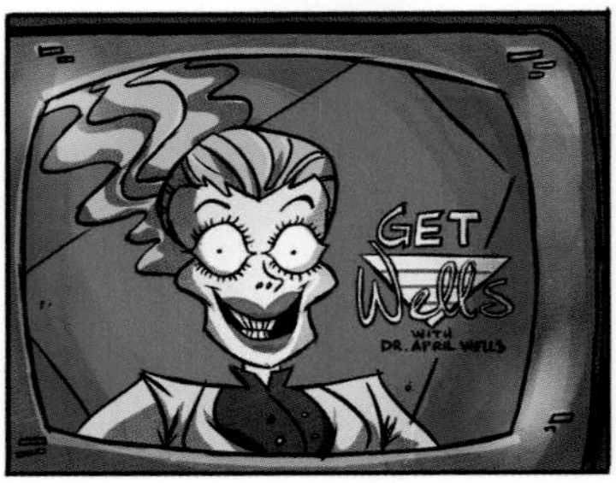
GET
Wells
WITH DR. APRIL WELLS

THOUGH. AFTER THINKING ABOUT WHAT KATE SAID, IT MADE MORE SENSE TO MAKE HIM SEEM A LITTLE MORE HUMAN, LIKE A LITTLE BOY.

WHEN IT CAME TO DR. WELLS, IN THE SCRIPT SHE REALLY COMES OFF AS THIS DR. PHIL-TYPE TALK-SHOW HOST MEETS CRUELLA DEVILLE CHARACTER, SO I PLAYED WITH THAT A BIT. I THINK IN A REVIEW SOMEONE MENTIONED THAT THEY DEFINITELY SAW HER BEING PLAYED BY HELENA BONHAM CARTER (DUH). SURPRISINGLY, IN THE END I WAS MORE INSPIRED BY CATHERINE O' HARA IN THE '90s OUTER LIMITS *EPISODE "THE REVELATIONS OF BECKA PAULSON." IT MADE HER PERFORMANCE IN* BEETLEJUICE *SEEM TAME.*

SARAH: I LOVED THAT YOU GUYS WERE THINKING IN LIKE, THREE DIMENSIONS. HOW IS THIS GOING TO WORK ON PAPER, BUT ALSO HOW WOULD IT WORK IN REAL LIFE, OR HOW WOULD PEOPLE COSPLAY IT. IT WAS SUPER INSPIRING, AND I KNEW EARLY ON WE WOULD BE A-OK ON THIS PROJECT!

DREW: *MY STYLE IS MADDENINGLY EXAGGERATED, BUT I THINK THE KEY TO MAKING THAT WORK WITH SOMETHING THAT WAS PORTRAYED WITH REAL PEOPLE IS STILL HAVING THE SENSE OF BELIEVABILITY. I WAS PRETTY IMPRESSED WITH HOW THE CHARACTERS EVOLVED INTO THEIR OWN PERSONALITIES THE MORE KATE WROTE THEM. THEY REALLY FELT LIKE THEY WERE ALIVE.*

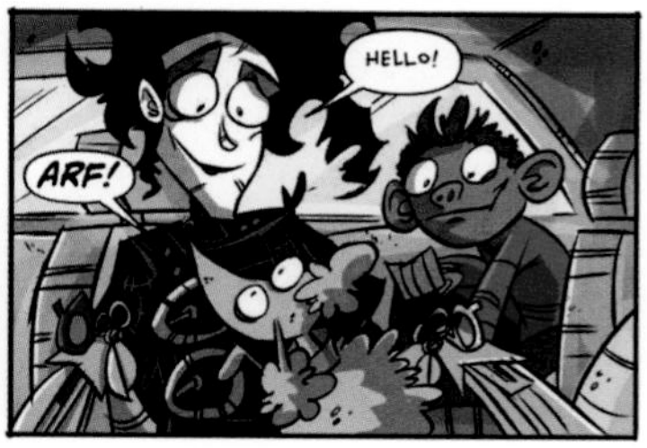
HELLO!
ARF!

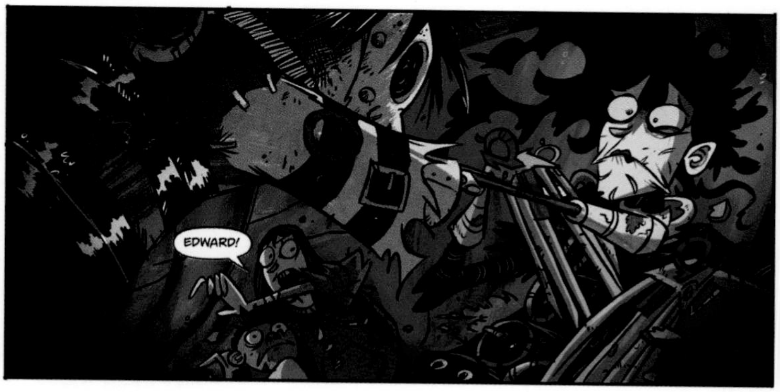
EDWARD!

SARAH: LET'S TAKE A MOMENT TO TALK ABOUT YOUR LEAST FAVORITE CHARACTER... SIMON THE DOG. I HAVE ONE QUESTION: DREW, WHY??

DREW: *IT'S FUNNY, KATE HAD ASKED ME IF IT WOULD BE OK FOR ELI TO KILL HIM IN, I THINK IT WAS, IN ISSUE #2 AND I WAS REALLY AGAINST IT. WE HAD SHOWN THE UNFORTUNATE DEMISE OF THE RAT IN THE FIRST ISSUE, SO IT FELT LIKE WE WERE JUST REPEATING OURSELVES. PERSONALLY I'M NOT A FAN OF HARMING ANIMALS FOR THE SAKE OF SHOCK VALUE. HORROR MOVIES TEND TO DO THIS AND I WANTED TO STEER CLEAR OF THAT. BUT THEN I NOTICED SIMON WAS GOING TO BE A RECURRING CHARACTER AND I IMMEDIATELY REGRETTED MY DECISION. I FIND DOGS IMPOSSIBLE TO DRAW. I HAVE TROUBLE WRAPPING MY HEAD AROUND HOW DOGS DOG.*

SARAH: SERIOUSLY?! I WOULD NOT KNOW THAT FROM YOUR DRAWINGS. WHAT ELSE DO YOU HATE TO DRAW?

DREW: *REALLY? I MEAN, SIMON GOES FROM LOOKING LIKE A DERANGED POODLE IN ISSUE #2 TO LOOKING LIKE THE FAMILY DOG BY THE END. WHAT ELSE DO I "HATE" TO DRAW? HRM — HORSES. BUT THEY DON'T EXIST REALLY, SO I'M OK.*

SARAH: OH, THANK GOD, HORSES ARE TERRIFYING. YOU'VE MADE ME SO HAPPY.

LET'S TALK ABOUT HOW YOU WOULD APPROACH EACH ISSUE. YOU'D GET THE SCRIPT, AND IN THE BEGINNING, WE'D ALL JUMP ON THE PHONE TOGETHER AND GO OVER YOUR THUMBNAILS. I THINK THAT WAS SUPER HELPFUL TO SORT OF GET THE FOUNDATION SET ON THE BOOK. WHAT ELSE CAN YOU TELL ME ABOUT HOW YOU'D TACKLE EACH SCRIPT?

DREW: *WELP, I WOULD GET THE SCRIPT, GIVE IT A GOOD SOLID READ, FIND A NICE DARK CORNER TO HAVE A NERVOUS BREAKDOWN, READ THE SCRIPT AGAIN, DO SOME REALLY TINY SCRIBBLES WHICH BOTH YOU AND KATE HAD THE AMAZING ABILITY OF BEING ABLE TO DECIPHER. WHEN WE FIRST STARTED, IT WAS REALLY HELPFUL TO ME TO GO INTO THE FINISHED ART WITH A SENSE OF CONFIDENCE THAT I WAS ON THE RIGHT TRACK. EVEN THOUGH KATE'S SCRIPTS WERE CRYSTAL CLEAR, SOMETIMES IT'S HARD TO GET WHAT A WRITER'S THINKING BEHIND A PARTICULAR MOTIVATION AND SINCE TWO OF THE MAIN CHARACTERS, EDWARD AND ELI, DIDN'T SPEAK, I REALLY WANTED TO GET THE ACTING JUST RIGHT.*

AFTER YOU AND KATE CONFIRMED THAT I WAS INDEED A REAL PERSON WHO COULD DRAW A THING, I MOVED ON TO PENCILING AND INKING. THANKFULLY WE HAD JEREMY COLWELL AND RIKKI SIMONS (WITH HELP FROM TAVISHA

WOLFGARTH-SIMONS) TO MAKE THAT MESS ALL BEAUTIFUL WITH THEIR COLORINGS!

SARAH: AH YES, WE ARE IN THEIR DEBT FOR SURE. BUT, LET'S BE HONEST... YOU WANTED TO COLOR IT ALL YOURSELF!!! HOWEVER, AS WE QUICKLY LEARNED... THE MONTHLY COMICS SCHEDULE IS A SON OF A BITCH.

DREW: I'M THE INSANE KIND OF PERSON WHO CREATIVELY NEEDS TO HAVE MY HAND IN EVERYTHING. I WANT TO BE A PART OF IT ALL. I LOVE THE PROCESS AND TELLING STORIES BUT OBVIOUSLY TIME IS A FACTOR. KATE TOLD ME ONCE, DURING ONE OF MY FITS OF "PERFECTION"—INDUCED INSANITY THAT THERE ARE SOME THINGS I JUST NEED TO LET GO. I'M INDEBTED TO JEREMY AND ESPECIALLY RIKKI AND TAVI, WHO WERE ABSOLUTELY MY HEROES. THEY DESERVE A LOT OF CREDIT FOR MAKING THIS COMIC AS MAGICAL AND DREAMLIKE AS IT IS.

SARAH: AW, DREW, I'M SO HAPPY TO HAVE HAD THIS EXPERIENCE WITH YOU!

I'M REALLY HOPING THIS ISN'T THE LAST WE SEE OF THIS EDWARD... READERS, LET IDW KNOW YOU WANT TO SEE MORE! I DON'T WANT TO KEEP YOU TOO LONG ON THIS

INTERVIEW... DO YOU HAVE A STORY YOU'D LIKE TO SHARE, OR AN EXPERIENCE IN THIS CREATIVE PROCESS THAT MIGHT BE HELPFUL FOR OTHER COMIC WRITERS AND ARTISTS?

DREW: IF I HAVE TO BE HONEST, ESPECIALLY AFTER HAVING DRAWN THE "BIG SCENE" (YOU KNOW THE ONE, SARAH), I STILL GET A BIT CHOKED UP THINKING THIS MIGHT BE THE LAST TIME I GET TO DRAW POOR EDWARD IN COMIC FORMAT. THE BEST WAY TO DESCRIBE IT IS THE FEELING OF HAVING TOYS YOU BORROWED FOR A YEAR AND THEN BEING TOLD IT'S TIME TO GIVE THEM BACK. THERE'S ALL THESE AMAZING MEMORIES YOU HAVE BUT ALSO THIS FEELING OF SADNESS AND JUST REALLY HOPING YOU DIDN'T ACCIDENTALLY BREAK ONE OF THEM.

SARAH: I WILL FIGHT TO MAKE SURE IT ISN'T THE LAST TIME!

DREW: I HOPE SO. I STILL THINK THERE'S STORIES TO BE TOLD IN THIS WORLD. I SURE DIDN'T DRAW THOSE CIRCUS POSTERS FOR NOTHING! IF YOU WOULD HAVE TOLD ME A YEAR AGO THAT I WOULD BE WORKING ON A SEQUEL TO TIM BURTON'S MOST BELOVED AND CHERISHED STORY, MY HEAD WOULD HAVE SPUN AROUND. IT HAS BEEN A DREAM, A JOY AND A DELIGHT TO WORK WITH YOU GUYS AND IDW ON SCISSORHANDS. I AM EXTREMELY GRATEFUL TO HAVE HAD THE OPPORTUNITY TO PLAY IN THE SNOW GLOBE WORLD OF EDWARD AND I HOPE THAT THE FANS, NEW AND OLD, ENJOYED THEMSELVES AND ARE NOW SOBBING THEMSELVES TO SLEEP JUST LIKE MANY OF US DID WHEN WE WATCHED THE MOVIE FOR THE FIRST TIME. I ESPECIALLY HOPE MR.

BURTON IS PLEASED WITH THE LOVE AND CARE WE TOOK WITH HIS CHARACTERS. FOR ME PERSONALLY, IT'S BEEN A LESSON THAT THOSE THINGS THAT YOU THINK WILL NEVER HAPPEN, MAY INDEED HAPPEN. EXCEPT FOR EVER SEEING A HORSE BECAUSE WE ALL KNOW HORSES DON'T EXIST.

I'M REALLY HAPPY WITH WHAT KATE AND I, WITH THE HELP OF ALL THESE AMAZING CREATIVE TYPES, ACCOMPLISHED. I LEARNED A LOT AND WILL DEFINITELY BE BRINGING THAT TO THE WEBCOMIC COMIC I WORK ON WITH JOCELYN GAJEWAY, MY BLACKS DON'T MATCH!, WHICH WE'LL BE STARTING AGAIN AFTER AN ALL-TOO-LONG HIATUS OVER AT WWW.DREWRAUSCH.COM. DID THAT SEEM LIKE A SHAMELESS SELF-PROMOTION? YEAH, YEAH IT DID. I'M SO SORRY.

SARAH: AND I THINK THAT'S THE TAKEAWAY MESSAGE FROM THIS INTERVIEW: THANK GOD HORSES DON'T EXIST. BUT SERIOUSLY, THANK YOU, DREW, FOR TAKING THE TIME TO DO THIS INTERVIEW. BUT MORE IMPORTANT, THANK YOU FOR HELPING BRING EDWARD BACK TO US, AND RE-INTRODUCING US TO THIS GREAT, BIG WORLD OF HIS.

DREW: BEFORE I GO CREEPING BACK INTO THE EMPTY HOLLOW I CALL MY STUDIO, I JUST WANT TO DEDICATE THIS SERIES TO MONSTERS, THE TWILIGHT ZONE, TALES FROM THE CRYPT, CREEPSHOW, GOOSEBUMPS, COURAGE THE COWARDLY DOG, THE OUTER LIMITS AND THE ABC'S OF DEATH. THESE SILLY HORROR ANTHOLOGIES GOT ME THROUGH THE LONG NIGHTS AND EVEN LONGER DAYS. AND A SPECIAL THANK-YOU TO ALL THE FANS WHO HUNG OUT

FOR THIS RIDE INTO FAIRYTALE SPOOKINESS – IT HAS BEEN A PLEASURE. STAY BATTY, MY FRIENDS!

SG LET'S TURN OUR ATTENTION TO COLORS. AS DREW MENTIONED, WE WERE LUCKY TO HAVE THE TALENTS OF JEREMY COLLWELL AND RIKKI SIMONS ON THIS SERIES. LET'S CHAT A BIT WITH OUR CURRENT COLORIST RIKKI, WHO, WITH THE HELP OF TAVISHA WOLFGARTH-SIMONS, BROUGHT EDWARD INTO FULL-COLOR-SPOOKY-VISION. ALSO, RIKKI AND TAVISHA BOTH CONTRIBUTED BEAUTIFUL EDWARDS FOR THIS EDITION OF CLIPPINGS!

SARAH: MANY FANS KNOW YOU FROM YOUR VOICE ACTOR WORK AS THE VOICE OF GIR, FROM *INVADER ZIM*. HOWEVER, YOU ADDITIONALLY CONTRIBUTED TO THAT SHOW WITH YOUR ART, BY PAINTING BACKGROUNDS FOR THE ANIMATION OF THE SHOW. CAN YOU TALK A LITTLE BIT ABOUT HOW YOU CAME TO PULL DOUBLE DUTY ON *ZIM*?

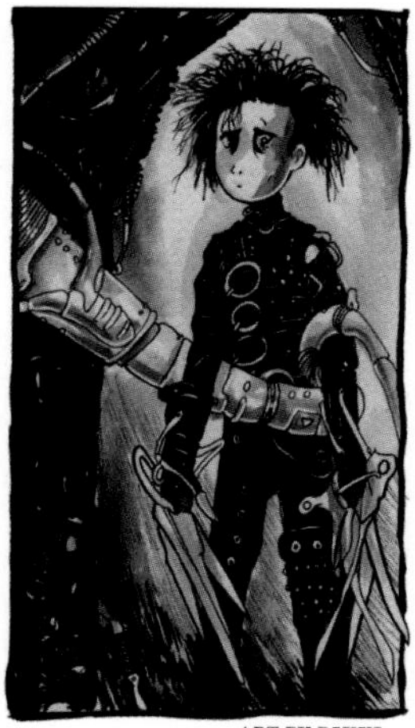

ART BY RIKKI

RIKKI: *IN THE 1990S, I WAS DOING BACKGROUND ACTING IN MOVIES, AND AT THE SAME TIME WRITING AND COLORING COMIC BOOKS. I HAD A SERIES WITH TAVISHA CALLED* SUPER INFORMATION HIJINX: REALITY CHECK! ZIM *CREATOR JHONEN VASQUEZ LIKED THE WAY I COLORED IT AND ASKED ME IF I WOULD WORK ON THE*

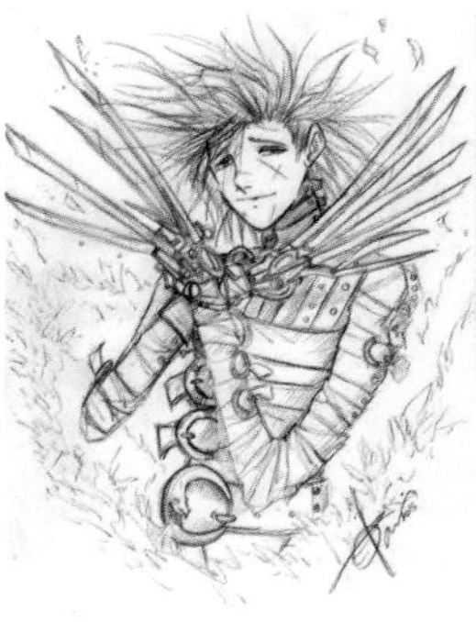

ART BY TAVISHA

COLOR FOR A SHOW HE WAS PITCHING TO NICKELODEON. WHILE HE WAS DEVELOPING THE PILOT, I WAS LIVING WITH HIM FOR ABOUT A MONTH COLORING HIS BOOK CALLED I FEEL SICK. *HE WAS HAVING DIFFICULTY FINDING A VOICE FOR GIR AND COMING HOME VERY GRUMPY EVERY NIGHT. I ASKED HIM IF I COULD TRY IT, AND HE SAID I PROBABLY COULDN'T SCREW IT UP ANYMORE THAN ANYONE ELSE, AND THEN HE GOT ME AN AUDITION. I DON'T THINK NICKELODEON WOULD HAVE AGREED TO THE AUDITION IF I WASN'T ALREADY DOING BACKGROUND ACTING. IN ANY CASE, I GOT THE VOICE PART FOR GIR, AND THE COLORING JOB. IT WAS A BUSY TIME! NOW I AM NOTHING. HOORAY!*

SARAH: CAN YOU TALK A LITTLE BIT ABOUT HOW YOU KNOW DREW, AND HOW YOU CAME TO CONTRIBUTE TO *EDWARD SCISSORHANDS*? I'D ESPECIALLY LIKE TO HEAR ABOUT HOW YOU APPROACH EACH PAGE, ESPECIALLY WHEN IT COMES TO LIGHTING AND USING THAT IN STORYTELLING. THAT'S ONE OF THE THINGS THAT REALLY STRUCK ME ABOUT YOUR PAGES.

RIKKI: *I CAN'T REMEMBER IF I MET DREW AT A CONVENTION OR THROUGH MUTUAL FRIENDS FIRST BUT I DO REMEMBER TURNING AROUND AND SUDDENLY SEEING HIS MOHAWK THERE. IT'S VERY TALL. HARD TO MISS. I THINK HIS MOHAWK*

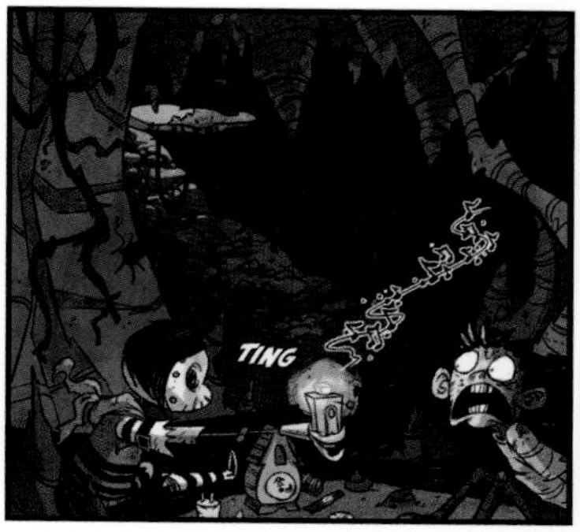
TING

TRICKED ME INTO COLORING EDWARD. IT'S VERY MESMERIZING.

I TEND TO BE A SURREALIST AT HEART AND I ENJOY THEATRICAL COLORS AND STRANGE MISTY LIGHTS WITH NO REAL BEARING ON REALITY. I THINK MY COLOR SENSE COMES FROM BEING NEARLY BLIND AS A CHILD AND NOT GETTING GLASSES UNTIL I WAS 10. I'M COMFORTABLE IN AN OTHERWORLDLY AND BLURRY LANDSCAPE. I TEND TO GRAVITATE BETWEEN VERY SATURATED HUES AND SOFT PASTELS. NOT SURE WHERE THAT CAME FROM. MAYBE I JUST LIKE EASTER.

SARAH: I HOPE THAT EVERYONE READING WILL GO AND CHECK OUT YOUR SITE TAVICAT.COM TO SEE THE WEBCOMICS THAT YOU AND TAVISHA WOLFGARTH-SIMONS COLLABORATE ON. PLEASE TELL US A BIT ABOUT THEM!

RIKKI: *THERE'S ABOUT 25 YEARS OF WORK AVAILABLE IN ONE FORM OR ANOTHER ON OUR SITE. MOST OF IT IS NOW IN PDF FORMAT SINCE A LOT OF THE BOOKS ARE OUT OF PRINT. TAVISHA IS HALF JAPANESE, AND HAS BEEN INFLUENCED BY MANGA GREATS LIKE OSAMU TEZUKA SINCE SHE WAS A LITTLE GIRL IN THE LATE 1960S, WHILE I TEND TO GRAVITATE BETWEEN MORE EARLY AMERICAN AND EUROPEANS, WINDSOR MCKAY AND TOVE JANSSON. TOGETHER, OUR WORKS HAVE DEVELOPED TO BE A SORT OF WHIMSICAL AND ABSURD COLLECTION OF*

STORIES. I'M NOT SURE WHERE WE'RE GOING WITH ALL OF IT, BUT WE DON'T SEEM TO BE STOPPING YET.

A DEPARTURE FROM OUR USUAL COMIC FORMAT HAS BEEN THE STRIP WE'VE BEEN DOING A FEW YEARS NOW ABOUT OUR CATS, CALLED @TAVICAT. IT'S A STRIP FORMAT, A SORT OF WALTER MITTY UNIVERSE OF COMPLETELY TRUE LIES ABOUT OUR CATS PIPPI AND FARGO. THEY GO TO SPACE A LOT. FARGO PASSED AWAY IN REAL LIFE A COUPLE OF YEARS AGO SO NOW WE TRY TO INCLUDE HIM AS AN ANGEL CAT. WE ALSO HAVE A NEW FANTASY CALLED THE SAD CIRCUS BY THE SEA *WHICH IS A SORT OF* HORTON HEARS A WHO *MEETS* MOOMINTROLL *TYPE GENRE. YOU KNOW, THE USUAL.*

SARAH: ANYTHING YOU'D LIKE TO TELL THE READERS (ESPECIALLY THE YOUNGER ONES) ABOUT WORKING IN THE CREATIVE FIELD?

RIKKI: *TAVISHA AND I DO A LOT OF THINGS. WE NEVER STICK TO ONE THING, BECAUSE IF WE DID WE WOULD DIE OF STARVATION. FOR MYSELF, I'M A SORT OF A MOVIES, TV, COMICS, ANIMATION, VOICE OVER, PROSE GNOME WHO CAN BE WEDGED INTO A VARIETY OF ART- AND STORY-RELATED JOBS, AND TOLD TO HAMMER AWAY UNTIL THEY'RE DONE. YOU HAVE TO BE DIVERSE WHEN IT COMES TO THIS TYPE OF WORK BECAUSE YOU NEVER KNOW WHEN SOMETHING WILL DRY UP. SO I GUESS YOU COULD SAY FOLLOW YOUR DREAMS, UNLESS THEY GO OFF A CLIFF. DON'T GO OFF A CLIFF. THAT'S BAD.*

- - - - - - - - - - - - - - - - - -

SARAH: SO, WE'VE LEARNED THAT HORSES DON'T EXIST, AND GOING OFF CLIFFS ARE BAD. NOTED. LAST BUT VERY MUCH NOT LEAST, I'D LIKE TO TALK A BIT WITH OUR SERIES LETTERER, TRAVIS LANHAM!

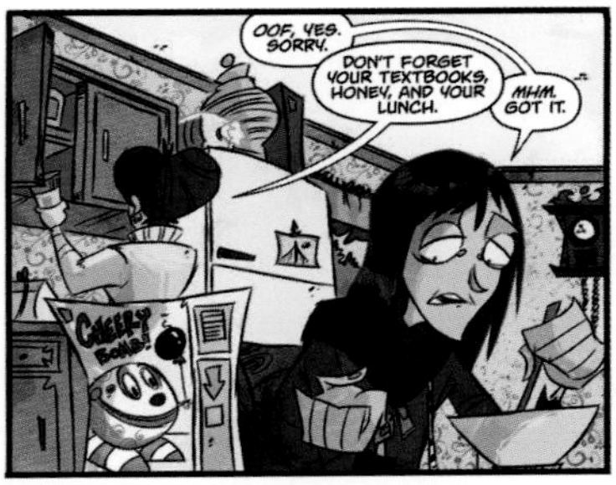
OOF, YES. SORRY.
DON'T FORGET YOUR TEXTBOOKS, HONEY, AND YOUR LUNCH.
MHM. GOT IT.

SARAH: WHEN YOU GET A NEW ASSIGNMENT, LIKE WHEN I ASKED YOU TO WORK ON *EDWARD*, HOW DO YOU APPROACH THE PROJECT?

TRAVIS: *WHEN YOU ASKED ME TO LETTER* EDWARD SCISSORHANDS, *I WAS REALLY HAPPY! I'M A BIG FAN OF THE MOVIE, AND I'M GLAD TO SEE HOW COOL THE COMIC HAS BECOME! THE FIRST THING I CONSIDER WHEN STARTING A NEW LETTERING ASSIGNMENT, IS THE ART AND WRITING STYLE OF THE BOOK. IT'S REALLY IMPORTANT AS A LETTERER THAT WHAT I CONTRIBUTE TO THE COMIC HELPS ADVANCE THE STORY, WITHOUT CLASHING WITH THE STYLE OF THE ARTIST OR THE TONE OF THE WRITING. THEN I CAN SET UP THE LETTERING STYLE GUIDE FOR THE SERIES. I'LL WORK WITH THE EDITOR AND THE TEAM TO BE SURE I'M HITTING ALL THE NOTES THEY'D LIKE TO SEE THROUGHOUT IN TERMS OF FONT CHOICES, SFX & CAPTION STYLES AND SO ON. ONCE THAT'S FINISHED, IT'S TIME TO LETTER THE BOOK!*

SARAH: CAN YOU TALK ABOUT HOW YOU SELECTED THE FONT STYLE FOR *EDWARD*?

TRAVIS: *THE IDEA FOR EDWARD'S LETTERING WAS TO BRING THAT SOFT-SPOKEN, UNIQUE VOCAL STYLE THAT WE ALL KNOW FROM* EDWARD SCISSORHANDS *TO THE COMIC BOOK PAGE. THE FONT I CHOSE HAS A BIT MORE OF A HAND-DRAWN AND LOOSE FEEL THAN THE FONT I USED FOR THE REGULAR DIALOGUE. ALSO, I KEPT HIS BALLOONS LARGER WITH MORE OPEN SPACE WITHIN THEM, TO TRY AND SET HIS STYLE APART FROM THE REST OF THE CHARACTERS IN THE SERIES. STILL, THE GOAL WAS TO KEEP THE LOOK SUBTLE, WITHOUT MAKING HIS STYLE TOO DISTINCTIVE OR HEAVY.*

SARAH: LETTERERS ARE OFTEN OVERLOOKED, BUT THEY ARE HUGELY IMPORTANT FOR A COMIC. CAN YOU TALK A BIT ABOUT WHY LETTERERS ARE SO IMPORTANT, AND ALSO WHO YOU LOOK UP TO AS A LETTERER?

TRAVIS: *I THINK LETTERING IS SUPER IMPORTANT TO COMICS, FOR SURE! WITHOUT LETTERING, NO ONE ON THE PAGES WOULD BE SAYING ANYTHING! WE HAVE TO COVER THE PAGE WITH A BUNCH OF BALLOONS, SFX, CAPTIONS, ETC, WITHOUT STEALING ATTENTION FROM THE ART WITHIN A SCENE... SO IT CAN BE TRICKY! WHEN YOU'RE READING A COMIC, YOUR EYES HAVE TO ACTUALLY SPEND A LOT OF TIME ON THE LETTERING, JUST TO READ THE STORY. SO, MAKING IT AS PROFESSIONAL, READABLE AND VISUALLY PLEASING AS POSSIBLE IS VERY IMPORTANT.*

THE LETTERERS I LOOK UP TO THE MOST ARE THE GUYS WHO TAUGHT ME HOW TO LETTER COMICS WHEN I WORKED AT DC COMICS AS A PRE-PRESS SERVICES ARTIST AND LATER AS A STAFF LETTERER. IN SPECIFIC, THE SUPER TALENTED NICK NAPOLITANO AND ROB LEIGH. I LOOKED UP TO THEM A BUNCH AS LETTERERS THEN... AND I STILL DO TODAY! IN ADDITION TO LETTERING, I HAVE A WEBCOMIC, CARL AND ZIP'S ADVENTURES THROUGH TIME!, *FOUND AT* **WWW.CARLANDZIP.COM**

- - - - - - - - - - - - - - - - - -

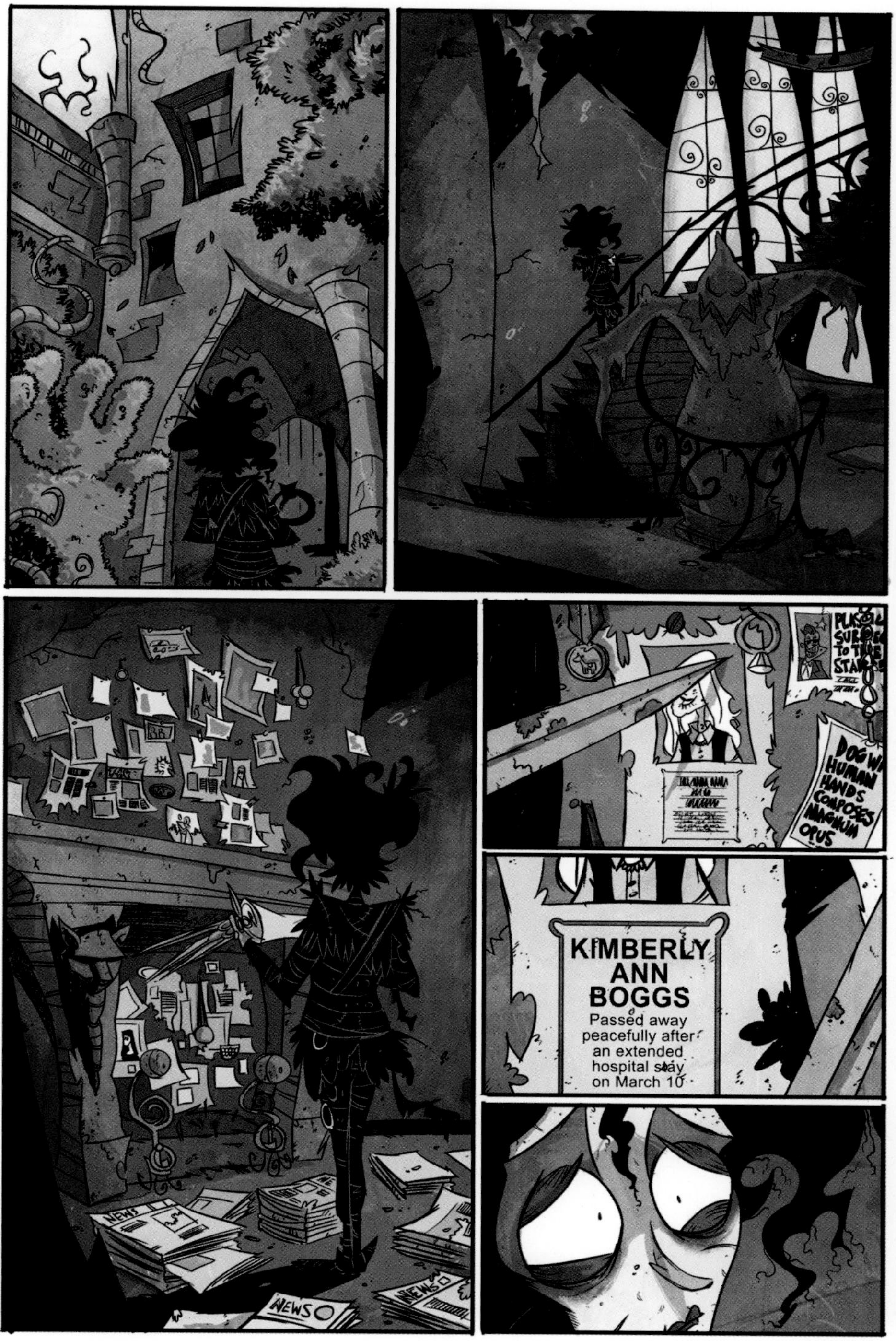
DOG WI
HUMAN
HANDS
COMPOSES
MAGNUM
OPUS
KIMBERLY
ANN
BOGGS
Passed away
peacefully after
an extended
hospital stay
on March 10
NEWS
NEWS

SARAH: BEFORE WE GO, READERS, A LAST THANK-YOU TO YOU ALL FOR THE SUPPORT ON THIS PROJECT. FROM THE CONTRIBUTIONS OF KATE, DREW, JEREMY, RIKKI, TAVISHA, AND TRAVIS... TO THE CONTRIBUTIONS OF PHOTOS AND STORIES FROM ALL OF YOU... THIS HAS BEEN A VERY SPECIAL PROJECT. IF YOU WANT TO SEE MORE EDWARD, LET IDW KNOW! LET YOUR LOCAL COMIC SHOP KNOW! SHOUT IT OUT ON SOCIAL MEDIA! WE'LL BE WATCHING... UNTIL NEXT TIME!

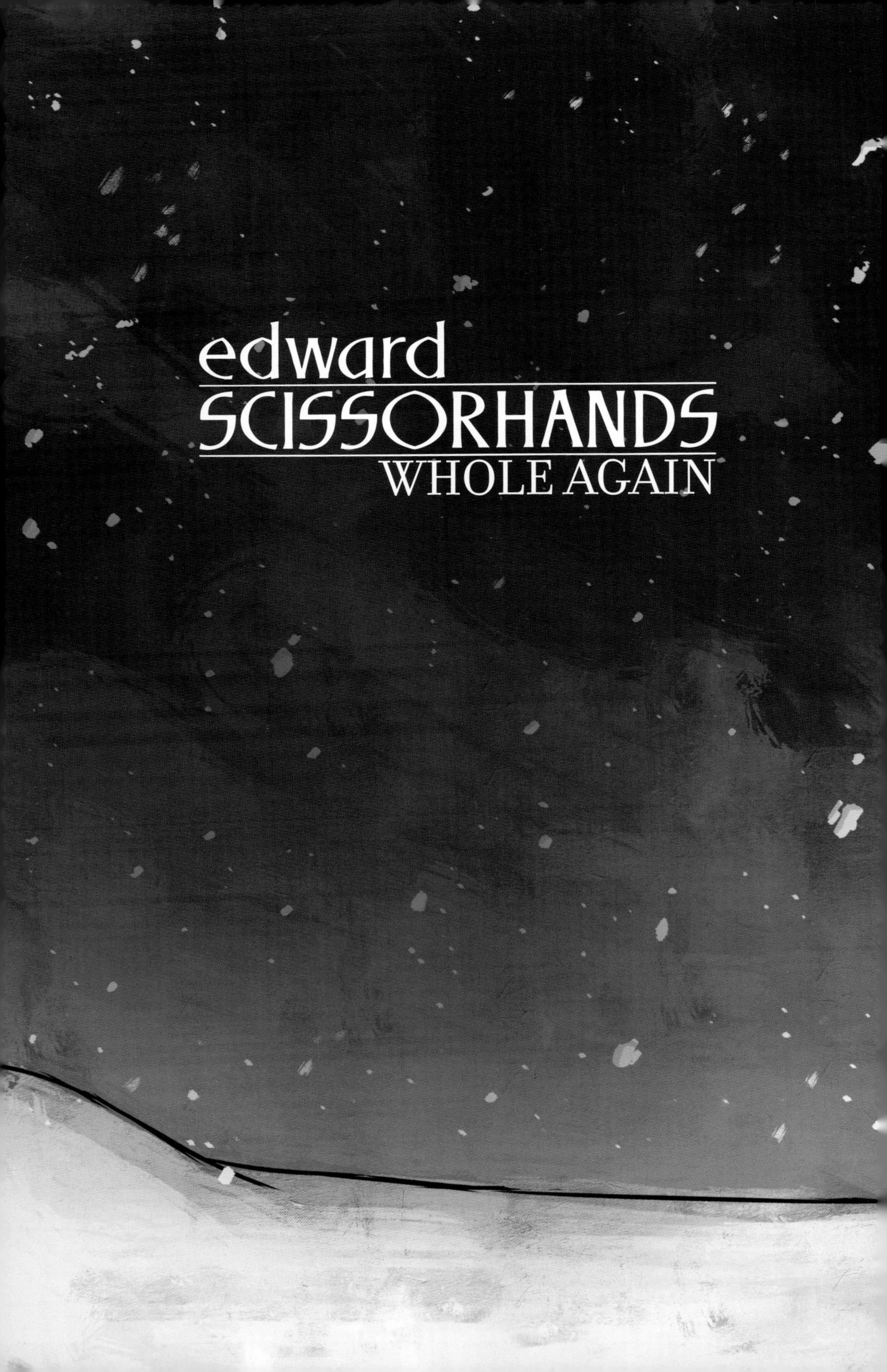
edward
SCISSORHANDS
WHOLE AGAIN